P9-EDQ-157

ON THEORETICAL SOCIOLOGY

ROBERT K. MERTON

On Theoretical Sociology

FIVE ESSAYS, OLD AND NEW

Including Part I of

SOCIAL THEORY AND SOCIAL STRUCTURE

THE FREE PRESS
A DIVISION OF MACMILLAN PUBLISHING CO., INC.
New York

COLLIER MACMILLAN PUBLISHERS
London

Printed in the United States of America

THE FREE PRESS
A Division of Macmillan Publishing Co., Inc.
866 Third Avenue, New York, New York 10022

Collier Macmillan Canada, Inc.
FIRST FREE PRESS PAPERBACK EDITION 1967

printing number
12 13 14 15 16 17 18 19 20

PREFACE

SINCE THE PUBLISHERS of *Social Theory and Social Structure* have told me that there is sufficient interest in Part I of that book to justify its separate publication, it is re-printed here without revision as Chapters III, IV, and V. But the short introduction to the larger book has been substantially expanded and appears as Chapters I and II of this book. A few words about these five chapters are needed to put them in perspective.

Chapter I states the case for the distinctive functions of histories of sociological theory and formulations of currently utilized theory. That current theory rests upon legacies of the past scarcely needs examination. But there is some value, I believe, in examining the intellectual requirements for a genuine history of sociological thought as more than a chronological series of synopses of sociological doctrine, just as there is value in considering just how current sociological theory draws upon antecedent theory.

Since a good deal of attention has been devoted to theory of the middle range in the past decades, there is reason to review its character and workings in the light of uses and criticisms of this type of theory that have developed during this time. Chapter II takes on this task.

Chapter III suggests a framework for the social theory described as functional analysis. It centers on a paradigm that codifies the assumptions, concepts and procedures that have been implicit (and occasionally, explicit) in functional interpretations developed in the fields of sociology, social psychology and social anthropology. If the large connotations of the word *discovery* are abandoned, then it can be said that the elements of the paradigm have mainly been discovered, not invented. They have been found partly by critically scrutinizing the researches and theoretical discussion of those who use the functional orientation to the study of society, and partly by reexamining my own studies of social structure.

The last two chapters summarize the types of reciprocal relations between theory and research now obtaining in sociological inquiry.

Chapter IV distinguishes the related but distinct types of inquiry encompassed by the often vaguely used term *sociological theory:* methodology or the logic of procedure, general orientations, analysis of concepts, *ex post facto* interpretations, empirical generalizations, and theory in the strict sense. In describing the interconnections among these —the fact that they are connected implies that they are also distinct— I emphasize the limitations as well as the functions of general orientations in theory, with which sociology has been more abundantly endowed than with sets of empirically confirmed specific uniformities derived from general theory. So, too, I emphasize and characterize the importance as well as the halfway character of the empirical generalization. In that chapter, it is suggested that these disparate generalizations can be collated and consolidated through the process of codification. They then become special cases of a general rule.

Chapter V examines the other part of this reciprocal relation between theory and research: the diverse kinds of impact of empirical research upon the development of sociological theory. Only those who merely read about empirical research rather than engage in it can continue to believe that the exclusive or even primary function of research is to test pre-established hypotheses. This represents an essential but narrow and far from exclusive function of such research, which plays a far more active role in the development of theory than is implied by this passive role. As the chapter states in detail, empirical research also initiates, reformulates, refocusses and clarifies sociological theory. And in the measure that empirical inquiry thus fructifies the development of theory, it is evident that the theorist who is remote from all research, of which he learns only by hearsay as it were, runs the risk of being insulated from the very experiences most likely to turn his attention in new and fruitful directions. His mind has not been prepared by experience. He is, above all, removed from the often noted experience of serendipity, the discovery through chance by a prepared mind of valid findings that were not looked for. Weber was probably right in subscribing to the view that one need not be Caesar in order to understand Caesar. But there is a temptation for us sociological theorists to act sometimes as though in order to understand Caesar, it is not necessary even to study Caesar.

Even a little book such as this one—part new, part old—benefits from collaboration. I owe special thanks to Barbara Bengen who applied her editorial talents to the first two chapters, to Dr. Harriet A. Zuckerman who criticized an early draft, and to Mrs. Mary Miles who converted a palimpsest into clear typescript. In preparing the introductory chapters, I was aided by a grant from the National Science Foundation.

R. K. M.

ACKNOWLEDGMENTS

NO MAN KNOWS fully what has shaped his own thinking. It is difficult for me to trace in detail the provenience of the conceptions set forth in this book, and to track down the reasons for their progressive modifications as I have worked with them over the years. Many social scientists have contributed to the development of these conceptions and whenever the source is known, reference is made in the numerous notes to the separate chapters. But among these, there are six to whom I owe an especial debt, though of varying degree and kind, and to them I want to pay tribute.

The earliest and greatest of these debts is slightly and too late acknowledged in the dedication of this book to Charles H. Hopkins. Because this man, the husband of my sister, lived, many lives were deepened in human dignity. As long as any of us whose lives touched his still live, he will live. It is with love and respect and gratitude that I dedicate this book to Hop, who learned for himself that he might teach others.

To my good friend, George Eaton Simpson, now of Oberlin College, I am grateful for having taken a brash sophomore in hand to make him *see* the intellectual excitement of studying the operation of systems of social relations. I could not easily have had a more propitious introduction to sociology.

Before he became absorbed in the study of historical movements on the grand scale as represented in his *Social and Cultural Dynamics*, Pitirim A. Sorokin helped me escape from the provincialism of thinking that effective studies of society were confined within American borders and from the slum-encouraged provincialism of thinking that the primary subject-matter of sociology was centered in such peripheral problems of social life as divorce and juvenile delinquency. I gladly acknowledge this honest debt, still not discharged.

To George Sarton, most esteemed among historians of science, I am thankful for friendship as well as guidance, and for the privilege of having been allowed to work the greater part of two years in his famed workshop at Harvard Library 189. Some small sign of his stimulus will be found in Chapter I of this book devoted to the requirements for a history of sociological theory.

Those who read the following pages will soon recognize the great debt I owe to my teacher and friend, Talcott Parsons, who so early in his teaching career conveyed his enthusiasm for analytical theory to so many. The measure of his calibre as a teacher is found in his having stirred up intellectual enthusiasm, rather than creating obedient disciples. In the intellectual intimacy afforded by the *small* graduate department of sociology at Harvard in the early 1930's, it was possible for a graduate student like myself, to have close and continued working relations with an instructor, like Dr. Parsons. It was indeed a collegium, today not easily found in departments numbering many score of graduate students and a small, hard-driven group of professors.

In recent years, while we have worked in double harness in the Columbia University Bureau of Applied Social Research, I have learned most from Paul F. Lazarsfeld. Since it is evident from our countless conversations that he has no conception of the full extent of my intellectual debt to him, I am especially happy to have this occasion for forcing it upon his attention in public. Not least valuable to me has been his sceptical curiosity which has compelled me to articulate more fully than I might otherwise have done my reasons for considering functional analysis the presently most promising, though not the only, theoretical orientation to a wide range of problems in human society. And above all, he has, through his own example, reinforced in myself the conviction that the great difference between social science and social dilettantism resides in the systematic and *serious*, that is to say, the intellectually responsible and austere, pursuit of what is first entertained as an interesting idea. This, I take it, is what Whitehead also means by the closing lines of the passage in the epigraph to this book.

There are four others who need little acknowledgment; one, because all who know me know my great obligation to her; the other three, because they will in due course discover for themselves the precise nature of my considerable obligation to them.

CONTENTS

I. On the History and Systematics of Sociological Theory *1*

II. On Sociological Theories of the Middle Range *39*

III. Manifest and Latent Functions *73*

IV. The Bearing of Sociological Theory on Empirical Research *139*

V. The Bearing of Empirical Research on Sociological Theory *156*

Index of Names *173*

Subject Index *177*

I ON THE HISTORY AND SYSTEMATICS OF SOCIOLOGICAL THEORY

"A science which hesitates to forget its founders is lost."

"It is characteristic of a science in its earlier stages . . . to be both ambitiously profound in its aims and trivial in its handling of details."

"But to come very near to a true theory, and to grasp its precise application, are two very different things, as the history of science teaches us. Everything of importance has been said before by somebody who did not discover it."

ALFRED NORTH WHITEHEAD,
The Organisation of Thought

ALTHOUGH THEY DRAW heavily upon the writings of past sociologists, these papers deal not with the history of sociological theory but with the systematic substance of certain theories with which sociologists now work. The distinction between the two is more than casual. Yet the two are often mingled in academic curricula and publications. Indeed, the social sciences in general, with the growing exception of psychology and economics, tend to merge current theory with its history to a far greater degree than do such sciences as biology, chemistry, or physics.[1]

THE ARTLESS MERGER OF HISTORY AND SYSTEMATICS

It is symbolically apt that sociologists tend to merge the history with the systematics of theory. For Auguste Comte, often described as the father of sociology, has also been described as the father of the history

1. This discussion draws upon an earlier paper discussing "the position of sociological theory," *American Sociological Review*, 1949, 13, 164-8. For apposite observations on the role of the history of social thought as distinct from that of currently sociological theory, see Howard Becker, "Vitalizing sociological theory," *ibid.*, 1954, 19, 377-88, esp. 379-81, and the recent emphatic and elaborately exemplified statement in Joseph Berger, Morris Zelditch, Jr. and Bo Anderson, *Sociological Theories in Progress* (Boston: Houghton Mifflin Company, 1966), ix-xii, and William R. Catton, *From Animistic to Naturalistic Sociology* (New York: McGraw Hill, 1966). A somewhat different view of the nature and functions of social theory will be found in Theodore Abel, "The present status of social theory," *American Sociological Review*, 1952, 17, 156-64 as well as in the discussion of this paper by Kenneth E. Bock and Stephen W. Reed, 164-7; and in Herbert Blumer, "What is wrong with social theory?," *ibid.*, 1954, 19, 3-10.

of science.[2] However, the attractive but fatal confusion of current sociological theory with the history of sociological ideas ignores their decisively different functions.

Suitable recognition of the difference between the history and systematics of sociology might result in the writing of authentic histories. These would have the ingredients and formal characteristics of the better histories of other sciences. They would take up such matters as the complex filiation of sociological ideas, the ways in which they developed, the connections of theory with the changing social origins and subsequent social statuses of its exponents, the interaction of theory with the changing social organization of sociology, the diffusion of theory from centers of sociological thought and its modification in the course of diffusion, and the ways in which it was influenced by changes in the environing culture and social structure. The distinction put into practice would, in short, make for a sociological history of sociological theory.

Yet sociologists retain a most parochial, almost Pickwickian conception of the history of sociological theory as a collection of critical summaries of past theories spiced with short biographies of major theorists. This helps to explain why almost all sociologists see themselves as qualified to teach and to write the "history" of sociological theory—after all, they are acquainted with the classical writings of an earlier day. But this conception of the history of theory is in fact neither history nor systematics, but a poorly thought-out hybrid.

In fact, this conception is an anomaly in contemporary intellectual work, and it signals a developing reversal of roles between sociologists and historians. For sociologists retain their narrow and shallow conception of the history of ideas at the very time that a new breed of special-

---

2. For example, by George Sarton, *The Study of the History of Science* (Cambridge: Harvard University Press, 1936), 3-4. The nomination of Comte or Marx or St. Simon or many others for the status of *the* father of sociology is partly a matter of opinion and partly the result of an unexamined assumption about how new disciplines emerge and crystallize. It remains an opinion because there are no generally acknowledged criteria for having fathered a science; the unexamined assumption is that there is typically *one* father for each science, after the biological metaphor. In fact the history of science suggests that polygenesis is the rule. However, there is little doubt that Comte in 1839 coined the term "sociology," the horrible hybrid that has ever since designated the science of society. Scholars then and today have protested the now domesticated barbarism. One of the innumerable examples of protest is the remark in 1852 by the talented and much neglected social theorist, George Cornewall Lewis: ". . . the main objection to a scientific word, formed partly of an English and partly of a Greek word, is, that it is unintelligible to a foreigner unacquainted with our language. M. Comte has proposed the word *sociology;* but what should we say to a German writer who used the word *gesellology,* or *gesellschaftology?*" The complaint is registered in Lewis' *A Treatise on the Methods of Observation and Reasoning in Politics* (London, 1852), II, 337n; as for the history of the word itself, see Victor Branford, "On the origin and use of the word sociology . . . ," *Sociological Papers* (London, 1905), I, 3-24 and L. L. Bernard and Jessie Bernard, *Origins of American Sociology* (New York: T. Y. Crowell, 1943), 249.

ized historians of science is drawing widely and deeply upon the sociology, psychology and politics of science for theoretical guides to their interpretations of the development of science.[3] The specialized history of science includes the intelligent but mistaken conceptions which made good sense at the time of their formulation but were later shattered by compelling empirical tests or replaced by conceptions more adequate to the enlarged facts of the case. It includes also the false starts, the now archaic doctrines and both the fruitless and fruitful errors of the past. The rationale for the history of science is to achieve an understanding of how things came to develop as they did in a certain science or in a complex of sciences, not merely to put synopses of scientific theory in chronological order. And above all, this sort of history is not designed to instruct today's scientist in the current operating theory, methodology or technique of his science. The history and systematics of scientific theory can be related precisely because they are first recognized to be distinct.

THE PUBLIC RECORD OF SOCIOLOGICAL THEORY

The sociologists and the historians of science have dramatically reversed roles in another, closely related way. The historians are energetically compiling the "oral history"[4] of the recent past in the sciences by conducting tape-recorded, focused interviews with major participants in that history; the sociologists still limit their attention to public documents. Here is another instance in which the colonized historians are outstripping the indigenous sociologists, to whom the historians are avowedly indebted for their interviewing techniques. In short, the historians of the physical and life sciences are coming to write analytical histories based in part on the *sociology* of science,[5] while the sociologists continue to see

---

3. The more consequential exponents of the new history of science include Charles Gillispie, Henry Guerlac, Rupert Hall, Marie Boas Hall, Thomas Kuhn, Everett Mendelsohn, Derek Price, Robert Schofield, L. Pearce Williams, and A. C. Crombie.

4. Invented by the historian Allan Nevins as a means of rescuing fugitive data about the historical present, oral history has drawn upon techniques of interviewing that are indigenous to field sociologists rather than historians, traditionally masters of gathering and assaying documentary materials. For a report on oral history, a mode of investigation which has spread far beyond its origin in Columbia University, see *The Oral History Collection of Columbia University* (New York: Oral History Research Office, 1964) v. 1 and yearly supplements.

As an example, the American Institute of Physics is compiling, under the direction of Charles Weiner, an oral and documentary history of nuclear physics; his techniques might well be emulated by sociologists concerned with the recent history of their own discipline.

5. For examples of the sociologically-tinged history of science, see the annual, *History of Science,* first published in 1962 under the editorship of A. C. Crombie and M. A. Hoskins; also Marshall Clagett, ed. *Critical Problems in the History of Science* (Madison: University of Wisconsin Press, 1959).

the history of sociological theory as a series of critical summaries of successive theoretical systems.

Given this restricted conception, it follows naturally that the crucial source materials for sociologists are the published writings describing these theoretical systems: for example, the writings of Marx, Weber, Durkheim, Simmel, Pareto, Sumner, Cooley, and others of less imposing stature. But this seemingly self-evident choice of source materials runs aground on the rock-bound difference between the finished versions of scientific work as they appear in print and the actual course of inquiry followed by the inquirer. The difference is a little like that between textbooks of 'scientific method' and the ways in which scientists actually think, feel and go about their work. The books on method present ideal patterns: how scientists *ought* to think, feel and act, but these tidy normative patterns, as everyone who has engaged in inquiry knows, do not reproduce the typically untidy, opportunistic adaptations that scientists make in the course of their inquiries. Typically, the scientific paper or monograph presents an immaculate appearance which reproduces little or nothing of the intuitive leaps, false starts, mistakes, loose ends, and happy accidents that actually cluttered up the inquiry. The public record of science therefore fails to provide many of the source materials needed to reconstruct the actual course of scientific developments.

The conception of the history of sociological ideas as a series of critical accounts of published ideas lags extraordinarily far behind long-recognized reality. Even before the evolutionary invention of the scientific paper, three centuries ago, it was known that the typically impersonal, bland and conventionalized idiom of science could communicate the barebone essentials of new scientific contributions but could not reproduce the actual course of inquiry. In other words, it was recognized even then that the history and systematics of scientific theory required distinct kinds of basic materials. At the very beginning of the seventeenth century Bacon at once observed and complained:

> That never any knowledge was delivered in the same order it was invented, no not in the mathematic, though it should seem otherwise in regard that the propositions placed last do use the propositions or grants placed first for their proof and demonstration.[6]

Ever since, perceptive minds have repeatedly and, it would seem, independently made the same kind of observation. Thus, a century later, Leibniz made much the same point in an off-the-record letter which has since become very much part of the historical record:

> Descartes would have us believe that he had read scarcely anything. That was a bit too much. Yet it is good to study the discoveries of others in a way

---

6. Francis Bacon, *The Works of Francis Bacon.* Collected and edited by James Spedding, Robert Leslie Ellis, and Douglas Denon Heath (Cambridge, England: Riverside Press, 1863), VI, 70.

that discloses to us the source of the discoveries and renders them in a sort our own. And I wish that authors would give us the history of their discoveries and the steps by which they have arrived at them. When they neglect to do so, we must try to divine these steps, in order to profit the more from their works. If the critics would do this for us in reviewing books [here, one must surely ask the great mathematician and philosopher: how?], they would render a great service to the public.[7]

In effect, what both Bacon and Leibniz are saying is that the raw materials needed for the history and for the systematics of science differ significantly. But since scientists ordinarily publish their ideas and findings not to help historians reconstruct their methods but to instruct their contemporaries and, hopefully, posterity about their contributions to science, they have largely continued to publish their work in logically cogent rather than historically descriptive fashion. This practice has continued to provide the same kind of observation made by Bacon and Leibniz. Almost two centuries after Leibniz, Mach noted that, to his mind, things had not changed for the better in the millennia since the emergence of Euclidean geometry. Scientific and mathematical expositions still tended toward logical casuistry rather than toward charting the actual paths of inquiry:

Euclid's system fascinated thinkers by its logical excellence, and its drawbacks were overlooked amid this admiration. Great inquirers, even in recent times, have been misled into following Euclid's example in the presentation of the results of their inquiries, and so into *actually concealing their methods of investigation,* to the great detriment of science.[8]

Yet in a way, Mach's observation is retrogressive. He fails to see what Bacon so clearly saw centuries before: that the record of science will inevitably differ according to whether it is intended to contribute to current systematic knowledge or to an improved historical understanding of how scientific work develops. But Mach, like Bacon and Leibniz, does imply that we cannot hope to reconstruct the actual history of scientific inquiry by attending solely to conventionalized published reports.

This same point was made recently by the physicist, A. A. Moles, who said that scientists are "professionally trained to conceal from themselves their deepest thought" and to "exaggerate unconsciously the rational aspect" of work done in the past.[9] What must be emphasized here is that this practice of glossing over the actual course of inquiry results largely from the mores of scientific publication which call for a passive idiom and format of reporting which imply that ideas develop without benefit

7. Gottfried Wilhelm Leibniz, *Philosophischen Schriften,* C. I. Gerhardt, ed. (Berlin, 1887), III, 568, in his letter to Louis Bourquet from Vienna, 22 March 1714.

8. Ernst Mach, *Space and Geometry,* trans. by T. J. McCormack (Chicago: Open Court Publishing Co., 1906), 113, italics supplied.

9. A. A. Moles, *La création scientifique* (Geneva, 1957) as quoted by Jacques Barzun, *Science: The Glorious Entertainment* (New York: Harper & Row, 1964), 93.

of human brain and that investigations are conducted without benefit of human hand.

This observation has been generalized by the botanist Agnes Arber, who notes that "the mode of presentation of scientific work is . . . moulded by the thought-prejudices of its period." But although styles of scientific reporting differ according to the prevailing intellectual commitments of the time, they all present a stylized reconstruction of the inquiry rather than faithfully describing its actual development. Thus Arber observes that in the Euclidean period, when deduction was highly prized, the actual course of inquiry was covered over "by the artificial method of stringing propositions on an arbitrarily chosen thread of deduction," in this way obscuring its empirical aspect. Today, the scientist "being under the domination of the inductive method, even if he has in fact reached his hypothesis by analogy, his instinctive reaction is to cover his traces, and to present *all* his work—not merely his proof—in inductive form, as though it were by this process that his conclusions had actually been reached."[10]

Agnes Arber notes that only in the non-scientific literature do we find efforts to record the reticular character of thought:

> Lawrence Sterne, and certain modern writers influenced by him in their technique [a clear enough allusion to such impressionists as James Joyce and Virginia Woolf], have visualized, and tried to convey in language, the complicated, non-linear behaviour of the human mind, as it darts to and fro, disregarding the shackles of temporal sequence; but few [scientists] would dare to risk such experiments.[11]

Nonetheless, more than just callow optimism suggests that the failure of sociology to distinguish between the history and systematics of theory will eventually be wiped out. First, some sociologists have recognized that the ordinary public record provides an insufficient basis for ferreting out the actual history of sociological theory and investigation. They have rounded this out by turning to other kinds of source materials: scientific notebooks and journals (*e.g.* Cooley), correspondence (*e.g.* Marx-Engels, Ross-Ward), autobiographies and biographies (*e.g.* Marx, Spencer, Weber and many others). Recent sociologists have occasionally begun to set forth candid chronicles of how their sociological inquiries were actually carried out, full of the particulars of intellectual and social influences, chance encounters with data and ideas, errors, oversights, departures

---

10. Agnes Arber, "Analogy in the history of science," *Studies and Essays in the History of Science and Learning offered in Homage to George Sarton*, ed. by M. F. Ashley Montagu (New York: Henry Schuman, 1944), 222-33 at 229.

11. Agnes Arber, *The Mind and the Eye: A Study of the Biologist's Standpoint* (Cambridge University Press, 1954), 46. Chapter Five, "The Biologist and the Written Word," and indeed the whole of this subtle, perceptive and profoundly informed book should be required study for the historians of every scientific discipline, not excluding sociology.

from the original design of inquiry, and all the other kinds of episodes that turn up in investigations but are seldom recorded in the published report.[12] Although only a beginning, chronicles of this sort greatly extend the practice initiated by Lester F. Ward in the six-volume *Glimpses of the Cosmos,*[13] of introducing each essay with an "historical sketch telling just when, where, how and why it was written."[13a]

Another promising sign is the appearance in 1965 of the *Journal of the History of the Behavioral Sciences,* the first journal devoted wholly to the history of these sciences (in contrast to the score or more of major journals and more than a hundred minor ones devoted to the history of the physical and life sciences). A third sign is the developing interest in studying the history of social investigation. Nathan Glazer, for example, has pointed the way in his authentically historical essay on "The Rise of Social Research in Europe," while Paul F. Lazarsfeld has inaugurated a program of special monographs devoted to the early development of empirical social research in Germany, France, England, Italy, the Low Countries, and Scandanavia.[14] And Alvin Gouldner sets an auspicious precedent for monographs that relate the environing social structure and culture to the development of social theory in his recent work on the social theory of Plato.[15] These are only a few of the many indications that sociologists are turning to distinctively historical and sociological analyses of the development of theory.

---

12. As examples: the detailed methodological appendix by William Foote Whyte to the enlarged edition of *Street Corner Society: The Social Structure of an Italian Slum* (Chicago: University of Chicago Press, 1955); E. H. Sutherland's account of the development of his theory of differential association in *The Sutherland Papers,* ed. by Albert Cohen, Alfred Lindesmith and Karl Schuessler (Bloomington: Indiana University Press, 1956); Edward A. Shils, "Primordial, Personal, Sacred and Civil Ties," *British Journal of Sociology,* June 1957, 130-145; Marie Jahoda, Paul F. Lazarsfeld and Hans Zeisel, *Die Arbeitslosen von Marienthal,* 2d unrevised edition (Bonn: Verlag für Demoskopie, 1960), with a new introduction by Lazarsfeld on the intellectual origins, climate of sociological and psychological thought and course of development of the research. In 1964, this concern with how it really was in various sociological inquiries was expressed in two collections of such accounts: Phillip E. Hammond, ed., *Sociologists at Work: The Craft of Social Research* (New York: Basic Books) and Arthur J. Vidich, Joseph Bensman and Maurice R. Stein, eds., *Reflections on Community Studies* (New York, John Wiley & Sons).

13. (New York and London: G. P. Putnam, 1913-18).

13a. For another example of the interplay between a sociologist's work, his life history and the social organization of the field, see the biographical essay by William J. Goode, Larry Mitchell, and Frank Furstenberg in *Selected Works of Willard W. Waller,* (in press).

14. Nathan Glazer, "The rise of social research in Europe," in *The Human Meaning of the Social Sciences,* Daniel Lerner, ed. (New York: Meridian Books, 1959), 43-72. See the first monograph published in the Lazarsfeld program: Anthony Oberschall, *Empirical Social Research in Germany 1848-1914* (Paris and The Hague: Mouton, 1965).

15. Alvin W. Gouldner, *Enter Plato: Classical Greece and the Origins of Social Theory* (New York: Basic Books, 1965).

CONTINUITIES AND DISCONTINUITIES IN SOCIOLOGICAL THEORY

Like other craftsmen, historians of ideas are exposed to various occupational hazards. One of the more exasperating and intriguing of these hazards turns up whenever historians try to identify historical continuities and discontinuities of ideas. The exercise is a little like walking a tightrope, because just a small departure from an upright posture is often enough for them to lose their balance. The historian of ideas runs the risk either of claiming to find a continuity of thought where it did not in fact exist or of failing to identify continuity where it did exist.[16] Observing the behavior of historians of ideas, one gets the distinct impression that, when they err at all, they tend toward the first kind of error. They are quick to claim a steady stream of precursors, anticipations, and adumbrations in many cases where more thorough investigation finds these to be figments.

It is understandable that sociologists should share this tendency with historians of science. For both generally adopt a model of the historical development of science as proceeding by increments of knowledge; in this view, occasional gaps occur only through failures to retrieve complete information from writings of the past. Not knowing previous work, later scientists make discoveries that turn out to be rediscoveries (that is, conceptions or findings which have been set forth before in every functionally relevant aspect). For the historian who has access to both the earlier and later versions of the discovery this occurrence indicates an intellectual, though not historical, continuity of which the later discoverer was unaware. Supporting this presumption of continuity is the fact that multiple independent discoveries and ideas occur in sciences, as abundant evidence testifies.[17]

---

16. An apt illustration of this point is the fact that I came upon much the same distinction as this in print some years after I had worked it out in detail in a course of public lectures. See the discussion of 'precursoritis' by Joseph T. Clark, S.J., "The philosophy of science and the history of science," in Clagett. *op. cit.*, 103-40, and the commentary on this paper by I. E. Drabkin, particularly at 152.

This coincidence of ideas is doubly apt since, for some time now, I have advanced the opinion that histories and sociologies of ideas exemplify some of the same historical and intellectual processes which they describe and analyze. For example, note the observation that the theory of multiple independent discoveries in science is confirmed by its own history since it has been periodically rediscovered over a span of generations. R. K. Merton, "Singletons and multiples in scientific discovery: a chapter in the sociology of science," *Proceedings of the American Philosophical Society*, October, 1961, 105, 470-86, at 475-7. See other cases of self-exemplifying hypotheses and theories indexed in R. K. Merton, *On the Shoulders of Giants* (New York: The Free Press, 1965; Harcourt, Brace & World, 1967).

17. For recent accounts that collate evidence to this effect gathered at least from the time of Francis Bacon to the time of William Ogburn and Dorothy Thomas and that supply additional systematic evidence, see Merton, "Singletons and multiples in scientific discoveries," *op. cit.* and "Resistance to the systematic study of multiple discoveries in science," *European Journal of Sociology*, 1963, 4, 237-82.

It does not follow, of course, that because some scientific ideas have been fully anticipated, all of them have. Historical continuity of knowledge does involve new increments in previous knowledge which have not been anticipated; there is, also, a measure of genuine discontinuity in the form of quantum jumps in the formulation of ideas and the discovery of empirical uniformities. Indeed, one step in advancing the sociology of science consists precisely of solving the problem of identifying the conditions and processes making for continuity and for discontinuity in science.

These problems of reconstructing the extent of continuity and discontinuity are indigenous to the entire history of science. But they take on a special character in those histories, such as the typical history of sociology, which are largely confined to chronologically arranged summaries of ideas. For in writings that exclude serious study of the interplay of ideas and social structure the alleged linkage between earlier and later ideas is put in the center of the stage. The historian of ideas, whether he recognizes it or not, is then committed to distinguishing the extent of similarity between earlier and later ideas, the range of differences being embraced by the terms rediscovery, anticipations, adumbrations and, at the extreme, adumbration*ism*.

1. Rediscovery and Prediscovery. Strictly speaking, multiple independent discoveries in science refer to substantively identical or functionally equivalent ideas and empirical findings set forth by two or more scientists, each unaware of the others' work. When these occur at about the same time they are called 'simultaneous' independent discoveries. Historians have not evolved generally accepted criteria of 'simultaneity,' but in practice, multiple discoveries are described as simultaneous when they occur within the span of a few years. When longer intervals separate functionally interchangeable discoveries, the later one is described as a *rediscovery.* Since historians of science have no established designation for the earlier one we shall adopt the term *prediscovery.*

It is no easy matter to establish the degree of similarity between independently developed ideas. Even in the more exact disciplines, such as mathematics, claims of independent multiple inventions are vigorously debated. The question is, how much overlap should be taken to constitute "identity"? A careful comparison of the non-Euclidean geometries invented by Bolyai and Lobachevsky, for example, maintains that Lobachevsky had developed five of the nine salient components of their overlapping conceptions more systematically, more fruitfully and in more detail.[18] So, too, it has been observed that no two of the twelve scientists who "grasped for themselves essential parts of the concept of energy and

18. B. Petrovievics, "N. Lobatschewsky et J. Bolyai: étude comparative d'un cas spécial d'inventeurs simultanés," *Revue Philosophique*, 1929, cviii, 190–214; and an earlier paper by the same author to the same effect for another case: "Charles Darwin und Alfred Russel Wallace: Beitrag zur höheren Psychologie und zur Wissenschaftsgeschichte," *Isis*, 1925, vii, 25-57.

its conservation" had precisely the same conception.[19] Nevertheless, by relaxing the criteria a bit, these are generally described as multiple independent discoveries. For the typically less precise formulations in much of the social sciences, it becomes even more difficult to establish the substantive identity or functional equivalence of independently evolved conceptions.

In place of a thoroughgoing comparison of earlier and later versions of the 'same' discovery, however, another kind of evidence seems presumptive if not compelling evidence of identity or equivalence: the report of a *later* discoverer that another had arrived there before him. Presumably, these reports are truthful; since the modern age of science puts a premium on originality (unlike earlier days in which ancient authority was deliberately claimed for new ideas), it is unlikely that discoverers would want to disclaim the originality of their own work. We find evidence of later discoverers themselves reporting prediscoveries in all the sciences. The highly inventive physicist, Thomas Young, for example, reported that "several circumstances unknown to the English mathematicians which I thought I had first discovered, I since find to have been discovered and demonstrated by the foreign mathematicians." Young in turn received an apology from Fresnel, who learned that he had inadvertently duplicated Young's work on the wave theory of light.[20] Similarly, Bertrand Russell remarked of his contributions to Whitehead's and his *Principia Mathematica* that "much of the work had already been done by Frege, but at first we did not know this."[21]

Every field of social science and the humanities as well has its own complement of cases in which later authors announce that their contribution has been anticipated, thus providing eloquent testimony to the fact of multiple discovery in these disciplines. Consider only this scattering of cases in point: Pavlov went out of his way to acknowledge that "the honour of having made the first steps along this path [of Pavlov's new method of investigation] belongs to E. L. Thorndike."[22] Freud, who gave evidence in print of his interest in priority of discovery on more than 150 occasions, reports that "I had found the essential characteristic and most significant part of my dream theory—the reduction of dream-

19. Thomas S. Kuhn, "Energy conservation as an example of simultaneous discovery." In Clagett, *op. cit.*, 321-56.

20. Alexander Wood, *Thomas Young: Natural Philosopher, 1773-1829* (Cambridge: University Press, 1954), 65, 188-9. Fresnel writes to Young: "When I submitted it [his memoir on the theory of light] to the Institute I did not know of your experiments and the deductions you drew from them, so that I presented as new explanations that which you had already given long ago."

21. Bertrand Russell, "My mental development," in James R. Newman, ed., *The World of Mathematics* (New York: Simon and Schuster, 1956), I, 388.

22. I. P. Pavlov, *Lectures on Conditioned Reflexes,* trans. by W. H. Gantt (New York: International Publishers, 1928), 39-40.

distortion to an inner conflict, a kind of inward dishonesty—later in a writer who was familiar with philosophy though not with medicine, the engineer J. Popper, who published his *Phantasien eines Realisten* under the name of Lynkeus."[23] R. G. D. Allen and J. R. Hicks, who had independently brought the modern economic theory of value to a culmination in 1934, took special pains to call public attention to their later uncovering of a prediscovery by the Russian economist, Eugen Slutsky, who had published in an Italian journal in 1915, a time when war took precedence over the ready circulation of ideas. Allen devoted an article to Slutsky's earlier theory and Hicks eponymously labelled the fundamental equation in the theory of values as "Slutsky's equation."[24]

The same pattern turns up among philosophers. Moore's *Principia Ethica,* possibly the most influential book in twentieth-century ethical theory, includes the by-now-familiar type of report: "When this book had been already completed, I found, in Brentano's 'Origin of the Knowledge of Right and Wrong,' opinions far more closely resembling my own, than those of any other ethical writer with whom I am acquainted." And then Moore goes on to summarize four major conceptions about which he writes wryly enough, "Brentano appears to agree with me completely."[25]

Reports of prior formulations extend even to such minor details as newly-minted figures of speech. Thus, David Riesman introduces the image of "the psychological gyroscope" and then goes on to report "that since writing the above I have discovered Gardner Murphy's use of the same metaphor in his volume *Personality.*"[26]

Coming upon a prediscovery of one's own idea can evidently be as disconcerting as coming unawares upon one's double in a crowd. The economist Edith Penrose no doubt speaks for uncounted numbers of other scientists and scholars when she announces that "after having laboriously worked out for myself what I took to be an important and 'original' idea, I have often had the disconcerting experience of subse-

---

23. Sigmund Freud, *Collected Papers,* trans. by Joan Riviere (London: Hogarth Press, 1949), I, 302. For a detailed account of Freud's involvement in anticipations, rediscoveries, prediscoveries and priorities, see Merton, "Resistance to the systematic study of multiple discoveries in science," *op. cit.,* 252-8.

24. R. G. D. Allen, "Professor Slutsky's Theory of Consumer Choice," *Review of Economic Studies,* February 1936, Vol. III, 2, 120; J. R. Hicks, *Value and Capital* (Oxford: Clarendon Press, 1946).

25. G. E. Moore, *Principia Ethica* (Cambridge University Press, 1903), x-xi. As a careful scholar, Moore also reports a basic difference between his ideas and Brentano's. He thus exemplifies a major component of the view being slowly developed here: that even an identity of certain ideas in two or more independently developed theories need not mean a thoroughgoing identity between the theories as wholes. Social and humanistic theories, and sometimes physical and biological theories, do not have such a tightknit logical coherence that identity of parts is equivalent to identity of the wholes.

26. David Riesman, in collaboration with Reuel Denney and Nathan Glazer, *The Lonely Crowd.* (New Haven: Yale University Press, 1950), 16, 6n.

quently finding the same idea better expressed by some other writer."[27]

Still another kind of evidence testifying to genuine rediscoveries is provided by the many scientists and scholars who discontinue a line of work when they find that it was forestalled by others. The latercomers would presumably be motivated to perceive even slight differences between the earlier work of others and their own; abandoning their line of inquiry indicates that, in their judgment, it had been carried out to a significant conclusion before them. Carl Spearman, for example, tells of his having evolved an elaborate theory of "correlation coefficients" to measure degrees of correlation only to find "that the greater part of my correlation theory had already been obtained—and much better—by other writers, especially by Galton and Udney Yule. Here again, then, a great deal of work had been wasted and the much believed original discovery was, as such, regretfully scrapped."[28] Forestalled inquiry applies also to details of scholarly research. As an example, the historian J. H. Hexter reports in his easy and forthright fashion that he had almost completed an appendix questioning "the thesis that in *Utopia* More dis-associated himself from the views on private property expressed by Hythloday when my colleague Prof. George Parks brought to my attention an excellent article dealing with that evidence by Edward L. Surtz. . . . The article makes such an appendix redundant."[29] Such publicly recorded instances of forestalled rediscoveries do not, of course, begin to exhaust what may be a vast number of unrecorded instances. Many scientists and scholars cannot bring themselves to report in print that they were forestalled, so that these cases are known only to a limited circle of close associates.[30]

2. Anticipations and Adumbrations. In his recent book,[31] the historian of science Thomas S. Kuhn has distinguished between "normal science" and "scientific revolutions" as phases in the evolution of science. Most published responses to the book have centered, just as Kuhn himself does, on those occasional leaps forward that mark the scientific revolu-

---

27. Edith Penrose, *The Theory of the Growth of the Firm* (New York: John Wiley, 1959), 2.

28. Carl Spearman, in *A History of Psychology in Autobiography,* Carl Murchison, ed. (New York: Russell and Russell, 1961), 322.

29. J. H. Hexter, *More's Utopia: The Biography of an Idea* (Princeton University Press, 1952), 34n. Hexter insists that he was anticipated in another aspect of his work as well: "My complete disagreement with Oncken's interpretation of More's intent in the *Utopia* and my considerable disagreement with his analysis of its composition doubles my chagrin at being anticipated by him on one point. My illusion that I was the first to notice a break in Book I of *Utopia* . . . was shattered by a subsequent reading of Oncken's introduction to the Ritter German translation." *Ibid.,* 13-14n.

30. For more evidence on this, see Merton, "Singletons and multiples in scientific discovery," *op. cit.,* 479 ff.

31. Thomas S. Kuhn, *The Structure of Scientific Revolutions* (Chicago: University of Chicago Press, 1962).

tion. But though these revolutions are the most dramatic moments in the development of science, most scientists most of the time are engaged in the work of "normal science," developing by cumulative increments the knowledge based on shared paradigms (more or less coherent sets of assumptions and imageries). Thus, Kuhn does not reject the long-standing conception that science grows mainly by increments, although his principal concern is to demonstrate that this is far from the whole story. But any reading of his work inferring that the accumulation of knowledge certified by the community of scientists is simply a myth would be flagrantly at odds with the historical record.

The view that much of science develops by accumulation of knowledge, though marked by mistaken forays, garden paths or temporary retrogressions, implies that most new ideas and findings have been anticipated or adumbrated. At any given time, there are approximations to what is soon to develop more fully. A suitable vocabulary is needed to designate varying degrees of resemblance between earlier and later formulations of scientific ideas and findings. We have examined one extreme: prediscoveries and rediscoveries, which involve substantive identity or functional equivalence. Anticipations refer to somewhat less of a resemblance, in which the earlier formulations overlap the later ones but do not focus upon and draw out the same set of implications. Adumbrations refer to an even smaller resemblance, in which earlier formulations have, quite literally, merely foreshadowed later ones, i.e. have only dimly and vaguely approximated the subsequent ideas, with practically none of their specific implications having been drawn and followed up.

The basic distinction between rediscovery and anticipations or adumbrations has been captured in Whitehead's apothegm affixed to the masthead of this chapter: "But to come very near to a true theory, and to grasp its precise application, are two very different things, as the history of science teaches us. Everything of importance has been said before by somebody who did not discover it." Whitehead would have been the first to appreciate the historical irony that in making this observation, he was anticipated though not preempted. The mathematician, logician and historian of ideas, Augustus de Morgan, for one example, had noted a generation before that "There has hardly ever been a great discovery in science, without its having happened that the germs of it have been found in the writings of several contemporaries or predecessors of the man who actually made it."[32] It required another masterful theorist using

32. Augustus de Morgan, *Essays on the Life and Work of Newton* (Chicago and London: The Open Court Publishing Co., 1914), 18. And for a later example, see the observation by today's dean of American psychologists, Edwin G. Boring, *A History of Experimental Psychology* (New York: Appleton-Century-Crofts, Inc., 1950, 2nd ed.), 4. "Nearly all great discoveries have had their anticipations which the historian digs up afterward."

near-Freudian figures of speech, to pin down a decisive difference between pre-discovery and anticipation: the one but not the other consists of pursuing an idea or finding seriously enough to make its implications evident.[33]

But historians of ideas often neglect these basic distinctions. The great frequency of genuine rediscoveries sometimes leads them to relax the standards of substantive identity or functional equivalence and to announce as "rediscoveries" formulations that were only dimly sensed in the past; at the extreme, historians dispense with such standards altogether and play the game of finding "anticipations" and "prediscoveries" all over the lot. This tendency to exaggerate the similarities and neglect the differences between earlier and later formulations is an occupational disease that afflicts many historians of ideas.

The newer historians of science, deeply disillusioned with the proclivity of their predecessors for conjuring up anticipations and adumbrations in the more exact sciences, may angrily deny the comparative diagnosis, but in fact the disease seems even more widespread and more acute among historians of the social sciences. The reasons for this are not hard to find. Take the history of sociology—an example that understandably interests us here. Through the generations, most sociological writing (including this introduction) has been in the style of the scientific essay. Unlike the long-established format of papers in the physical and biological sciences, it has only recently become established practice for papers in sociology to set out a compact statement of the problem, the procedures and instruments of investigation, the empirical findings, a discussion of these, and the theoretical implications of what was found.[34] Past sociological papers and particularly books were written in a style in which the basic concepts were seldom strictly defined, while the logic of procedure and the relationships between variables and the specific theory being developed remained largely implicit, in keeping with the long-established humanist tradition. This practice has had two consequences:

---

33. It is symbolically apt for Freud to have put the issue in this language: "I am well aware that it is one thing once or twice, or even oftener, to give words to an idea that comes in the form of a fleeting inspiration, and quite another to intend it seriously, to take it literally, to pursue it in spite of all difficulties into every detail and to win it a place among accepted truths. It is the difference between a casual flirtation and solemn matrimony with all its duties and difficulties. 'To be wedded to an idea' is not an uncommon figure of speech." Sigmund Freud, "On the history of the psycho-analytic movement," first published in 1914 and reprinted in *Collected Papers, op. cit.*, I, 287-359 at 296. This deeply personal essay devoted to the history of an idea is chock-full of observations germane to our immediate subject.

34. To keep the record straight, we are *not* saying or implying that the use of this format for sociological papers ensures their significance. Some papers that do adopt the format succeed only in demonstrating clearly that they are inconsequential, just as other papers that retain the style of the scientific essay sometimes manage to convey far more of consequence for our understanding of man in society. The issue here is not the relative scientific merit of differing styles of sociological writing but the attributes of the sociological essay that encourage historians of sociology to read anticipations and adumbrations into its development.

First, underlying basic concepts and ideas easily slip from view since they are not expressly tagged or defined and so some of them are in fact later rediscovered. Second, the vagueness of earlier formulations tempts the historian of ideas into easy identifications of prediscoveries in cases where closer analysis finds only dim and inconsequential resemblance.

These ambiguities place upon historians of ideas the heavy burden of distinguishing between genuine anticipations and pseudo-anticipations, in which resemblance is typically confined to an incidental use of some of the same words as the later version, infused by the historian with meanings drawn from later knowledge. The distinction between genuine and pseudo-anticipations is anything but clearcut: Yet if the historian gives way to indolence and allows any degree of resemblance between old and new formulations to pass as anticipations, he is in fact writing the mythology of ideas, not their history.

As with prediscoveries, presumptive evidence of a genuine anticipation is provided when the later scientist himself maintains that others before him have set forth certain aspects of his idea. Thus, Gordon Allport decisively formulated the principle of functional autonomy: that forms of behavior become, under specifiable conditions, ends or goals in themselves, although they were begun for some other reason. The essential point is that behavior can maintain itself even though it is not reinforced by the originating drive or motive. When Allport first formulated this influential and, in some quarters, controversial conception,[35] he was quick to indicate earlier intimations of it: Woodworth's observation that psychological mechanisms may be transformed into drives; Stern's observation that phenomotives can become transformed into genomotives; Tolman's observation that "means-objects" may "set up in their own right." These qualify as anticipations rather than prediscoveries since the earlier versions overlapped the later one only in part and, more significantly, they did not draw out many of the logical implications and empirical manifestations expressly stated by Allport. That is why Allport's formulation changed the course of the history of functional autonomy whereas the anticipations did not. This sort of difference is lost in histories of ideas that are primarily concerned with allocating 'credit' for contributions, for they tend to merge prediscoveries and anticipations into a shapeless blur. In contrast, histories of ideas that are primarily concerned with reconstructing the actual course of scientific development take note of the crucial difference between early approximations to an idea and later formulations that leave their mark on that idea's development by inducing their authors or others to follow them up systematically.

35. Gordon W. Allport, "The functional autonomy of motives," *American Journal of Psychology,* 1937, 50, 141-56. Allport's references to anticipations have been noted by Calvin S. Hall and Gardner Lindzey, *Theories of Personality* (New York: John Wiley & Sons, 1957), 270-1.

When a scientist comes upon an early and forgotten formulation, pauses to find it instructive and *then himself follows it up,* we have an authentic case of historical continuity of ideas, despite the lapse of some years. But contrary to the story-book version of scientific inquiry, this pattern seems to be infrequent. What is more common is that an idea is formulated definitely enough and emphatically enough that it cannot be overlooked by contemporaries, and it then becomes easy to find anticipations or adumbrations of it. But what is decisive for a theory of the history of ideas is the fact that these earlier intimations remain in oblivion and are not systematically followed up by anyone until the new and temporarily definitive formulation brings them back into the limelight.

Identifications of prediscoveries, anticipations, and adumbrations may be prompt or delayed. The prompt discoveries come about through the sheer number of lookouts in the social system of scientists or scholars. When a newly formulated idea or empirical finding is published, there is likely to be a handful of scientists who have already run across the earlier version of the idea, although they did not employ it in their work. When their memory of this earlier version is activated by the new formulation, these scientists then report the prediscovery, anticipation, or adumbration to others in the system. (The pages of the journal *Science* are peppered with letters to the scientific fraternity that exemplify this pattern.)

Delayed identification occurs when the earlier version had quickly sunk into oblivion. Perhaps it had been published in some obscure journal, or tucked away in a paper on another subject, or confined to an unpublished laboratory notebook, journal or letter. A discovery is for a time regarded as altogether new by contemporaries. But once they are thoroughly familiar with this new idea, some scientists or scholars will recognize formulations that resemble the new one as they *subsequently* reread earlier works. It is in this sense that the past history of a science is continually being recast by its subsequent history.

Allport's formulation of functional autonomy as a psychological principle exemplifies the second pattern of discovery. Now that Allport has impressed the principle upon us, we are alerted to any version of it as we read writings of an earlier day. Thus, thanks to Allport, I can report in re-reading J. S. Mill that he had intimated the same principle back in 1865: "It is only when our purposes have become independent of the feelings of pain or pleasure from which they originally took their rise, that we are said to have a confirmed character."[36] The point is, however, that I had not paused over Mill's observation when I had first encountered it since I was not then sensitized by acquaintance with Allport's formulation. Or I can report that in 1908 Simmel had anticipated Allport's principle in sociological terms:

---

36. John Stuart Mill, *A System of Logic* (London: Longmans, Green, 1865), 423.

It is a fact of the greatest sociological importance that innumerable relationships preserve their sociological structure unchanged, even after the feeling or practical occasion, which originally gave rise to them, has ended. . . . The rise of a relationship, to be sure, requires a certain number of positive and negative conditions, and the absence of even one of them may, at once, preclude its development. Yet once started, it is by no means always destroyed by the subsequent disappearance of that condition which earlier, it could not have overcome. What has been said of [political] states—that they are maintained only the means by which they are founded—is only a very incomplete truth, and anything but an all-pervasive principle of sociation generally. Sociological connectedness, no matter what its origin, develops a self-preservation and autonomous existence of its form that are independent of its initially connecting motives.[37]

Both Mill's and Simmel's formulations represent authentic anticipations of Allport's principle. They explicitly state part of the same idea, they do not apply the idea sufficiently to impress it upon their contemporaries (this, despite Simmel's characterization of it as "a fact of the greatest sociological importance") and, most of all, their earlier formulations were not picked up and developed in the interval between their enunciation and Allport's statement of functional autonomy. Indeed, had they been followed up in that interval, Allport would have had no occasion to formulate the principle; at most, he would simply have amplified it.

This case provides a parable for the appropriate treatment of anticipations in the history of ideas. Coming upon the Mill and Simmel anticipations after having become alerted to them by the Allport formulation, the authentic historian of ideas would at once identify the crucial historical problem: why were the earlier intimations neglected by the authors, their contemporaries and immediate successors? He would note that there was no *immediate* and inexorable progression of this idea, just as he would note its eventual re-emergence as a focus of empirical research. This historian would try to identify the intellectual and social contexts within which the idea appeared in its earlier form and the changes in those contexts that gave added weight to it in its later and more developed form. He would, in short, attend to both the similarities *and* the differences (1) among the several formulations of the idea, (2) in the extent to which it fit into other theoretical constructions of the time, and (3) in the contexts which affected its historical fate.

But as we know, historians of sociology commonly fall far short of these austere requirements for analyzing anticipations and adumbrations. Often, they appear to take pleasure—sometimes, being human, a perverse pleasure—in digging up anticipations, real or fancied, of recently formu-

---

37. George Simmel, *Soziologie* (Leipzig: Duncker & Humblot, 1908), 582-3, faithfully translated by Kurt H. Wolff in *The Sociology of Georg Simmel* (New York: The Free Press, 1950), 380-1.

lated conceptions. This self-contained task is not difficult, as a few illustrations show:

The Primary Group. As is well known, Cooley's formulation of the primary group in 1909 left an immediate and lasting impression on the sociological analysis of group life. Some years later, an historian of sociology called attention to the appearance in the same year of a book by Helen Bosanquet which dealt with the interaction among members of the family as a social process influencing the personality of each member. The historian goes on to note that Small and Vincent had, in 1894, entitled a chapter of their *Introduction to the Study of Society,* "The Primary Social Group: The Family." Later on, however, the biographer of Cooley reviewed the entire matter and significantly concluded that "Labels are one thing; generally accepted contents for them are another. Cooley gave the concept meaningful content; this is the important thing." Even more to the point, he adds that it was Cooley's formulation, not the others, that generated much study and research on the primary group. Alerted by Cooley's influential formulation, we can now note that the *term* "primary group" ("primäre Masse") was independently and briefly introduced in 1921 by Freud who, from all available evidence, was unacquainted with the existence of Cooley.[38] But Cooley's conception was a much more significant seedbed of sociological research and inquiry than was Freud's term "primary group."

The Looking-glass Self: Cooley's classic formulation of this concept designates the social process through which our self-images are shaped by perceptions of other people's imagery of us. As is well known, because Cooley himself tells us so, this formulation amplified the earlier conceptions advanced by the psychologists William James and James Mark Baldwin. We see here a clear instance of cumulative increments in theory that have continued to the present day. As is less well-known, recent research in the Soviet Union on the development of self and socialization is derived from a remark by Marx that in understanding one's self, each person looks at another as a mirror. As was evidently unknown both in Kiev and in Ann Arbor, Adam Smith had adopted the metaphor of a mirror formed from the opinions of us held by others that enables us to become the spectators of our own behavior. In Smith's words:

38. As is now well known from Cooley's own testimony, the discussion of the primary group in his *Social Organization* was introduced only as an after-thought and did not appear in the original draft at all. The historian who notes simultaneous independent discussions of the idea and an anticipation of the term is Floyd N. House, *The Range of Social Theory* (New York: Holt, 1929), 140-1. Cooley's biographer who, in the course of his defense, hits upon salient aspects of anticipations for the history of thought is Edward C. Jandy, *Charles Horton Cooley: His Life and His Social Theory* (New York: The Dryden Press, 1942), 171-81. Freud's use of the term and the partial overlap of his conception with Cooley's will be found in his *Massenpsychologie und Ich-Analyse* (Leipzig, Wien, Zurich: Internationaler Psychoanalytischer Verlag, 1921), 76, as follows: "Eine solche primäre Masse ist eine Anzahl von Individuen, die ein und dasselbe Objekt an die Stelle ihres Ichideals gesetzt und sich infolgedessen in ihrem Ich miteinander identifiziert haben" (all this in print spaced out for emphasis). And since the English translation by James Strachey substitutes the word 'group' throughout the translation for the "rather more comprehensive German 'Masse', this passage emerges, without any intent to ape Cooley, as "A primary group of this kind is a number of individuals who have substituted one and the same object for their ego ideal and have consequently identified themselves with one another in their ego." The term "primary group" is Cooley's, but the distinctive theoretical formulation is unmistakably Freud's.

"This is the only looking-glass by which we can in some measure, with the eyes of other people, scrutinize the propriety of our own conduct." Extending the metaphor almost in the language of William James, Leslie Stephen writes at the end of the last century that "we have to take into account not merely the primary but the secondary reflections; and, indeed, we must imagine two opposite mirrors, reflecting images in indefinite succession." Here, on the face of it, are multiple independent formulations of the idea in quite different theoretical traditions. But these episodes are merely the raw material for analysis of the evolution of an idea, not an end-point at which the multiple, partly overlapping versions of the idea simply happened to occur.[39]

I offer a number of swiftly assembled, undeveloped allusions to prediscoveries, anticipations, adumbrations and pseudo-anticipations in sociology and psychology in order to make the double point that (1) these are easy enough to come by and (2) they easily degenerate into an antiquarianism that does not advance the *history* of sociological theory at all but merely duplicates that battle between advocates of the Ancients and the Moderns which used up so much intellectual energy in the seventeenth and eighteenth centuries:

Shakespeare ostensibly anticipating Freud on wishful thinking and rationalization in Henry IV: "thy wish was father, Harry, to that thought."

Epictetus, to say nothing of Schopenhauer and many others, presumably anticipating what I have described as the Thomas Theorem that men's definitions of situations affect their consequences: "What disturbs and alarms man are not the things, but his opinions and fancies about the things."[40]

Sumner ostensibly anticipating Lippmann's concept of stereotypes when he writes, in the *Folkways*, that the mores "are stereotyped."

Spencer writing that "the attraction of cities is directly as the mass and inversely as the distance," and so ostensibly anticipating Stouffer's theory of intervening opportunities—another wholly verbal rather than substantive similarity.

Veblen's notion of "trained incapacity" (picked up, developed and applied by later sociologists), ostensibly anticipated by Philip Hamerton in his long-forgotten book published in 1873, when he writes of "mental refusals" [inhibitions] as indicating "no congenital incapacity, but [only] that the mind

39. Cooley's still enduring formulation appeared in his *Human Nature and the Social Order* (New York: Scribner, 1902), 183-4. Jandy, *op. cit.*, 108-26, reconstructs Cooley's extension of the idea and George Mead's extension in turn. The independent source of the idea in Marx was attested by the social psychologists at the Institute of Psychology in Kiev who knew their Marx well but had heard nothing of Cooley and Mead (based on interviews by Henry Riecken and myself in 1961). Leslie Stephen picked up Adam Smith's metaphor in his *History of English Thought in the Eighteenth Century* (New York: G. P. Putnam's Sons, 1902, 3d ed.), I, 74-75.

40. Born in the same year and ultimately finding their way to the lively atmosphere of sociological inquiry that marked the University of Chicago in the first third of this century, W. I. Thomas and George H. Mead use almost identical language in formulating the theorem—Thomas in general terms, Mead in a more restricted way. Thus Thomas say, "If men define situations as real, they are real in their consequences." Mead says, "If a thing is not recognized as true, then it does not function as true in the community." *Movements of Thought in the Nineteenth Century* (University of Chicago Press, 1936), 29.

has been incapacitated by its acquired habits and its ordinary occupations" thus producing an "acquired unfitness." (*The Intellectual Life*)

John Stuart Mill anticipating in a general rule the specific case of the Hawthorne effect, identified a century later: in experiments, "the effect may have been produced not by the change, but by the means employed to produce the change. The possibility, however, of this last supposition generally admits of being conclusively tested by other experiments."

Aristotle adumbrating G. H. Mead's concept of "significant others" when he writes in *Rhetoric* that "the people before whom we feel shame are those whose opinion of us matters to us . . . etc. . ."

A specific example of the self-fulfilling prophecy set forth in the seventeenth century by the French philosopher and scientist, Pierre Gassendi, who argued that astrological predictions about the fate of individuals contribute to their own realization by their stimulating or depressing effect upon these individuals.

As an example of the broad class of cases in which it is alleged that proverbs fully capture widely adopted sociological ideas, the case of the reflected self-image adopted by a deviant ensuing in deviant behavior: "call one a thief and he will steal."

This quickly assembled collection of instances, which any literate sociologist could multiply at will, only shows the ease with which actual or seeming anticipations and adumbrations can be identified as soon as a theoretical idea or empirical finding is set forth. Such attributions do not make for an understanding of the historical development of thought. Like the investigation of multiple discoveries in the physical and biological sciences, fruitful historical inquiry requires detailed analysis both of the theoretical substance of the earlier and later versions *and* of the conditions making for observed continuities or discontinuities of thought. An excellent example of such inquiry is J. J. Spengler's painstaking examination of Lovejoy's claim that Mandeville's *Fable of the Bees* (1714) had fully anticipated all of Veblen's principal ideas advanced in *The Theory of the Leisure Class*.[41] Rather than taking superficial resemblance as evidence enough, Spengler subjects the two sets of ideas to thoroughgoing analysis, thus exhibiting the profound differences as well as the occasional similarities between them. In doing so, he shows how initially small but functionally consequential differences of formulation eventuate in different theoretical implications which are then followed up and developed by successors.

3. *Adumbrationism.* The identification of prediscoveries, anticipations, or adumbrations discussed in the preceding section is built into the information channels of the social system of science and scholarship; no concentrated effort is made to unearth them. *Adumbrationism,* however, refers to the dedicated, deliberate search for all manner of earlier versions of scientific or scholarly ideas. At the extreme, the adumbra-

41. J. J. Spengler, "Veblen and Mandeville Contrasted," *Weltwirtschaftliches Archiv: Zeitschrift des Instituts für Weltwirtschaft an der Universität Kiel,* 1959, 82, 3-67.

tionist describes the faintest shadow of resemblance between earlier and later ideas as virtual identity.

The sources of this motivated search vary greatly. In some cases, it appears to come from a commitment to proving that there is really nothing new under the sun. The quest then presents the profoundly human spectacle of scholars and scientists arguing that everything of consequence must have been discovered before, while each is sedulously trying to make new discoveries designed to advance his discipline.[42] In other cases, the search is sparked by chauvinistic allegiances. When a new formulation is set forth by a scientist of an alien nationality or an alien school of thought or, more generally, by a member of *any* outgroup, the adumbrationist is motivated to find some seeming anticipation or foreshadowing in an intellectually congenial ancestor in order to restore the appropriate distribution of honor within the system. In still other cases, the search seems to be motivated by hostility toward the contemporary discoverer who will presumably be taken down quite a few pegs by being confronted with adumbrations of his proclaimed new contribution. But adumbrationism becomes most pronounced when it is institutionalized in the creed-and-practice of downgrading the "Moderns" in favor of the "Ancients," of taking from the quick and giving to the dead.[43]

Whatever the motives of the adumbrationist, which at best can only be most tentatively inferred from his writings, the observable pattern remains much the same. In fact adumbrationism can be expressed in the form of a credo:

> The discovery is not true;
> If true, it is not new;
> If both new and true, it is not significant.

Victims of the adumbrationist and detached observers of his behavior have both identified variations of this set of canons. Often scarred by the broadsides of the adumbrationist, William James brought himself to describe "the classic stages of a theory's career": it is first "attacked as absurd; then it is admitted to be true, but obvious and insignificant; finally it is seen to be so important that its adversaries claim that they themselves discovered it."[43] Again, provoked by the "misunderstanders" of his pragmatist account of truth, James plaintively protested the insincerity of the opposition "which has already begun to express itself in

---

42. Scholars and scientists, like other men, often engage in behavior that denies the very assumptions they are trying to confirm. Whitehead refers to a behaviorist in the 1920s who announced that his purpose was to demonstrate that purpose has no significant part in human behavior.

43. The Battle of the Ancients and Moderns is of notoriously long duration. The report on this senseless battle-turned-into-interminable-war with which I am most closely familiar is that by Merton, *On the Shoulders of Giants*.

43. William James, *Pragmatism: A New Name for Some Old Ways of Thinking* (New York: Longmans, Green, 1907), 198.

the stock phrase that 'what is new is not true, and what is true not new' . . . If we said nothing in any degree new, why was our meaning so desperately hard to catch? [And then, in a masterful understatement] The blame cannot be laid wholly upon our obscurity of speech, for in other subjects we have attained to making ourselves understood."[44]

While victims hotly protest adumbrationism, historians of science coolly observe it. So, George Sarton, in his recent time the dean among the world's historians of science, observed that

> violent objection to a discovery, especially to one which is as disturbing as it is great, generally passes through two stages. The first stage is that of denial, best represented by the Parisian anti-circulators: Harvey's theory is wrong, it is plain nonsense, etc. When that position becomes untenable, the second stage begins: The discovery is all right, but Harvey did not make it; it was made by many other people before him. . . It was Van der Linden's originality, as the foremost Hippocratist of his day, to claim . . . 'There cannot be the shadow of a doubt that the circulation of the blood was known to Hippocrates!' This is a good illustration of the philological mind at work, mistaking words for realities.[45]

The adumbrationist is also at work in the humanities, where he has been given the harsh-sounding title of *Quellenforscher* (or source-hunter). Saintsbury has identified a fitting representative of the breed: Gerard Langbaine, "the somewhat famous author of the *Account of the English Dramatic Poets.*" The English critic does not maintain even a semblance of detachment in his pen-portrait of the French adumbrationist:

> Having some reading and a good memory, he discovers that poets do not as a rule invent their matter, and it seems to him a kind of victory over them to point out where they got it. As a mere point of history there is of course nothing to object to in this: it is sometimes interesting, and need never be offensive. But, as a matter of fact, it too often is made so, and is always made so in Langbaine. . . 'Had Mr. W. put on his spectacles he would have found it printed thus.' &c., &c. . . I am afraid that Dante, if he had known Langbaine, would have arranged a special *bolgia* for him; and it would not have lacked later inhabitants.[46]

Adumbrationism in the humanities and the physical sciences has its emphatic counterpart in the social sciences. Adumbrationism in sociology

---

44. William James, *The Meaning of Truth: A Sequel to 'Pragmatism'* (New York: Longmans, Green, 1909), 181.

45. George Sarton, "Johannes Antonides Vander Linden (1609-1664) Medical Writer and Bibliographer," in *Science, Medicine and History: Essays on the Evolution of Scientific Thought and Medical Practice, Written in Honour of Charles Singer,* collected and edited by E. Ashworth Underwood (London: Oxford University Press, 1953), II, 15. For just one other example of this pattern described by an historian, see A. R. Hall, *The Scientific Revolution, 1500-1800* (London: Longmans, Green, 1954), 255 ff. which outlines the reception of Newton's theory of light in much the same series of stages.

46. George Saintsbury, *A History of Criticism and Literary Taste in Europe from the Earliest Texts to the Present Day* (Edinburgh and London: William Blackwood & Sons, 1909), II, 400-1.

for example has its own roots. Although we lack comparative monographic studies, the early modern development of sociology does not seem in fact to be as cumulative as that of the physical and life sciences.[47] The predilection in the nineteenth century and, in some quarters, today for sociologists to develop their own "systems of sociology" means that these are typically laid out as competing systems of thought rather than consolidated into a cumulative product. This tendency diverts attention from historical analysis of the development of theory toward showing that the allegedly new system is not new after all. The history of ideas then becomes an arena for claims and counter-claims to a kind of originality that is uncharacteristic of the growth of science. The less marked the degree of accumulation, the greater the tendency to search for similarities between past and present thought and, by easy extension, to end up in adumbrationism.

Histories of sociology move in and out of this shadowy realm. To a varying extent,[48] they oscillate between the two basic assumptions we have described about how sociology develops: on one side adumbrationism; on the other, the position that sociology grows through occasional new orientations and through increments of knowledge gained through inquiry guided by these orientations—sometimes involving *documented* prediscoveries, anticipations, and adumbrations.

Perhaps no other historian of sociological theory has addressed himself as thoroughly to the matter of prediscoveries, anticipations, and adumbrations as Pitirim A. Sorokin, in his massive work, *Contemporary Sociological Theories*,[49] still in active use forty years after its first publication. Organized by schools of sociological thought and designed "to connect the present sociology with its past," the book prefaces its account of each school with a list of precursors. Possibly because it refers in varying detail to more than a thousand authors, the book deploys widely differing criteria of identity between earlier and later ideas.

---

47. We are *not* suggesting that the model of development in the physical and life sciences is one of steady, inexorable continuity and cumulation. The history of these sciences is of course marked by many rediscoveries coming years or even generations after the prediscovery was lost to view. But such breaks in continuity, subsequently repaired by independent rediscoveries that alert observers to earlier forgotten versions, are less frequent and less consequential there than in the social sciences.

48. A methodical analysis of the following contemporary histories of sociological theory reveals great variability in this respect: N. S. Timasheff, *Sociological Theory: Its Nature and Growth* (New York: Doubleday & Co., 1955); Dan Martindale, *The Nature and Types of Sociological Theory* (Boston: Houghton Mifflin Co., 1960); Harry E. Barnes and Howard Becker, *Social Thought from Lore to Science* (Washington: Harran Press, 1952, 2nd ed.); Charles P. Loomis and Zona K. Loomis, *Modern Social Theorists* (New York: D. Van Nostrand, 1961); Harry Elmer Barnes, ed. *An Introduction to the History of Sociology* (Chicago: University of Chicago Press, 1948); Lewis A. Coser and Bernard Rosenberg, *Sociological Theory* (New York: Macmillan, 1964, 2d ed.).

49. New York and London: Harper & Brothers, 1928.

At one extreme are the assertions that ancient writings—the *Sacred Books of the East*, Confucius, Taoism, etc.—contain "all the essentials" of ideas found in contemporary sociologistic or psychological schools; the latter are described as "mere repetition" or as "nothing but" repetition. (*e.g.* pp. 5n, 26n, 309, 436–7). In part, resemblances consist of references in the earlier classics to certain 'factors' in social life that are also discussed in later works: for example, the *Sacred Books* "stress the role" played by "the factors of race, selection and heredity" (p. 219); "the fact that since immemorial times thinkers were aware of the important role played by 'economic factors' in human behavior, social organization, social processes. . . ." (p. 514), *etc.* In part, the observation that a school of thought is very old becomes invidious. Thus, the formal school (Simmel, Tönnies, von Wiese) claiming to be new, is described "as a very old school, perhaps even older than any other school of social science" (p. 495); the economic school, chiefly the repudiated ideas of Marx and Engels, is described "as old as human thought itself" (p. 523); while the psycho-sociologistic "theory that belief, especially a magical or religious belief, is the most efficient factor in human destiny is perhaps the oldest form of social theory" (p. 662).

Also embedded in Sorokin's book, on the other hand, is the conception that these ancient ideas were significantly developed in later works, which are not "mere repetition." This is expressed in ambivalent observations of the following kind: ". . . neither Comte, nor Winiarsky, nor anybody else among the sociologists of the end of the nineteenth century, can claim the privilege of originating the above, or *practically any other theory.* They have *only* been *developing* that which was known many centuries, even thousands of years ago." (p. 368n, italics inserted). Or again: the sociologistic school, "like almost all contemporary sociological systems, originated in the remote past. Since that time *with variations* the principles of the school may be traced throughout the history of social thought." (p. 437; italics inserted).

This transitional formulation allows the possibility of significant new departures in the history of sociological thought. Thus, E. De Roberty is described as "one of the earliest pioneers in sociology" (p. 438); Kovalevsky "elaborated his [demographic] theory independently from Loria three years earlier" (p. 390n); the brilliant Tarde "left many *original* plans, ideas and theories" (p. 637); recent studies of public opinion "have clarified our knowledge of the phenomena to a considerable degree" (p. 706); Giddings is a "pioneer of American and world sociology" (p. 727n); and, as a final example of incremental development, "social physiology . . . in this way, step by step, . . . has been broadened, and at the present moment we are at the beginnings of the first attempts to construct a general, but factual theory of social mobility." (p. 748)

This tendency to discrminate among degrees of resemblance between older and more recent theories becomes much more marked in Sorokin's companion volume, *Sociological Theories of Today*,[50] published a generation later. Some of what were described as prediscoveries in the earlier work are now treated in effect as anticipations, and previously identified anticipations, as adumbrations. The new work remains as adamantly critical as its predecessor, but it nevertheless conveys, with occasional backsliding, a sense of growth and development in theory. Two instances, highlighted by italics, illustrate this shift in perspective.

Spengler and Danilevsky: From Prediscovery to Anticipation

Thus were O. Spengler's theories anticipated by half a century. Indeed, *in all its essential characteristics* Spengler's work is a *mere repetition* of the social speculations of Leontieff and Danilevsky [and since Danilevsky preceded Leontieff by four years, presumably Leontieff's work too is a "mere repetition."] (*Contemporary Sociological Theories*, p. 26n, italics added.)

As a "mere repetition," Spengler's work would seem superfluous, having nothing to distinguish it from the work of predecessors. But Sorokin's later and more discriminating judgment indicates otherwise:

Spengler's *Der Untergang des Abendlandes*, published in 1918, has proved to be one of the most influential, controversial, and durable masterpieces of the first half of the twentieth century in the fields of cultural sociology, the philosophy of history, and German philosophy. Though in its total character *The Decline of the West* is *quite different* from Danilevsky's work, nevertheless its basic conceptual framework resembles Danilevsky's in all important points. . . . The many pages that Spengler devotes to a detailed analysis of these transformations [in the cycle of social forms or systems] are *fresh*, penetrating, and *classic*. . . Despite its defects, *The Decline of the West* is likely to survive as one of the most important works of the first half of the twentieth century. (*Sociological Theories of Today*, pp. 187, 196–7.)

Marx-Engels and their Predecessors: from Adumbrationism to Anticipation

As far as the originality and the content of the theory of Marx's materialistic conception of history is concerned (but not that of Marx's practical influence) at the present moment. . . there seems to be *no possibility to claim that Marx added any single new idea in this field or gave a new and scientifically better synthesis of the ideas which existed before him.* (*CST*, 520n; italics inserted)

In this earlier work Sorokin continues to reiterate that neither the specific ideas nor the synthesis of Marx and Engels had a shred of originality; he then concludes with the classic credo of the adumbrationist:

First, from a purely scientific point of view, so far as its sound elements are concerned, there is nothing in their theory that was not said by earlier authors; second, what is really original is far from being scientific; third, the only merit of the theory is that it in a somewhat stronger and exaggerated form generalized the ideas given before the time of Marx. . . . There is no reason even for

50. New York: Harper & Row, 1966.

regarding their scientific contributions as something above the average. (*CST*, 545).

In his later work, Sorokin, while still highly critical of Marxian theory and still properly insistent that it did not develop *ex nihilo*,[51] is ready to grant it a distinctive intellectual (and not merely a political) role.

> Karl Marx and Friedrich Engels, by their division of sociocultural relations into two main classes, the 'relations of production [which] constitute the economic structure of society,' and the 'ideological superstructure,' . . . gave a *new life and full development* to the economic variation of the dichotomic theories. Almost all recent theories of this kind represent *variations and elaborations* on the Marx-Engels division. . . . Marx's theory is in fact a prototype of all the other—later—theories surveyed. (*STT*, 289, 296; italics inserted)

If Sorokin's later book is an archetype, we may be witnessing a shift toward more discriminating conceptions of the development of sociological ideas. This is all to the good. If adumbrationism is scrapped, sociologists will be free to concentrate on identifying the *specific* respects in which newer developments of ideas build upon past ones in order to analyze the character and conditions of continuities in sociological knowledge.

HUMANISTIC AND SCIENTIFIC ASPECTS OF SOCIOLOGY

The contrast between the orientation of the sciences toward the great classical works and that of the humanities has often been noticed. It stems from profound differences in the kind of selective accumulation that takes place in civilization (which includes science and technology) and in culture (which includes the arts and value-configurations).[52] In

---

51. Marx's own theory of the historical development of science and thought, of course, assumes that *ex nihilo nihil fit*. As Marx put it in his well-known attempt to discriminate between the corpus of earlier thought and his own additions to it: ". . . no credit is due to me for discovering the existence of classes in modern society, nor yet the struggle between them. Long before me bourgeois historians had described the historical development of this class struggle and bourgeois economists, the economic anatomy of the classes. What I did that was new was to prove: (1) that the *existence of classes* is only bound up with *particular, historic phases in the development of production;* (2) that the class struggle necessarily leads to the *dictatorship of the proletariat;* (3) that this dictatorship itself only constitutes the transition to the *abolition of all classes* and to a *classless society*. . . ." In his letter to Joseph Wedemeyer, March 5, 1852, printed in Marx, *Selected Works* (Moscow: Co-operative Publishing Society, 1935), I, 377. We need not accept Marx's self-appraisal at face value; two of these three contributions were dubious projections into the future and, as the later Sorokin testifies, Marx contributed to more than the theory of social class. The point is that both the Marx letter and the later Sorokin try to discriminate between sheer rediscovery and analytical or synthetic increments that advance knowledge.

52. The distinction among processes of society, culture and civilization was emphasized by Alfred Weber, "Prinzipielles zur Kultursoziologie: Gesellschaftsprozess, Zivilisationsprozess und Kulturbewegung," *Archiv für Sozialwissenschaft und Sozialpolitik*, 1920, 47, 1-49. See the similar analysis by R. M. MacIver, *Society: Its Struc-*

the more exact sciences, the selective accumulation of knowledge means that classical contributions made by men of genius or great talent in the past are largely developed in later work, often by men of distinctly smaller talent.

The severest test of truly cumulative knowledge is that run-of-the-mill minds can solve problems today which great minds could not begin to solve earlier. An undergraduate student of mathematics knows how to identify and solve problems which defied the best powers of a Leibniz, Newton or Cauchy.[53]

Because the theory and findings of the fairly remote past are largely incorporated into cumulative present knowledge in the more exact sciences, commemoration of the great contributors of the past is substantially reserved to the history of the discipline; scientists at their workbenches and in their papers make use primarily of the more recent contributions, which have developed these earlier discoveries. The result of this practice is that earlier and often much weightier scientific contributions tend to be obliterated (though not without occasional and sometimes significant exceptions) by incorporation into later work.

In the humanities, by direct contrast, each classical work—each poem, drama, novel, essay, or historical work—tends to remain a part of the direct experience of succeeding generations of humanists. As Derek Price has put it in instructive imagery: "the cumulating structure of science has a texture full of short-range connexions like knitting, whereas the texture of a humanistic field of scholarship is much more of a random network with any point being just as likely to be connected with any other."[54] In short, firsthand acquaintance with classics plays a small role in the work of the physical and life scientists and a very large one in the work of humanistic scholars.

Kessler, another student of information systems in science, has put the point in deliberately provocative if not exasperating language:

---

ture and Changes (New York: Long & Smith, 1931), 225-36 and the later discussion by R. K. Merton, "Civilization and Culture," *Sociology and Social Research,* Nov.-Dec. 1936, 21, 103-113. And for an illustration of the tendency to blend the history and the systematics of theory, see brief reviews of the concepts "culture" and "civilization" as used by Herder, Humboldt, Guizot, E. Du Bois-Reymond, Wundt, Ferguson, Morgan, Tylor, Buckle, Gothein, etc. in the following works: Paul Barth, *Die Philosophie der Geschichte als Soziologie* (Leipzig: Reisland, 1922), 597-613; H. S. Stoltenberg, "Seele, Geist und Gruppe," *Schmollers Jahrbuch,* 1929, LV, 105 ff.; R. Eucken, *Geschichte und Kritik der Grundbegriffe der Gegenwart* (Leipzig: 1878), 187 ff. Sorokin provides a critical review of this framework of analysis in his *Sociological Theories of Today,* Chapter 10.

53. Charles C. Gillispie, *The Edge of Objectivity: An Essay in the History of Scientific Ideas* (Princeton University Press, 1960), 8. ". . . every college freshman knows more physics than Galileo knew, whose claim is higher than any other's to the honor of having founded modern science, and more too than Newton did, whose mind was the most powerful ever to have addressed itself to nature."

54. Derek J. de Solla Price, "The scientific foundations of science policy," *Nature,* April 17, 1965, 206, No. 4981, 233-8.

Even the masterpieces of scientific literature will in time become worthless except for historical reasons. This is a basic difference between the scientific and belletristic literature. It is inconceivable for a serious student of English literature, for example, not to have read Shakespeare, Milton and Scott. A serious student of physics, on the other hand, can safely ignore the original writings of Newton, Faraday and Maxwell.[55]

Kessler's language is designed to raise the hackles of the reader. And indeed, from the standpoint of humanism and the history of science, this statement appears to be an expression of latter-day barbarism. It is hard for many of us to distinguish our historical and commemorative interest in the pathbreaking works of science from our interest in advancing a contemporary science that requires little direct acquaintance with Newton's *Principia* or Lavoisier's *Traité*. Yet the same observation as Kessler's was eloquently advanced by one of the founding fathers of modern sociology. In language that personalizes the fateful process of incorporation and extension in science, Max Weber observes:

In science, each of us knows that what he has accomplished will be antiquated in ten, twenty, fifty years. That is the fate to which science is subject; it is the very *meaning* of scientific work, to which it is devoted in a quite specific sense, as compared with other spheres of culture for which in general the same holds. Every scientific 'fulfillment' raises new 'questions'; it *asks* to be 'surpassed' and outdated. Whoever wishes to serve science has to resign himself to this fact. Scientific works certainly can last as 'gratifications' because of their artistic quality, or they may remain important as a means of training. Yet they will be surpassed scientifically—let that be repeated—for it is our common fate and, more, our common goal. We cannot work without hoping that others will advance further than we have. In principle, this progress goes on *ad infinitum*.[56]

Sociologists, poised between the physical and life scientists and the humanists, are subject to cross-pressures in their orientation toward the classic contributions and do not take easily to the commitment described by Weber. Only a few sociologists adapt to these pressures by acting wholly the scientific role suggested by Weber or the humanistic one. Perhaps the majority oscillate between the two, and a few try to consolidate them. These efforts to straddle scientific and humanistic orientations typically lead to merging the systematics of sociological theory with its history.

That the social sciences stand between the physical sciences and the humanities in their cumulation of knowledge is dramatically confirmed by so-called citation studies which compare the distributions of dates of publications *cited* in the several fields. The findings are notably con-

55. M. M. Kessler, "Technical information flow patterns," *Proceedings,* Western Joint Computer Conference, May 9, 1961, 247-57.

56. Max Weber, *From Max Weber: Essays in Sociology,* translated and edited by H. H. Gerth and C. Wright Mills (New York: Oxford University Press, 1946), 138; the extract is, of course, from his enduring eloquent affirmation of "science as a vocation."

sistent. In the physical sciences—represented by such journals as *The Physical Review* and the *Astrophysical Journal*—some 60% to 70% of the citations refer to publications appearing within the preceding five years. In the humanities—represented by such journals as the *American Historical Review, Art Bulletin* and the *Journal of Aesthetics and Art Criticism*—the corresponding figures range from 10% to 20%. In between are the social sciences—represented by such journals as the *American Sociological Review*, the *American Journal of Sociology* and the *British Journal of Psychology*—where from 30% to 50% of the citations refer to publications of the preceding five years.[57] Other studies of citation patterns testify that these findings are typical in their main outlines.

In one way, sociology adopts the orientation and practice of the physical sciences. Research moves from the frontiers advanced by the cumulative work of past generations; sociology is, in this precise sense, historically short-sighted, provincial and effective. But in another way, sociology retains its kinship with the humanities. It is reluctant to abandon a firsthand acquaintance with the classical works of sociology and pre-sociology as an integral part of the experience of the sociologist *qua* sociologist. Every contemporary sociologist with a claim to sociological literacy has had direct and repeated encounters with the works of the founding fathers: Comte, Marx and Spencer, Durkheim, Weber, Simmel and Pareto, Sumner, Cooley and Veblen, and the rest of the short list of talented men who have left their indelible stamp on sociology today. Since I have long shared the reluctance to lose touch with the classics, even before finding a rationale for it, and since to a degree I continue to share it, this may be reason enough for speculating about its character and sources.

ERUDITION VERSUS ORIGINALITY

No great mystery shrouds the affinity of sociologists for the works of their predecessors. There is a degree of immediacy about much of the sociological theory generated by the more recent members of this distinguished lineage, and current theory has a degree of resonance to many of the still unsolved problems identified by the earlier forerunners.

However, interest in classical writings of the past has also given rise

57. I am indebted to Derek J. de Solla Price for access to his still-unpublished data based on 154 batches of journals in various fields. The abundance of citation studies includes: P. E. Burton and R. W. Keebler, " 'Half-life' of some scientific and technical literatures," *American Documentation*, 1960, 11, 18-22; R. N. Broadus, "An analysis of literature cited in the American Sociological Review," *American Sociological Review*, June 1952, 17, 355-6 and "A citation study for sociology," *The American Sociologist*, February 1967, 2, 19-20; Charles E. Osgood and Louis V. Xhignesse, "Characteristics of bibliographical coverage in psychological journals published in 1950 and 1960," Institute of Communications Research, University of Illinois, March 1963. Discriminating citation-studies must of course distinguish between citations to research studies and to 'raw data'—i.e. historical documents, poems and other literature of the distant past which humanists critically re-examine.

to intellectually degenerative tendencies in the history of thought. The first is an uncritical reverence toward almost any statement made by illustrious ancestors. This has often been expressed in the dedicated but, for science, largely sterile exegesis of the commentator. It is to this practice that Whitehead refers in the epigraph to this chapter: "A science which hesitates to forget its founders is lost." The second degenerative form is banalization. For one way a truth can become a worn and increasingly dubious commonplace is simply by being frequently expressed, preferably in unconscious caricature, by those who do not understand it. (An example is the frequent assertion that Durkheim assigned a great place to coercion in social life by developing his conception of 'constraint' as one attribute of social facts.) Banalization is an excellent device for drying up a truth by sponging upon it.

In short, the study of classical writings can be either deplorably useless or wonderfully useful. It all depends on the form that study takes. For a vast difference separates the anemic practices of mere commentary or banalization from the active practice of following up and developing the theoretical leads of significant predecessors. It is this difference that underlies the scientists' ambivalence toward extensive reading in past writings.

This ambivalence of scientists has historical and psychological roots. From the beginning of modern science, it was argued that scientists should know the work of their predecessors in order to build on what had gone before and to give credit where credit was due. Even the most vocal prophet of anti-scholasticism, Francis Bacon, took this for granted: "When a man addresses himself to discover something, he first seeks out and sees before him all that has been said about it by others; then he begins to meditate for himself. . . ."[58] This practice has since been institutionalized in the format of scientific papers which calls for a summary of the theory and investigations that bear upon the problems in hand. The rationale for this is as clear as it is familiar: ignorance of past work often condemns the scientist to discovering for himself what is already known. As Sorokin has put the case for our own field:

> Not knowing that a certain theory has been developed long ago, or that a certain problem has been carefully studied by many predecessors, a sociologist may easily devote his time and energy to the discovery of a new sociological America after it was discovered long ago. Instead of a comfortable crossing of the scientific Atlantic in the short period of time necessary for the study of what has been done before, such a sociologist has to undergo all the hardships of Columbus to find, only after his time and energy are wasted, that his discovery has been made long ago, and that his hardships have been useless. Such a finding is a tragedy for a scholar, and a waste of valuable ability for society and sociology.[59]

---

58. Francis Bacon, *Novum Organum* (London: George Routledge & Sons, n.d.) Aphorism LXXXII, page 105.

59. Sorokin, *Contemporary Sociological Theories,* xviii-xix.

The same case has often been stated for other fields of science. That genius of physics, Clerk Maxwell, (who had a deep avocational interest in the social science of his day) remarked early in his scientific career: "I have been reading old books of optics, and find many things in them far better than what is new. The foreign mathematicians are discovering for themselves methods which were well known at Cambridge in 1720, but are now forgotten."[60]

Since the policy and in part the practice of searching the antecedent literature have been long institutionalized in science, they require no further documentation. But the counter-emphasis—little institutionalized yet often put into practice—requires extensive documentation if we are to understand the ambivalence of scientists toward erudition.

Through at least the last four centuries, eminent men of science have warned of the alleged dangers of erudition. The historical roots of this attitude are embedded in the revolt against the scholasticism of the commentator and exegetist. Thus, Galileo gives his clarion call:

> . . . a man will never become a philosopher by worrying forever about the writings of other men, without ever raising his own eyes to nature's works in the attempt to recognize there the truths already known and to investigate some of the infinite number that remain to be discovered. This, I say, will never make a man a philosopher, but only a student of other philosophers and an expert in their works.[61]

William Harvey echoes this thought (in language that deeply impressed Clerk Maxwell, himself caught up in the ambivalence toward erudition):

> For whosoever they be that read authors, and do not, by the aid of their own senses, abstract true representations of the things themselves (comprehended in the author's expressions), they do not represent true ideas, but deceitful idols and phantasmas; by which means they frame to themselves certain shadows and chimaeras, and all their theory and contemplation (which they call science) represents nothing but waking men's dreams and sick men's phrensies.[62]

In due course, the ambivalence toward erudition was converted by some into a choice between scholarship and original scientific work. By the end of the seventeenth century, Temple, the defender of the Ancients, who knew of science only by hearsay, was prepared to satirize the Moderns on this score:

> If these speculations should be true, then I know not what advantages we can pretend to modern Knowledge, by any we receive from the Ancients. Nay, 'tis possible men may lose rather than gain by them, may lessen the Force

60. Lewis Campbell and William Garnett, *The Life of James Clerk Maxwell* (London: Macmillan and Co., 1884), 162.

61. *Le Opere di Galileo Galilei,* Edizione Nazione (Firenze: Tipographia di G. Barbèra, 1892), III, i. 395.

62. Campbell and Garnett, *op. cit.,* 277.

and Growth of their Genius by constraining and forming it upon that of others, may have less Knowledge of their own for contenting themselves with that of those before them. . . Besides who can tell whether learning may not even weaken Invention in a man that has great advantages from Nature and Birth, whether the weight and number of so many other mens thoughts and notion may not suppress his own, or hinder the motion and agitation of them from which all invention arises.[63]

What Temple, in his ample ignorance of scientists, thought laughable was taken quite seriously by great scientists of a later day. Their ambivalence toward erudition is expressed in so many words. For example, a Claude Bernard assumes that a man of science must know the work of his predecessors. But, he goes on to say, the reading of even such "useful scientific literature . . . must not be carried too far, lest it dry up the mind and stifle invention and scientific originality. What use can we find in exhuming worm-eaten theories or observations made without proper means of investigation?" In a word, "misconceived erudition has been, and still is, one of the greatest obstacles to the advancement of experimental science."[64]

Minds of the calibre of Bernard's could evidently handle this ambivalence with comparative ease by selectively reading the writings directly relevant to their own experimental and theoretical work. The mathematician, Littlewood, like Bernard himself, has coped with the problem by turning first to his own ideas and *then* checking on the antecedent literature before publishing his results.[65] In doing so, Bernard and Littlewood have come full circle to the practice advocated by savants and scientists of an earlier day.[66]

---

63. Sir William Temple's *Essays on Ancient and Modern Learning,* edited by J. E. Spingarn (Oxford: Clarendon Press, 1909), 18.

64. Claude Bernard, *An Introduction to the Study of Experimental Medicine* (New York: Henry Schuman, 1949; first published in 1865), 145, 141.

65. J. E. Littlewood, *A Mathematician's Miscellany* (London: Methuen Publishing Co., 1953), 82-3. "It is of course good policy, and I have often practised it, to *begin* without going too much into the existing literature." (italics inserted). Charles Richet, *The Natural History of a Savant,* trans. by Sir Oliver Lodge (New York: George H. Doran Co., 1927), 43-4, formulates the policy in these words: "The well-informed worker . . . may know too much about what has been printed by others to be truly original himself. Perhaps it would be better never to publish an experiment except after profound study of the appropriate bibliography, and yet not to encumber oneself with too much knowledge before experimenting."

66. Dr. E. Bernard in a letter to John Collins, 3 April 1671: "Books and experiments do well together, but separately they betray an imperfection, for the illiterate is anticipated unwittingly by the labours of the ancients, and the man of authors deceived by story instead of science." Stephen Peter Rigaud, ed. *Correspondence of Scientific Men of the 17th Century* (Oxford: at the University Press, 1841), I, 158. And on the interplay of erudition and personal observation, see the 17th and 18th century physician, John Freind: "Every physician will make and ought to make, observations from his own experience; but will be able to make a better judgment and juster observations by comparing what he reads and what he sees together. It is neither an affront to any man's understanding, nor a cramp to his genius, to say that both the one and the other may be usefully employed, and happily improved in searching and examining into the opinions and methods of those who lived before

Others have dealt with their ambivalence by largely abandoning the effort to become versed in the antecedent literature in order to get on with their own work. The social sciences have their own complement of such adaptations. Long ago, Vico was ready to quote with pleasure Hobbes' observation that if he had read as much as other men he would have known as little.[67] Herbert Spencer—of whom it can be said that never before had anyone written so much with so little knowledge of what others before him had written on the same wide range of subjects—elevated both his hostility toward authority and his illness (he was dizzied by reading) into a philosophy of investigation that gave little room to acquaintance with predecessors.[68] And Freud, repeatedly and quite self-consciously, maintained the policy of working up his clinical data and theory without recourse to antecedent work. As he put it on one occasion, "I am really very ignorant about my predecessors. If we ever meet up above they will certainly treat me ill as a plagiarist. But it is such a pleasure to investigate the thing itself instead of reading the literature about it." And again: "In later years I have denied myself the very great pleasure of reading the works of Nietzsche from a deliberate resolve not to be hampered in working out the impressions received in psychoanalysis by any sort of expectation derived from without. I have to be prepared, therefore—and am so, gladly—to forego all claim to priority in the many instances in which laborious psycho-analytic investigation can merely confirm the truths which this philosopher recognized intuitively."[69]

It was a founding father of sociology who managed to carry this sort of adaptation to the tension between erudition and originality to its inept extreme. During the dozen years he devoted to writing the *Course of Positive Philosophy*, Comte followed the "principle of cerebral hygiene"—he washed his mind clean of everything but his own ideas by the simple tactic of not reading anything even remotely germane to his subject. As he proudly put it in a letter to A. B. Johnson: "For my part, I read nothing except the great poets ancient and modern. The cerebral hygiene is exceedingly salutary to me, particularly in order to maintain

---

him, especially considering that no one is tied up from judging for himself, or obliged to give into the notions of any author, any further than he finds them agreeable to reason, and reducible to practice. No one therefore need fear that his natural sagacity, whatever it is, should be perplexed or misled by reading." *History of Physic* (London: 1725-6), I, 292.

67. *The Autobiography of Giambattista Vico*. Translated by Max Harold Fisch and Thomas Goddard Bergin (Ithaca, New York: Great Seal Books, 1963).

68. *Autobiography of Herbert Spencer*. (New York: D. Appleton & Co., 1904).

69. The first observation comes from Freud's letter to Pfister, 12 July 1909; the second from his "History of the Psychoanalytic Movement," *Collected Papers*, I, 297. Freud was prescient in supposing that all manner of anticipations of his work would later be dredged up; for a compilation of these, both remote and close, see Lancelot Law Whyte, *The Unconscious Before Freud* (New York: Basic Books, Inc., 1960).

the originality of my peculiar meditations."[70] Thus we find Comte making the ultimate—and, at this extreme, absurd—distinction between the history and the systematics of sociology; as historian of science, he tried to reconstruct the development of science through a relatively extensive reading of the classics, while as originator of the positivist *system* of sociological theory, he devoutly ignored immediately antecedent ideas—not least, those of his onetime master, Saint-Simon—in order to achieve a pickwickian kind of originality.

As we have seen, the historically recurring tension between erudition and originality is a problem yet to be solved. Since the seventeenth century, scientists have warned that erudition often encourages mere scholastic commentary on earlier writings instead of new empirical investigation and that a deep involvement with earlier ideas hobbles originality by producing inflexible sets of mind. But despite these dangers, great scientists have been able to combine erudition and original inquiry for the advancement of science either by reading only the immediately prior research devoted to their problem which presumably incorporates the relevant cumulative knowledge of the past, or by exploring more remote sources only after their inquiry has been brought to a head. However, an extreme effort to emancipate oneself from antecedent ideas—as made by Comte—can deteriorate into the conscientious neglect of all the pertinent theory of the past and an artificial distinction between the history and systematics of theory.

THE FUNCTIONS OF CLASSICAL THEORY

Not even a founding father should be allowed to caricature the fundamental difference we have been investigating between authentic history and the systematics of sociological theory. For the distinction we have been emphasizing resembles Comte's little or not at all. A genuine *history* of sociological theory must extend beyond a chronologically ordered set of critical synopses of doctrine; it must deal with the interplay between theory and such matters as the social origins and statuses of its exponents, the changing social organization of sociology, the changes that diffusion brings to ideas, and their relations to the environing social and cultural structure. We want now to sketch out some distinctive functions for systematic theory of a thorough grounding in the classical formulations of sociological theory.

The condition of the physical and life sciences remains considerably different from that of the social sciences and of sociology in particular. Though the physicist *qua* physicist has no need to steep himself in Newton's *Principia* or the biologist *qua* biologist to read and re-read Darwin's *Origin of Species*, the sociologist *qua* sociologist rather than

70. The letter was addressed to Alexander Bryan Johnson and is printed in the new edition of his remarkable *Treatise on Language*, ed. by David Rynin (Berkeley: University of California Press, 1959), 5-6.

as historian of sociology, has ample reason to study the works of a Weber, Durkheim, and Simmel and, for that matter, to turn back on occasion to the works of a Hobbes, Rousseau, Condorcet or Saint-Simon.

The reason for this difference has been examined here in detail. The record shows that the physical and life sciences have generally been more successful than the social sciences in retrieving relevant cumulative knowledge of the past and incorporating it in subsequent formulations. This process of obliteration by incorporation is still rare in sociology. As a result, previously unretrieved information is still there to be usefully employed as new points of departure. The present uses of past theory in sociology are still more complex as evidenced by the range of functions served by citations of classical theory.

One type of citation involves neither mere commentary on the classics nor the use of authority to establish credentials for current ideas. Instead this form of citation represents moments of affinity between our own ideas and those of our predecessors. More than one sociologist has had the self-deflating experience of finding that his independent discovery is unwittingly a *rediscovery*, and, moreover, that the language of the classical prediscovery, long lost to view, is so crisp, so eloquent, or so implicative as to make his own version only second-best. In the ambivalent state of misery over having been preempted and joy at the beauty of the earlier formulation, he cites the classical idea.

Differing only by a nuance are citations to classical writings that come about when the reader, stocked with his own ideas, finds in the earlier book precisely what he already had in mind. The idea, still hidden from other readers, is noted precisely because it is congenial to the reader who has developed it himself. It is often assumed that to cite an earlier source *necessarily* means that the idea or finding in that citation first came to mind upon the reading of it. Yet the evidence often indicates that the earlier passage is noted only because it agrees with what the reader has already developed on his own. What we find here is that unlikely sounding event: a dialogue between the dead and the living. These do not differ much from dialogues between contemporary scientists in which each is delighted as he discovers that the other agrees with what was until then an idea held in solitude and perhaps even suspect. Ideas take on new validity when they are independently expressed by another, either in print or in conversation. The only advantage of coming upon it in print is that one knows there has been no inadvertent contagion between the book or article and one's own prior formulation of the same idea.

Sociologists conduct "dialogues" with classical formulations in still another way. A contemporary sociologist often comes upon a discussion in the classics questioning an idea that he was ready to affirm as sound. Reflections that ensure are sobering. The later theorist, forced to consider that he just might be mistaken, re-examines his idea and if he finds it is in fact defective, reformulates it in a version that profits from the unrecorded dialogue.

A fourth function of the classics is that of providing a model for intellectual work. Exposure to such penetrating sociological minds as those of Durkheim and Weber helps us to form standards of taste and judgment in identifying a *good* sociological problem—one that has significant implications for theory—and to learn what constitutes an apt theoretical solution to the problem. The classics are what Salvemini liked to call *libri fecondatori*—books which sharpen the faculties of exacting readers who give them their undivided attention. It is this process, presumably, that led the great and youthful Norwegian mathematician Niels Abel, to record in his notebook: "It appears to me that if one wants to make progress in mathematics, one should study the masters and not the pupils."[71]

Finally, a classical sociological book or paper worth reading at all is worth re-reading periodically. For part of what is communicated by the printed page changes as the result of an interaction between the dead author and the live reader. Just as the *Song of Songs* is different when it is read at age 17 and at age 70, so Weber's *Wirtschaft und Gesellschaft* or Durkheim's *Suicide* or Simmel's *Soziologie* differ when they are read at various times. For, just as new knowledge has a retroactive effect in helping us to recognize anticipations and adumbrations in earlier work, so changes in current sociological knowledge, problems, and foci of attention enable us to find *new* ideas in a work we had read before. The new context of recent developments in our own intellectual life or in the discipline itself bring into prominence ideas or hints of ideas that escaped notice in an earlier reading. Of course, this process requires intensive reading of the classics—the kind of concentration evidenced by that truly dedicated scholar (described by Edmund Wilson) who, interrupted at his work by a knock on the door, opened it, strangled the stranger who stood there, and then returned to his work.

As an informal check on the potentially creative function of re-reading the classics, we need only examine the marginalia and notes we have taken on a classical work which has been read and then re-read years later. If the book has precisely the same things to say to us the second time, we are suffering from severe intellectual stagnation, or the classical work has less intellectual depth than has been attributed to it, or both unhappy conditions obtain.

What is a familiar experience in the intellectual life of the individual sociologist can become prevalent for entire generations of sociologists. For as each new generation accumulates its own repertoire of knowledge and thus becomes sensitized to new theoretical problems, it comes to

71. The extract from Abel's notebook is recorded in Oystein Ore, *Niels Henrik Abel: Mathematician Extraordinary* (Minneapolis: University of Minnesota Press, 1957), 138.

see much that is 'new' in earlier works, however often these works have been previously examined. There is much to be said for the re-reading of older works—particularly in an imperfectly consolidated discipline such as sociology—providing that this study consists of something more than that thoughtless mimicry through which mediocrity expresses its tribute to greatness. Re-reading an older work through new spectacles allows contemporary sociologists to find fresh perceptions that were blurred in the course of firsthand research and, as a result, to consolidate the old, half-formed insight with newly developing inquiry.

All apart from reading the masters for the purposes of writing a history of sociological theory, then, acquaintance and reacquaintance with the classics have a variety of functions. These range from the direct pleasure of coming upon an aesthetically pleasing and more cogent version of one's own ideas, through the satisfaction of independent confirmation of these ideas by a powerful mind, and the educative function of developing high standards of taste for sociological work to the interactive effect of developing new ideas by turning to older writings within the context of contemporary knowledge. Each function derives from the imperfect retrieval of past sociological theory that has not yet been fully absorbed in subsequent thought. For that reason, sociologists in our time must continue to behave unlike their contemporaries in the physical and life sciences and devote more of themselves to close familiarity with their not-so-distant classical predecessors. But if they are to be effective rather than merely pious, if they are to *use* earlier formulations of theory rather than simply commemorate them, they must distinguish between the scholastic practice of commentary and exegesis and the scientific practice of extending antecedent theory. And most important, sociologists must distinguish between the distinctive tasks of developing the history of sociological theory and developing its current systematics.

II ON SOCIOLOGICAL THEORIES OF THE MIDDLE RANGE

LIKE SO MANY WORDS that are bandied about, the word theory threatens to become meaningless. Because its referents are so diverse—including everything from minor working hypotheses, through comprehensive but vague and unordered speculations, to axiomatic systems of thought—use of the word often obscures rather than creates understanding.

Throughout this book, the term *sociological theory* refers to logically interconnected sets of propositions from which empirical uniformities can be derived. Throughout we focus on what I have called *theories of the middle range:* theories that lie between the minor but necessary working hypotheses that evolve in abundance during day-to-day research[1] and the all-inclusive systematic efforts to develop a unified theory that will explain all the observed uniformities of social behavior, social organization and social change.[2]

Middle-range theory is principally used in sociology to guide empirical inquiry. It is intermediate to general theories of social systems which are too remote from particular classes of social behavior, organization and change to account for what is observed and to those detailed orderly descriptions of particulars that are not generalized at all. Middle-range theory involves abstractions, of course, but they are close enough to observed data to be incorporated in propositions that permit empirical testing. Middle-range theories deal with delimited aspects of social phenomena, as is indicated by their labels. One speaks of a theory

1. "A 'working hypothesis' is little more than the common-sense procedure used by all of us everyday. Encountering certain facts, certain alternative explanations come to mind and we proceed to test them." James B. Conant, *On Understanding Science* (New Haven: Yale University Press, 1947), 137, n. 4.

2. This discussion draws upon and expands a critique of Parsons' paper on the position of sociological theory at the 1947 meetings of the American Sociological Society as briefly published in the *American Sociological Review,* 1949, 13, 164-8. It draws also upon subsequent discussions: R. K. Merton, "The role-set: problems in sociological theory," *The British Journal of Sociology,* June 1957, 8, 106-20, at 108-10; R. K. Merton, "Introduction" to Allen Barton, *Social Organization under Stress: A Sociological Review of Disaster Studies* (Washington, D.C.: National Academy of Sciences—National Research Council, 1963), xvii-xxxvi, at xxix-xxxvi.

of reference groups, of social mobility, of role-conflict and of the formation of social norms just as one speaks of a theory of prices, a germ theory of disease, or a kinetic theory of gases.

The seminal ideas in such theories are characteristically simple: consider Gilbert on magnetism, Boyle on atmospheric pressure, or Darwin on the formation of coral atolls. Gilbert *begins* with the relatively simple idea that the earth may be conceived as a magnet; Boyle, with the simple idea that the atmosphere may be conceived of as a 'sea of air'; Darwin, with the idea that one can conceive of the atolls as upward and outward growths of coral over islands that had long since subsided into the sea. Each of these theories provides an image that gives rise to inferences. To take but one case: if the atmosphere is thought of as a sea of air, then, as Pascal inferred, there should be less air pressure on a mountain top than at its base. The initial idea thus suggests specific hypotheses which are tested by seeing whether the inferences from them are empirically confirmed. The idea itself is tested for its fruitfulness by noting the range of theoretical problems and hypotheses that allow one to identify new characteristics of atmospheric pressure.

In much the same fashion, the theory of reference groups and relative deprivation starts with the simple idea, initiated by James, Baldwin, and Mead and developed by Hyman and Stouffer, that people take the standards of significant others as a basis for self-appraisal and evaluation. Some of the inferences drawn from this idea are at odds with common-sense expectations based upon an unexamined set of 'self-evident' assumptions. Common sense, for example, would suggest that the greater the actual loss experienced by a family in a mass disaster, the more acutely it will feel deprived. This belief is based on the unexamined assumption that the magnitude of objective loss is related linearly to the subjective appraisal of the loss and that this appraisal is confined to one's own experience. But the theory of relative deprivation leads to quite a different hypothesis—that self-appraisals depend upon people's comparisons of their own situation with that of other people perceived as being comparable to themselves. This theory therefore suggests that, under specifiable conditions, families suffering serious losses will feel *less* deprived than those suffering smaller losses if they are in situations leading them to compare themselves to people suffering even more severe losses. For example, it is people in the area of greatest impact of a disaster who, though substantially deprived themselves, are most apt to see others around them who are even more severely deprived. Empirical inquiry supports the theory of relative deprivation rather than the common-sense assumptions: "the feeling of being relatively *better off* than others *increases with objective loss* up to the category of highest loss" and only then declines. This pattern is reinforced by the tendency of public communications to focus on "the *most extreme sufferers* [which] tends to fix them as a reference group against which even other sufferers can compare themselves favorably." As the inquiry develops, it is found that these patterns of self-appraisal in turn affect the distribution of morale in the community of survivors and their motivation to help others.[3] Within a particular *class* of behavior, therefore, the theory of relative deprivation directs us to a set of hypotheses that can be empirically tested. The confirmed conclusion can then be put simply enough: when few are hurt to much the same extent, the pain and loss of each seems great; where many are hurt in greatly varying degree, even fairly large losses seem small as they are compared with far larger ones. The probability that comparisons will be made is affected by the differing visibility of losses of greater and less extent.

The specificity of this example should not obscure the more general character of middle-range theory. Obviously, behavior of people confronted with a mass disaster is only one of an indefinitely large array of particular situations to which the theory of reference groups can be instructively applied, just as is the case with the theory of change in social stratification, the theory of authority, the theory of institutional interdependence, or the theory of anomie. But it is equally clear that such middle-range theories have not been logically *derived* from a single all-embracing theory of social systems, though once developed they may be consistent with one. Furthermore, each theory is more than a mere empirical generalization—an isolated proposition summarizing observed uniformities of relationships between two or more variables. A theory comprises a set of assumptions from which empirical generalizations have themselves been derived.

Another case of middle-range theory in sociology may help us to identify its character and uses. The theory of role-sets[4] begins with an image of how social status is organized in the social structure. This image is as simple as Boyle's image of the atmosphere as a sea of air or Gilbert's image of the earth as a magnet. As with all middle-range theories, however, the proof is in the using not in the immediate response to the originating ideas as obvious or odd, as derived from more general theory or conceived of to deal with a particular class of problems.

Despite the very diverse meanings attached to the concept of *social status,* one sociological tradition consistently uses it to refer to a position in a social system, with its distinctive array of designated rights and obligations. In this tradition, as exemplified by Ralph Linton, the related concept of *social role* refers to the behavior of status-occupants that is oriented toward the patterned expectations of others (who accord the rights and exact the obligations). Linton, like others in this tradition, went on to state the long recognized and basic observation that each person in society inevitably occupies multiple statuses and that each of these statuses has its associated role.

---

3. Barton, *op. cit.,* 62-63, 70-72, 140, and the Introduction, xxiv-xxv.
4. The following pages draw upon Merton, "The role-set," *op. cit.*

It is at this point that the imagery of the role-set theory departs from this long-established tradition. The difference is initially a small one—some might say so small as to be insignificant—but the shift in the angle of vision leads to successively more fundamental theoretical differences. Role-set theory begins with the concept that each social status involves not a single associated role, but an array of roles. This feature of social structure gives rise to the concept of role-set: that complement of social relationships in which persons are involved simply because they occupy a particular social status. Thus, a person in the status of medical student plays not only the role of student *vis-à-vis* the correlative status of his teachers, but also an array of other roles relating him diversely to others in the system: other students, physicians, nurses, social workers, medical technicians, and the like. Again, the status of school teacher has its distinctive role-set which relates the teacher not only to the correlative status, pupil, but also to colleagues, the school principal and superintendent, the Board of Education, professional associations and, in the United States, local patriotic organizations.

Notice that the role-set differs from what sociologists have long described as 'multiple roles.' The latter term has traditionally referred not to the complex of roles associated with a single social status but to the various social statuses (often, in different institutional spheres) in which people find themselves—for example, one person might have the diverse statuses of physician, husband, father, professor, church elder, Conservative Party member and army captain. (This complement of distinct statuses of a person, each with its own role-set, is a status-set. This concept gives rise to its own array of analytical problems which need not be considered here.)

Up to this point, the concept of role-set is *merely* an image for thinking about a component of the social structure. But this image is a beginning, not an end, for it leads directly to certain analytical problems. The notion of the role-set at once leads to the inference that social structures confront men with the task of articulating the components of countless role-sets—that is, the functional task of managing somehow to organize these so that an appreciable degree of social regularity obtains, sufficient to enable most people most of the time to go about their business without becoming paralyzed by extreme conflicts in their role-sets.

If this relatively simple idea of role-set has theoretical worth, it should generate distinctive problems for sociological inquiry. The concept of role-set does this.[5] It raises the general but definite problem of identify-

5. For an early version of this developing idea, see Merton, "The social-cultural environment and *anomie*," in Helen L. Witmer and Ruth Kotinsky, editors, *New Perspective for Research on Juvenile Delinquency:* Report on a conference on the relevance and interrelations of certain concepts from sociology and psychiatry for delinquency, held May 6 and 7, 1955 (Washington, D.C.: U.S. Department of Health, Education, and Welfare, 1956), 24-50, at 47-48.

ing the social mechanisms—that is, the social processes having designated consequences for designated parts of the social structure—which articulate the expectations of those in the role-set sufficiently to reduce conflicts for the occupant of a status. It generates the further problem of discovering how these mechanisms come into being, so that we can also explain why the mechanisms do not operate effectively or fail to emerge at all in some social systems. Finally, like the theory of atmospheric pressure, the theory of role-set points directly to relevant empirical research. Monographs on the workings of diverse types of formal organization have developed empirically-based theoretical extensions of how role-sets operate in practice.[6]

The theory of role-sets illustrates another aspect of sociological theories of the middle range. They are frequently consistent with a variety of so-called systems of sociological theory. So far as one can tell, the theory of role-sets is not inconsistent with such broad theoretical orientations as Marxist theory, functional analysis, social behaviorism, Sorokin's integral sociology, or Parsons' theory of action. This may be a horrendous observation for those of us who have been trained to believe that systems of sociological thought are logically close-knit and mutually exclusive sets of doctrine. But in fact, as we shall note later in this introduction, comprehensive sociological theories are sufficiently loose-knit, internally diversified, and mutually overlapping that *a given theory of the middle range,* which has a measure of empirical confirmation, can often be subsumed under comprehensive theories which are themselves discrepant in certain respects.

This reasonably unorthodox opinion can be illustrated by reexamining the theory of role-sets as a middle-range theory. We depart from the traditional concept by assuming that a single status in society involves, not a single role, but an array of associated roles, relating the status-occupant to diverse others. Second, we note that this concept of the role-set gives rise to distinctive theoretical problems, hypotheses, and so to empirical inquiry. One basic problem is that of identifying the social mechanisms which articulate the role-set and reduce conflicts among roles. Third, the concept of the role-set directs our attention to the structural problem of identifying the social arrangements which integrate

---

6. If we are to judge from the dynamics of development in science, sketched out in the preceding part of this introduction, theories of the middle range, being close to the research front of science, are particularly apt to be products of multiple and approximately simultaneous discovery. The core idea of the role-set was independently developed in the important empirical monograph, Neal Gross, Ward S. Mason and A. W. McEachern, *Explorations in Role Analysis: Studies of the School Superintendency Role* (New York: John Wiley & Sons, Inc., 1958). Significant extensions of the theory coupled with empirical investigation will be found in the monographs: Robert L. Kahn et al., *Organizational Stress: Studies in Role Conflict and Ambiguity* (New York: John Wiley & Sons, 1964), see 13-17 and *passim;* Daniel Katz and Robert L. Kahn, *The Social Psychology of Organizations* (New York: John Wiley & Sons, 1966) 172 ff. and *passim.*

as well as oppose the expectations of various members of the role-set. The concept of multiple roles, on the other hand, confines our attention to a different and no doubt important issue: how do *individual* occupants of statuses happen to deal with the many and sometimes conflicting demands made of them? Fourth, the concept of the role-set directs us to the further question of how these social mechanisms come into being; the answer to this question enables us to account for the many concrete instances in which the role-set operates ineffectively. (This no more assumes that all social mechanisms are functional than the theory of biological evolution involves the comparable assumption that no dysfunctional developments occur.) Finally, the logic of analysis exhibited in this sociological theory of the middle-range is developed wholly in terms of the elements of social structure rather than in terms of providing concrete *historical descriptions* of particular social systems. Thus, middle-range theory enables us to transcend the mock problem of a theoretical conflict between the nomothetic and the idiothetic, between the general and the altogether particular, between generalizing sociological theory and historicism.

From all this, it is evident that according to role-set theory there is always a *potential* for differing expectations among those in the role-set as to what is appropriate conduct for a status-occupant. The basic source of this potential for conflict—and it is important to note once again that on this point we are at one with such disparate general theorists as Marx and Spencer, Simmel, Sorokin and Parsons—is found in the structural fact that the other members of a role-set are apt to hold various social positions differing from those of the status-occupant in question. To the extent that members of a role-set are diversely located in the social structure, they are apt to have interests and sentiments, values and moral expectations, differing from those of the status-occupant himself. This, after all, is one of the principal assumptions of Marxist theory as it is of much other sociological theory: social differentiation generates distinct interests among those variously located in the structure of the society. For example, the members of a school board are often in social and economic strata that differ significantly from the stratum of the school teacher. The interests, values, and expectations of board members are consequently apt to differ from those of the teacher who may thus be subject to conflicting expectations from these and other members of his role-set: professional colleagues, influential members of the school board and, say, the Americanism Committee of the American Legion. An educational essential for one is apt to be judged as an educational frill by another, or as downright subversion, by the third. What holds conspicuously for this one status holds, in identifiable degree, for occupants of other statuses who are structurally related through their role-set to others who themselves occupy differing positions in society.

As a theory of the middle range, then, the theory of role-sets begins with a concept and its associated imagery and generates an array of theoretical problems. Thus, the assumed structural basis for potential disturbance of a role-set gives rise to a double question (which, the record shows, has not been raised in the absence of the theory): which social mechanisms, if any, operate to counteract the theoretically assumed instability of role-sets and, correlatively, under which circumstances do these social mechanisms fail to operate, with resulting inefficiency, confusion, and conflict? Like other questions that have historically stemmed from the general orientation of functional analysis, these do not assume that role-sets invariably operate with substantial efficiency. For this middle-range theory is not concerned with the historical generalization that a degree of social order or conflict prevails in society but with the analytical problem of identifying the social mechanisms which produce a greater degree of order or less conflict than would obtain if these mechanisms were not called into play.

TOTAL SYSTEMS OF SOCIOLOGICAL THEORY

The quest for theories of the middle range exacts a distinctly different commitment from the sociologist than does the quest for an all-embracing, unified theory. The pages that follow assume that this search for a total system of sociological theory, in which observations about every aspect of social behavior, organization, and change promptly find their preordained place, has the same exhilarating challenge and the same small promise as those many all-encompassing philosophical systems which have fallen into deserved disuse. The issue must be fairly joined. Some sociologists still write as though they expect, here and now, formulation of *the* general sociological theory broad enough to encompass the vast ranges of precisely observed details of social behavior, organization, and change and fruitful enough to direct the attention of research workers to a flow of problems for empirical research. This I take to be a premature and apocalyptic belief. We are not ready. Not enough preparatory work has been done.

An historical sense of the changing intellectual contexts of sociology should be sufficiently humbling to liberate these optimists from this extravagant hope. For one thing, certain aspects of our historical past are still too much with us. We must remember that early sociology grew up in an intellectual atmosphere[7] in which vastly comprehensive systems of philosophy were being introduced on all sides. Any philosopher of the eighteenth and early nineteenth centuries worth his salt had to develop his own philosophical system—of these, Kant, Fichte, Schelling, Hegel

7. See the classical work by John Theodore Merz, *A History of European Thought in the Nineteenth Century* (Edinburgh and London: William Blackwood, 1904), 4 vols.

were only the best known. Each system was a personal bid for the definitive overview of the universe of matter, nature and man.

These attempts of philosophers to create total systems became a model for the early sociologists, and so the nineteenth century was a century of sociological systems. Some of the founding fathers, like Comte and Spencer, were imbued with the *esprit de système*, which was expressed in their sociologies as in the rest of their wider-ranging philosophies. Others, such as Gumplowicz, Ward, and Giddings, later tried to provide intellectual legitimacy for this still "new science of a very ancient subject." This required that a general and definitive framework of sociological thought be built rather than developing special theories designed to guide the investigation of specific sociological problems within an evolving and provisional framework.

Within this context, almost all the pioneers in sociology tried to fashion his own system. The multiplicity of systems, each claiming to be the genuine sociology, led naturally enough to the formation of schools, each with its cluster of masters, disciples and epigoni. Sociology not only became differentiated from other disciplines, but it became internally differentiated. This differentiation, however, was not in terms of specialization, as in the sciences, but rather, as in philosophy, in terms of total systems, typically held to be mutually exclusive and largely at odds. As Bertrand Russell noted about philosophy, this total sociology did not seize "the advantage, as compared with the [sociologies] of the system-builders, of being able to tackle its problems one at a time, instead of having to invent at one stroke a block theory of the whole [sociological] universe."[8]

Another route has been followed by sociologists in their quest to establish the intellectual legitimacy of their discipline: they have taken as their prototype systems of scientific theory rather than systems of philosophy. This path too has sometimes led to the attempt to create total systems of sociology—a goal that is often based on one or more of three basic misconceptions about the sciences.

The first misinterpretation assumes that systems of thought can be effectively developed before a great mass of basic observations has been accumulated. According to this view, Einstein might follow hard on the heels of Kepler, without the intervening centuries of investigation and systematic thought about the results of investigation that were needed to prepare the terrain. The systems of sociology that stem from this tacit assumption are much like those introduced by the system-makers in medicine over a span of 150 years: the systems of Stahl, Boissier de Sauvages, Broussais, John Brown and Benjamin Rush. Until well into the nineteenth century eminent personages in medicine thought it necessary to develop a theoretical system of disease long before the

8. Bertrand Russell, *A History of Western Philosophy* (New York: Simon and Schuster, 1945), 834.

antecedent empirical inquiry had been adequately developed.[9] These garden-paths have since been closed off in medicine but this sort of effort still turns up in sociology. It is this tendency that led the biochemist and avocational sociologist, L. J. Henderson, to observe:

A difference between most system-building in the social sciences and systems of thought and classification in the natural sciences is to be seen in their evolution. In the natural sciences both theories and descriptive systems grow by adaptation to the increasing knowledge and experience of the scientists. *In the social sciences, systems often issue fully formed from the mind of one man.* Then they may be much discussed if they attract attention, but *progressive adaptive modification as a result of the concerted efforts of great numbers of men is rare.*[10]

The second misconception about the physical sciences rests on a mistaken assumption of historical contemporaneity—*that all cultural products existing at the same moment of history have the same degree of maturity*. In fact, to perceive differences here would be to achieve a sense of proportion. The fact that the discipline of physics and the discipline of sociology are both identifiable in the mid-twentieth century does not mean that the achievements of the one should be the measure of the other. True, social scientists today live at a time when physics has achieved comparatively great scope and precision of theory and experiment, a great aggregate of tools of investigation, and an abundance of technological by-products. Looking about them, many sociologists take the achievements of physics as the standard for self-appraisal. They want to compare biceps with their bigger brothers. They, too, want to *count*. And when it becomes evident that they neither have the rugged physique nor pack the murderous wallop of their big brothers, some sociologists despair. They begin to ask: is a science of society really possible unless we institute a total system of sociology? But this perspective ignores the fact that between twentieth-century physics and twentieth-century sociology stand billions of man-hours of sustained, disciplined, and cumulative research. Perhaps sociology is not yet ready for its Einstein because it has not yet found its Kepler—to say nothing of its Newton, Laplace, Gibbs, Maxwell or Planck.

Third, sociologists sometimes misread the actual state of theory in the physical sciences. This error is ironic, for physicists agree that they have not achieved an all-encompassing system of theory, and most see little prospect of it in the near future. What characterizes physics is an array of special theories of greater or less scope, coupled with the historically-

9. Wilfred Trotter, *Collected Papers* (Oxford University Press), 1941, 150. The story of the system-makers is told in every history of medicine; for example, Fielding H. Garrison, *An Introduction to the History of Medicine* (Philadelphia: Saunders, 1929) and Ralph H. Major, *A History of Medicine* (Oxford: Blackwell Scientific Publications, 1954), 2 vols.

10. Lawrence J. Henderson, *The Study of Man* (Philadelphia: University of Pennsylvania Press, 1941) 19-20, italics supplied; for that matter, the entire book can be read with profit by most of us sociologists.

grounded hope that these will continue to be brought together into families of theory. As one observer puts it: "though most of us hope, it is true, for an all embracive future theory which will unify the various postulates of physics, we do not wait for it before proceeding with the important business of science."[11] More recently, the theoretical physicist, Richard Feynman, reported without dismay that "today our theories of physics, the laws of physics, are a multitude of different parts and pieces that do not fit together very well."[12] But perhaps most telling is the observation by that most comprehensive of theoreticians who devoted the last years of his life to the unrelenting and unsuccessful search "for a unifying theoretical basis for all these single disciplines, consisting of a minimum of concepts and fundamental relationships, from which all the concepts and relationships of the single disciplines might be deprived by logical process." Despite his own profound and lonely commitment to this quest, Einstein observed:

> The greater part of physical research is devoted to the development of the various branches in physics, in each of which the object is the theoretical understanding of more or less restricted fields of experience, and in each of which the laws and concepts remain as closely as possible related to experience.[13]

These observations might be pondered by those sociologists who expect a sound general system of sociological theory in our time—or soon after. If the science of physics, with its centuries of enlarged theoretical generalizations, has not managed to develop an all-encompassing theoretical system, then *a fortiori* the science of sociology, which has only begun to accumulate empirically grounded theoretical generalizations of modest scope, would seem well advised to moderate its aspirations for such a system.

UTILITARIAN PRESSURES FOR TOTAL SYSTEMS OF SOCIOLOGY

The conviction among some sociologists that we must, here and now, achieve a grand theoretical system not only results from a misplaced comparison with the physical sciences, it is also a response to the ambiguous position of sociology in contemporary society. The very uncertainty about whether the accumulated knowledge of sociology is adequate to meet the large demands now being made of it—by policy-makers, reformers and reactionaries, by business-men and government-

---

11. Henry Margenau, "The basis of theory in physics," unpublished ms., 1949, 5-6.

12. Richard Feynman, *The Character of Physical Law* (London: Cox & Wyman Ltd., 1965), 30.

13. Albert Einstein, "The fundamentals of theoretical physics," in L. Hamalian and E. L. Volpe, eds. *Great Essays by Nobel Prize Winners* (New York: Noonday Press, 1960), 219-30 at 220.

men, by college presidents and college sophomores—provokes an overly-zealous and defensive conviction on the part of some sociologists that they must somehow be equal to these demands, however premature and extravagant they may be.

This conviction erroneously assumes that a science must be adequate to meet *all* demands, intelligent or stupid, made of it. This conviction is implicitly based on the sacrilegious and masochistic assumption that one must be omniscient and omnicompetent—to admit to less than total knowledge is to admit to total ignorance. So it often happens that the exponents of a fledgling discipline make extravagant claims to total systems of theory, adequate to the entire range of problems encompassed by the discipline. It is this sort of attitude that Whitehead referred to in the epigraph to this book: "It is characteristic of a science in its earlier stages . . . to be both ambitiously profound in its aims and trivial in its handling of details."

Like the sociologists who thoughtlessly compared themselves with contemporary physical scientists because they both are alive at the same instant of history, the general public and its strategic decision-makers often err in making a definitive appraisal of social science on the basis of its ability to solve the urgent problems of society today. The misplaced masochism of the social scientist and the inadvertent sadism of the public both result from the failure to remember that social science, like all science, is continually developing and that there is no providential dispensation providing that at any given moment it will be adequate to the entire array of problems confronting men. In historical perspective this expectation would be equivalent to having forever prejudged the status and promise of medicine in the seventeenth century according to its ability to produce, then and there, a cure or even a preventative for cardiac diseases. If the problem had been widely acknowledged—look at the growing rate of death from coronary thrombosis!—its very importance would have obscured the *entirely independent question* of how adequate the medical knowledge of 1650 (or 1850 or 1950) was for solving a wide array of other health problems. Yet it is precisely this illogic that lies behind so many of the practical demands made on the social sciences. Because war and exploitation and poverty and racial discrimination and psychological insecurity plague modern societies, social science must justify itself by providing solutions for all of these problems. Yet social scientists may be no better equipped to solve these urgent problems today than were physicians, such as Harvey or Sydenham, to identify, study, and cure coronary thrombosis in 1655. Yet, as history testifies, the inadequacy of medicine to cope with this particular problem scarcely meant that it lacked powers of development. If everyone backs only the sure thing, who will support the colt yet to come into its own?

My emphasis upon the gap between the practical problems assigned to the sociologist and the state of his accumulated knowledge and skills does not mean, of course, that the sociologist should not seek to develop increasingly comprehensive theory or should not work on research directly relevant to urgent practical problems. Most of all, it does not mean that sociologists should deliberately seek out the pragmatically trivial problem. Different sectors in the spectrum of basic research and theory have different probabilities of being germane to particular practical problems; they have differing potentials of relevance.[14] But it is important to re-establish an historical sense of proportion. The urgency or immensity of a practical social problem does not ensure its immediate solution.[15] At any given moment, men of science are close to the solutions of some problems and remote from others. It must be remembered that necessity is only the mother of invention; socially accumulated knowledge is its father. Unless the two are brought together, necessity remains infertile. She may of course conceive at some future time when she is properly mated. But the mate requires time (and sustenance) if he is to attain the size and vigor needed to meet the demands that will be made upon him.

This book's orientation toward the relationship of current sociology and practical problems of society is much the same as its orientation toward the relationship of sociology and general sociological theory. It is a developmental orientation, rather than one that relies on the sudden mutations of one sociologist that suddenly bring solutions to major social problems or to a single encompassing theory. Though this orientation makes no marvellously dramatic claims, it offers a reasonably realistic assessment of the current condition of sociology and the ways in which it actually develops.

TOTAL SYSTEMS OF THEORY AND THEORIES OF THE MIDDLE RANGE

From all this it would seem reasonable to suppose that sociology will advance insofar as its major (but not exclusive) concern is with developing theories of the middle range, and it will be retarded if its primary attention is focussed on developing total sociological systems. So it is that in his inaugural address at the London School of Economics, T. H.

---

14. This conception is developed in R. K. Merton, "Basic research and potentials of relevance," *American Behavioral Scientist*, May 1963, VI, 86-90 on the basis of my earlier discussion, "The role of applied social science in the formation of policy," *Philosophy of Science*, 1949, 16, 161-81.

15. As can be seen in detail in such works as the following: Paul F. Lazarsfeld, William Sewell and Harold Wilensky, eds., *The Uses of Sociology* (New York: Basic Books, in press); Alvin W. Gouldner and S. M. Miller, *Applied Sociology: Opportunities and Problems* (New York: The Free Press, 1965); Bernard Rosenberg, Israel Gerver and F. William Howton, *Mass Society in Crisis: Social Problems and Social Pathology* (New York: The Macmillan Company, 1964); Barbara Wootton, *Social Science and Social Pathology* (New York: The Macmillan Company, 1959).

Marshall put in a plea for sociological "stepping-stones in the middle distance."[16] Our major task today is to develop special theories applicable to limited conceptual ranges—theories, for example, of deviant behavior, the unanticipated consequences of purposive action, social perception, reference groups, social control, the interdependence of social institutions—rather than to seek immediately the total conceptual structure that is adequate to derive these and other theories of the middle range.

Sociological theory, if it is to advance significantly, must proceed on these interconnected planes: (1) by developing special theories from which to derive hypotheses that can be empirically investigated and (2) by evolving, not suddenly revealing, a progressively more general conceptual scheme that is adequate to consolidate groups of special theories.

To concentrate entirely on special theories is to risk emerging with specific hypotheses that account for limited aspects of social behavior, organization and change but that remain mutually inconsistent.

To concentrate entirely on a master conceptual scheme for deriving all subsidiary theories is to risk producing twentieth-century sociological equivalents of the large philosophical systems of the past, with all their varied suggestiveness, their architectonic splendor, and their scientific sterility. The sociological theorist who is *exclusively* committed to the exploration of a total system with its utmost abstractions runs the risk that, as with modern décor, the furniture of his mind will be bare and uncomfortable.

The road to effective general schemes in sociology will only become clogged if, as in the early days of sociology, each charismatic sociologist tries to develop his own general system of theory. The persistence of this practice can only make for the balkanization of sociology, with each principality governed by its own theoretical system. Though this process has periodically marked the development of other sciences—conspicuously, chemistry, geology and medicine—it need not be reproduced in sociology if we learn from the history of science. We sociologists can look instead toward progressively comprehensive sociological theory which, instead of proceeding from the head of one man, gradually consolidates theories of the middle range, so that these become special cases of more general formulations.

Developments in sociological theory suggest that emphasis on this orientation is needed. Note how few, how scattered, and how unimpressive are the specific sociological hypotheses which are *derived* from a master conceptual scheme. The proposals for an all-embracing theory run so far ahead of confirmed special theories as to remain unrealized programs rather than *consolidations* of theories that at first seemed discrete. Of course, as Talcott Parsons and Pitirim Sorokin (in his *Sociological*

---

16. The inaugural lecture was delivered 21 February 1946. It is printed in T. H. Marshall, *Sociology at the Crossroads* (London: Heinemann, 1963), 3-24.

Theories of Today) have indicated, significant progress has recently been made. The gradual convergence of streams of theory in sociology, social psychology and anthropology records large theoretical gains and promises even more.[17] Nonetheless, a large part of what is now described as sociological theory consists of *general orientations toward data, suggesting types of variables which theories must somehow take into account, rather than clearly formulated, verifiable statements of relationships between specified variables.* We have many concepts but fewer confirmed theories; many points of view, but few theorems; many "approaches" but few arrivals. Perhaps some further changes in emphasis would be all to the good.

Consciously or unconsciously, men allocate their scant resources as much in the production of sociological theory as they do in the production of plumbing supplies, and their allocations reflect their underlying assumptions. Our discussion of middle range theory in sociology is intended to make explicit a policy decision faced by all sociological theorists. Which shall have the greater share of our collective energies and resources: the search for confirmed theories of the middle range or the search for an all-inclusive conceptual scheme? I believe—and beliefs are of course notoriously subject to error—that theories of the middle range hold the largest promise, *provided that* the search for them is coupled with a pervasive concern with consolidating special theories into more general sets of concepts and mutually consistent propositions. Even so,

---

17. I attach importance to the observations made by Talcott Parsons in his presidential address to the American Sociological Society subsequent to my formulation of this position. For example: "At the *end* of this road of increasing frequency and specificity of the islands of theoretical knowledge lies the ideal state, scientifically speaking, where *most* actual operational hypotheses of empirical research are directly derived from a general system of theory. On any broad front, . . . only in physics has this state been attained in *any* science. We cannot expect to be anywhere nearly in sight of it. But it does not follow that, distant as we are from that goal, steps in that *direction* are futile. Quite the contrary, *any* real step in that direction is an advance. Only at this *end* point do the islands merge into a continental land mass.

At the very least, then, general theory can provide a broadly orienting framework [*n.b.*] . . . It can also serve to codify, interrelate and make available a vast amount of existing empirical knowledge. It also serves to call attention to gaps in our knowledge, and to provide canons for the criticism of theories and empirical generalizations. Finally, even if they cannot be systematically derived [*n.b.*], it is indispensable to the systematic clarification of problems and the fruitful formulation of hypotheses." (italics supplied)

Parsons, "The prospects of sociological theory," *American Sociological Review,* February 1950, 15, 3-16 at 7. It is significant that a general theorist, such as Parsons, acknowledges (1) that in fact general sociological theory seldom provides for specific hypotheses to be derived from it; (2) that, in comparison with a field such as physics, such derivations for most hypotheses are a remote objective; (3) that general theory provides only a general orientation and (4) that it serves as a basis for codifying empirical generalizations and specific theories. Once all this is acknowledged, the sociologists who are committed to developing general theory do not differ significantly in principle from those who see the best promise of sociology today in developing theories of the middle range and consolidating them periodically.

we must adopt the provisional outlook of our big brothers and of Tennyson:

> Our little systems have their day;
> They have their day and cease to be.

POLARIZED RESPONSES TO THEORIES OF THE MIDDLE RANGE

Since the policy of focusing on sociological theories of the middle range was advocated in print, the responses of sociologists have understandably been polarized. By and large, it appears that these responses were largely governed by sociologists' own patterns of work. Most sociologists who had been engaged in theoretically oriented empirical research gave assent to a policy which merely formulated what had already been working philosophy. Conversely, most of those who were committed to the humanistic study of the history of social thought or who were trying to develop a total sociological theory here and now described the policy as a retreat from properly high aspirations. The third response is an intermediate one. It recognizes that an emphasis on middle-range theory does not mean exclusive attention to this kind of theorizing. Instead, it sees the development of more comprehensive theory as coming about through consolidations of middle-range theories rather than as emerging, all at once, from the work of individual theorists on the grand scale.

THE PROCESS OF POLARIZATION

Like most controversies in science, this dispute over the allocation of intellectual resources among different kinds of sociological work, involves social conflict and not merely intellectual criticism.[18] That is, the dispute is less a matter of contradictions between substantive sociological ideas than of competing definitions of the role of the sociologist that is judged most effective at this time.

This controversy follows the classically identified course of social conflict. Attack is followed by counter-attack, with progressive alienation between the parties to the conflict. In due course, since the conflict is public, it becomes a status-battle more than a search for truth. Attitudes become polarized, and then each group of sociologists begins to respond largely to stereotyped versions of what the other is saying. Theorists of the middle range are stereotyped as mere nose-counters or mere fact-finders or as merely descriptive sociographers. And theorists aiming at general theory are stereotyped as inveterately speculative, entirely un-

---

18. The following pages draw upon Merton, "Social conflict in styles of sociological work," *Transactions*, Fourth World Congress of Sociology, 1961, 3, 21-46.

concerned with compelling empirical evidence or as inevitably committed to doctrines that are so formulated that they cannot be tested.

These stereotypes are not entirely removed from reality; like most stereotypes, they are inflexible exaggerations of actual tendencies or attributes. But in the course of social conflict, they become self-confirming stereotypes as sociologists shut themselves off from the experience that might force them to be modified. Sociologists of each camp develop highly selective perceptions of what is actually going on in the other. Each camp sees in the work of the other primarily what the hostile stereotype has alerted it to see, and it then promptly takes an occasional remark as an abiding philosophy, an emphasis as a total commitment. In this process, each group of sociologists becomes less and less motivated to study the work of the other, since it is patently without truth. They scan the out-group's writings just enough to find ammunition for new fusillades.

The process of reciprocal alienation and stereotyping is probably reinforced by the great increase in published sociological writings. Like many other scientists and scholars, sociologists can no longer 'keep up' with what is being published in the field. They must become more and more selective in their reading. And this increased selectivity readily leads those who are initially hostile to a particular kind of sociological work to give up studying the very publications that might have led them to abandon their stereotype.

These conditions tend to encourage polarization of outlook. Sociological orientations that are *not* substantively contradictory are regarded as if they were. According to these all-or-none positions, sociological inquiry must be statistical *or* historical; either the great issues and problems of the time must be the sole objects of study *or* these refractory matters must be avoided altogether because they are not amenable to scientific investigation; and so on.

The process of social conflict would be halted in midcourse and converted into intellectual criticism if a stop were put to the reciprocal contempt that often marks these polemics. But battles among sociologists ordinarily do not occur in the social context that is required for the non-reciprocation of affect to operate with regularity. This context involves a jointly recognized differentiation of status between the parties, at least with respect to the issue at hand. When this status-differentiation is present—as with the lawyer and his client or the psychiatrist and his patient—a technical norm attached to the more authoritative status in the relationship prevents the reciprocity of expressed feelings. But scientific controversies typically take place within a company of equals (however much the status of the parties might otherwise differ) and, moreover, they take place in public, subject to the observation of peers. So rhetoric is met with rhetoric, contempt with contempt, and the intellectual issues become subordinated to the battle for status.

Furthermore, there is little room in these polarized controversies for the uncommitted third party who might convert social conflict into intellectual criticism. True, some sociologists will not adopt the all-or-none position that is expected in social conflict. But typically, these would-be noncombatants are caught in the crossfire between the hostile camps. They become tagged either as "mere eclectics," thus making it unnecessary for the two camps to examine what this third position asserts or how valid it is; or, they are labeled "renegades" who have abandoned the doctrinal truths; or perhaps worst of all, they are mere middle-of-the-roaders or fence-sitters who, through timidity or expediency, flee from the fundamental conflict between unalloyed sociological good and unalloyed sociological evil.

But polemics in science have both their functions and dysfunctions. In the course of social conflict, cognitive issues become warped as they are pressed into the service of scoring off the other fellow. Nevertheless, when the conflict is regulated by a community of peers, even polemics with their distortions which use up the energies of those engaged in mock intellectual battles, may help to redress accumulative imbalances in science. There is no easy way to determine the optimum utilization of resources in a field of science, partly because of ultimate disagreement over the criteria of the optimum.[19] Social conflict tends to become marked in sociology whenever a particular line of investigation—say, of small groups or world societies—or a particular set of ideas—say, functional analysis or Marxism—or a particular mode of inquiry—say, social surveys or historical sociology—has engrossed the attention and energies of a rapidly increasing number of sociologists. This line of development might have become popular because it has proved effective for dealing with certain intellectual or social problems or because it is ideologically congenial. The currently unpopular fields or types of work are left with fewer recruits of high caliber, and with diminished accomplishments, this kind of work becomes less attractive. Were it not for such conflict, the reign of theoretical orthodoxies and imbalances in the distribution of sociological work would be even more marked than they are. Thus noisy claims that neglected problems, methods, and theoretical orientations merit more concerted attention—even when these claims are accompanied by extravagant attacks on the prevailing line of development —may help to diversify sociological work by curbing the tendency to concentrate on a narrow range of problems. Greater heterodoxy in turn

19. The physicist and student of science policy, Alvin M. Weinberg, has instructively addressed himself to this problem. See Chapter III, "The Choices of Big Science," in his book, *Reflections on Big Science* (Cambridge, Mass.: The M.I.T. Press, 1967).

increases the prospect of scientifically productive ventures, until these develop into new orthodoxies.

ASSENT TO THE POLICY OF MIDDLE-RANGE THEORY

As we noted earlier, resonance to the emphasis on middle-range theory is most marked among sociologists who are themselves engaged in theoretically oriented empirical research. That is why the policy of sociological theories of the middle range has taken hold today whereas earlier versions—which we shall presently examine—did not. In a fairly precise sense of the familiar phrase, "the time was not ripe." That is, until the last two or three decades, with conspicuous exceptions, sociologists tended to be far more devoted either to the search for all-embracing, unified theory or to descriptive empirical work with little theoretical orientation altogether. As a result, pleas for the policy of middle-range theory went largely unnoticed.

Yet, as I have noted elsewhere,[20] this policy is neither new nor alien; it has well-established historical roots. More than anyone else before him, Bacon emphasized the prime importance of "middle axioms" in science:

> The understanding must not however be allowed to jump and fly from particulars to remote axioms and of almost the highest generality (such as the first principles, as they are called, of arts and things), and taking stand upon them as truths that cannot be shaken, proceed to prove and frame the middle axioms by reference to them; which has been the practice hitherto; the understanding being not only carried that way by a natural impulse but also by the use of syllogistic demonstration trained and inured to it. But then, and then only, may we hope well of the sciences, when in a just scale of ascent, and by successive steps not interrupted or broken, we rise from particulars to lesser axioms; and then to middle axioms, one above the other; and last of all to the most general. For the lowest axioms differ but slightly from bare experience, while the highest and most general (which we now have) are notional and abstract and without solidity. But the middle are the true and solid and living axioms, on which depend the affairs and fortunes of men; and above them, last of all, those which are indeed the most general; such I mean as are not abstract, but of which those intermediate axioms are really limitations.[21]

Bacon, in turn, cites a more ancient version:

> And Plato, in his *Theaetetus*, noteth well: 'That particulars are infinite, and the higher generalities give no sufficient direction;' and that the pith of all sciences, which maketh the artsman differ from the inexpert, is in the middle

20. Merton, "The role-set," *British Journal of Sociology*. June 1957, 108.

21. Bacon, *Novum Organum*, Book I, Aphorism CIV; see also Book I, Aphorisms LXVI and CXVI. Herbert Butterfield remarks that Bacon thus seems in "a curious but significant way . . . to have foreseen the structure that science was to take in the future." *The Origins of Modern Science, 1300-1800* (London: G. Bell & Sons, 1949), 91-92.

propositions, which in every particular knowledge are taken from tradition and experience.[22]

Just as Bacon cites Plato as his predecessor, so John Stuart Mill and George Cornewall Lewis cite Bacon as theirs. Although differing with Bacon on the mode of logic connecting "most general laws" with "middle principles," Mill nevertheless echoes him in these words:

Bacon has judiciously observed that the *axiomata media* of every science principally constitute its value. The lowest generalizations, until explained by and resolved into the middle principles of which they are the consequences, have only the imperfect accuracy of empirical laws; while the most general laws are too general, and include too few circumstances, to give sufficient indication of what happens in individual cases, where the circumstances are almost always immensely numerous. In the importance, therefore, which Bacon assigns, in every science, to the middle principles, it is impossible not to agree with him. But I conceive him to have been radically wrong in his doctrine respecting the mode in which these *axiomata media* should be arrived at . . . [i.e. Bacon's inveterate addiction to total induction, with no place at all provided for deduction][23]

Writing at almost the same time as Mill, but, as the historical record shows, without having the same impact on contemporaries, Lewis draws upon Bacon to make a case for "limited theories" in political science. He advances the further idea that a large number of valid theorems can be developed by restricting observation to designated *classes* of communities:

. . . we are enabled to form limited theories, to predicate general tendencies, and prevailing laws of causation, which might not be true, for the most part, if extended to all mankind, but which have a presumptive truth if confined to certain nations . . .
. . . it is possible to enlarge the region of speculative politics, consistently with the true expression of facts, by narrowing the range of observation, and by confining ourselves to a limited class of communities. By the adoption of this method, we are enabled to increase the number of true political theorems which can be gathered from the facts, and, at the same time, to give them more fulness, life, and substance. Instead of being mere jejune and hollow generalities, they resemble the *Media Axiomata* of Bacon, which are generalized expressions of fact, but, nevertheless, are sufficiently near to practice to serve as guides in the business of life.[24]

Though these early formulations differ in detail—the contrast between Bacon and Mill is particularly conspicuous—they all emphasize

22. Francis Bacon, *The Advancement of Learning*, in *Works*, ed. by Basil Montague (London: William Pickering, 1825), II, 177; see also 181.
23. John Stuart Mill, *A System of Logic* (London: Longmans, Green and Co., 1865) 454-5; Mill explicitly applies the same conception to laws of social change as middle principles, *ibid.*, 520.
24. George Cornewall Lewis, *A Treatise on the Methods of Observation and Reasoning in Politics*, *op. cit.*, II, 112, 127; see also 200, 204-5.

the strategic importance of a graded series of empirically confirmed intermediate theories.

After those early days, similar, though not identical, formulations were advanced by Karl Mannheim, in his concept of "*principia media*"; by Adolf Löwe, in his thesis that "sociological middle principles" connect the economic with the social process; and by Morris Ginsberg, in his examination of Mill's treatment of middle principles in social science.[25] At the moment, then, there is evidence enough to indicate that theories of the middle range in sociology have been advocated by many of our intellectual ancestors. But to modify the adumbrationist's credo, if the working philosophy embodied in this orientation is not altogether new, it is at least true.

It is scarcely problematic that Bacon's widely known formulations were not adopted by sociologists for there were no sociologists around to examine the pertinence of his conceptions. It is only slightly more problematic that Mill's and Lewis's formulations, almost 250 years later, produced little resonance among social scientists; the disciplines were then only in their beginnings. But why did the formulations of Mannheim, Löwe, and Ginsberg, as late as the 1930s, evoke little response in the sociological literature of the period immediately following? Only after similar formulations by Marshall and myself in the late 1940s do we find widespread discussion and application of this orientation to sociological theory. I suspect, although I have not done the spadework needed to investigate the question, that the widespread resonance of middle-range theory in the last decades results in part from the emergence of large numbers of sociological investigators carrying out research that is both empirically based and theoretically relevant.

A small sampling of assent to the policy of middle-range theory will illustrate the basis of resonance. Reviewing the development of sociology over the past four decades, Frank Hankins concludes that:

> middle-range theories seem likely . . . to have the greater explicative significance [than total sociological theories]. Here much has been done relating to

---

25. These formulations have recently been earmarked by Seymour Martin Lipset in his Introduction to the American edition of T. H. Marshall, *Class, Citizenship and Social Development* (New York: Doubleday, 1964), xvi. The citations are to Karl Mannheim, *Mensch und Gesellschaft in Zeitalter des Umbaus* (Leiden, 1935) and *Man and Society in an Age of Reconstruction* (New York: Harcourt, Brace & Co., 1950), 173–90; Adolf Löwe, *Economics and Sociology* (London: Allen & Unwin, 1935) and Morris Ginsberg, *Sociology* (London: Thornton Butterworth Ltd., 1934). Just as this book goes to press, there comes to my attention a detailed account of these same historical antecedents together with an exacting critique: C. A. O. van Nieuwenhuijze, *Intelligible Fields in the Social Sciences* (The Hague: Mouton & Co., 1967), Chapter I: "The Quest for the Manageable Social Unit—Is There a Middle Range?" This work raises a number of serious questions about theories of the middle range, all of which, in my opinion, are clarifying and none of which is beyond an equally serious answer. But since this book is now in production, this opinion must remain unsupported by the detailed analysis that Nieuwenhuijze's discussion amply deserves.

mass communication, class stratification, bureaucracy, small groups of various types, and other important aspects of the social totality. [And then, in the polarizing fashion of all or none, Hankins concludes] It may be we shall find that only such have realistic and practical value.[26]

This resonance of middle range theory occurs among sociologists with a variety of general theoretical orientations, providing that they have a concern with the empirical relevance of theory. So, Arthur K. Davis, oriented toward Marxist theory, suggests that the case for

'theories of the middle range' in contrast to Parsons' more comprehensive approach, was well conceived . . . A middle-range focus—empirical analysis in a limited conceptual setting—appears to assure more securely the necessary continuous contact with empirical variables.[27]

A decade ago, Peter H. Rossi, a man deeply engaged in empirical research and an observer of the recent history of sociology, noted the complex consequences of an explicit formulation of the case for theories of the middle range:

The conception of 'theories of the middle range' achieved wide popoularity both among sociologists primarily oriented to research and among those conerned with theory. It is still too early to estimate the extent to which this idea will affect the relationships between theory and research in American sociology. So far, its acceptance has brought with it mixed blessings. On the negative side, researchers who have been vulnerable to the charge of being 'mere empiricists' have in this conception of theory a convenient way of raising the status of their work without changing its form. On the positive side, it has tended to raise the status of research which is guided by theoretical considerations of a limited nature, for example, the study of small groups. In the opinion of this reviewer, there is a great benefit to be derived ultimately from redirecting theoretical activity from broad, theoretical schemes to levels which are more closely linked to the present capabilities of our research technology.[28]

Of greatest interest in this set of observations is Rossi's abstention from a polar position. The concept of theories of the middle range has sometimes been misappropriated to justify altogether descriptive inquiries which reflect no theoretical orientation at all. But misuse of a conception is no test of its worth. In the end, Rossi, as a sociologist committed to systematic empirical research for its theoretical implications, supports this policy as one that captures the twin concern with empirical inquiry and theoretical relevance.

Durkheim's monograph, *Suicide,* is perhaps the classical instance of the use and development of middle-range theory. It is therefore not surprising that such sociologists in the Durkheimian tradition as Armand

26. Frank H. Hankins, "A forty-year perspective," *Sociology and Social Research,* 1956, 40, 391-8 at 398.

27. Arthur K. Davis, "Social theory and social problems," *Philosophy and Phenomenological Research,* Dec. 1957, 18, 190-208, at 194.

28. Peter H. Rossi, "Methods of social research, 1945–55," in *Sociology in the United States of America: A Trend Report,* ed. by Hans L. Zetterberg (Paris: Unesco, 1956), 21-34, at 23-24.

Cuvillier[29] should endorse this theoretical orientation. Cuvillier's discussion reminds us that middle range theory deals with both micro- and macro-sociological inquiry—with experimental studies of small groups as much as with the comparative analysis of specified aspects of social structure. That macrosociological investigations do not presuppose a total system of sociological theory is the position also taken by David Riesman who maintains that it is best to "be working in the middle range, to talk less of 'breakthrough' or of 'basic' research and to make fewer claims all round."[30]

It might be assumed that the enduring European traditions of working toward total systems of sociology would lead to repudiation of middle-range theory as a preferred orientation. This is not altogether the case. In examining the recent history of sociological thought and conjecturing about prospective developments, one observer has expressed the hope that "*las teorías del rango medio*" will reduce mere polemics among "schools of sociological thought" and make for their continuing convergence.[31] Others have carried out detailed analyses of the logical structure of this type of theory; notably, Filippo Barbano, in an extended series of monographs and papers devoted to "*theorie di media portata.*"[32]

Perhaps the most thoroughgoing and detailed analyses of the logical structure of middle-range theory have been developed by Hans L. Zetterberg in his monograph, *On Theory and Verification in Sociology*[33] and by Andrzej Malewski in his *Verhalten und Interaktion.*[34] Most important,

29. Armand Cuvillier, *Où va la sociologie française?* (Paris: Libraire Marcel Rivière & Cie, 1953) and *Sociologie et problèmes actuels* (Paris: Libraire Philosophique J. Vrin, 1958).

30. David Riesman, "Some observations on the 'older' and the 'newer' social sciences," in *The State of the Social Sciences,* ed. by L. D. White (Chicago: The University of Chicago Press), 319–39, at 339. Riesman's announced orientation should be read in the light of the remark by Maurice R. Stein, soon to be discussed, that middle range theory "downgrades" the "penetrating efforts at interpreting modern society made by such men as C. Wright Mills and David Riesman . . ."

31. Salustiano del Campo in *Revista de Estudios Politicos,* Jan.-Feb. 1957, 208-13.

32. The long list of such works by Barbano includes: *Teoria e ricerca nella sociologia contemporanea* (Milano: A. Giuffrè, 1955), esp. at 100–108; "La metodologia della ricerca nella sua impostazione teorica," *Sociologia,* July-Sept. 1958, 3, 282–95; "Attività e programmi di gruppi ricerca sociologica," *Il Politico,* 1957, 2, 371-92; "Strutture e funzioni sociali: l'emancipazione strutturale in sociologia," *Quaderni di Scienze Sociali,* April 1966, 5, 1-38. Along the same lines, see also: Gianfranco Poggi, "Momento tecnico e momento metodologica nella ricerca," *Bollettino delle Ricerche Sociale,* Sept. 1961, 1, 363-9.

33. Totowa, N.J.: The Bedminister Press, 1965, third enlarged edition. See also: Zetterberg, "Theorie, Forschung und Praxis in der Soziologie," in *Handbuch der empirischen Sozialforschung* (Stuttgart: Ferdinand Enke Verlag, 1961), I. Band, 64-104.

34. Translated from the Polish by Wolfgang Wehrstedt. Tübingen: J. C. B. Mohr (Paul Siebeck), 1967. His book lists the complete bibliography of singularly perceptive and rigorous papers by Malewski, one of the ablest of Polish sociologists, who cut his life short when only 34. Few others in our day have managed to develop with the same clarity and rigor the linkages between Marxist theory and determinate

both Zetterberg and Malewski transcend the polarizing tendency to regard middle-range theory as an array of unconnected special theories. They indicate, by both precept and detailed example, how special theories have been consolidated into successively enlarged sets of theory. This same orientation is manifested by Berger, Zelditch, Anderson and their collaborators, who regard theories of the middle range as applicable to all situations exhibiting specified aspects of social phenomena, and who go on to demonstrate the use of a variety of such theories.[35]

A systematic inventory of middle-range theories developed in the last few decades would run far beyond the compass of these pages. But perhaps a small and arbitrary sampling will show the diversity of problems and subjects with which they deal. The essential point is that these are empirically grounded theories—involving sets of confirmed hypotheses—and not merely organized descriptive data or empirical generalizations or hypotheses which remain logically disparate and unconnected. A cumulative set of such theories has emerged in the investigation of bureaucracies; notably by Selznick, Gouldner, Blau, Lipset-Trow-and-Coleman, Crozier, Kahn and Katz, and a long list of other investigators.[36] Raymond Mack has developed a middle-range theory of the occupational subsystem; Pellegrin, a theory of mobility into topmost positions in groups; Junkichi Abe, an intermediate theory based on both micro- and macrosociological data that relates patterns of deviant behavior to the structure of communities; Hyman, consolidation of empirical uniformities in public opinion into a composite theory and Hillery, a consolidation of demographic uniformities.[37]

There is, however, a far more significant basis for assessing the present orientation of sociologists toward theories of the middle range than this

---

theories of the middle range. See his article of major importance: "Der empirische Gehalt der Theorie des historischen Materialismus," *Kolner Zeitschrift für Soziologie und Sozialpsychologie,* 1959, 11, 281-305.

35. Berger, Zelditch and Anderson, *Sociological Theories in Progress, op. cit.,* at 29 and *passim.*

36. Philip Selznick, *TVA and the Grass Roots* (Berkeley: University of California Press, 1949); A. W. Gouldner, *Patterns of Industrial Bureaucracy* (Glencoe: The Free Press, 1954); P. M. Blau, *The Dynamics of Bureaucracy* (Chicago: University of Chicago Press, 1963, 2d ed.); S. M. Lipset, Martin Trow and James Coleman, *Union Democracy* (New York: The Free Press, 1956). A consolidation of the theoretical conclusions of these monographs is provided by James G. March and Herbert A. Simon, *Organizations* (New York: John Wiley, 1958), 36-52. As further major examples of middle-range theory in this field, see Michel Crozier, *The Bureaucratic Phenomenon* (Chicago: The University of Chicago Press, 1964); Kahn and Katz, *op. cit.*

37. Raymond Mack, "Occupational determinatedness: a problem and hypotheses in role theory," *Social Forces,* Oct. 1956, 35, 20-25; R. J. Pellegrin, "The achievement of high statuses," *Social Forces,* Oct. 1953, 32, 10-16; Junkichi Abe, "Some problems of life space and historicity through the analysis of delinquency," *Japanese Sociological Review,* July 1957, 7, 3-8; Herbert H. Hyman, "Toward a theory of public opinion," *Public Opinion Quarterly,* Spring 1957, 21, 54-60; George Hillery, "Toward a conceptualization of demography," *Social Forces,* Oct. 1958, 37, 45-51.

scanty list of examples. It is symbolic that Sorokin, though personally committed to developing sociological theory on the grand scale, repeatedly assigns a significant place to middle-range theory. In his most recent book, he periodically assesses current theoretical developments in terms of their capacity to account for "middle-range uniformities." For example, he reviews an array of statistical inquiries in sociology and finds them defective because they do "not give us general or 'middle-range' uniformities, causal laws, or formulas valid for all times and for different societies." Elsewhere Sorokin uses this criterion to appraise contemporary research which would be vindicated if it "has discovered a set of universal, or, at least . . . 'middle-range' uniformities applicable to many persons, groups, and cultures." And still elsewhere he describes selected typologies of cultural systems as acceptable if "like . . . 'middle-range generalizations' . . . they are not overstated and overgeneralized." In his overview of recent research in sociology, Sorokin distinguishes emphatically between "fact-finding" and "uniformities of a 'middle-range' generality." The first produces "purely local, temporary, 'informational' material devoid of general cognitive value." The second makes

> intelligible an otherwise incomprehensible jungle of chaotic historical events. Without these generalizations, we are entirely lost in the jungle, and its endless facts make little sense in their how and why. With a few main rules to guide us, we can orient ourselves in the unmapped darkness of the jungle. Such is the cognitive role of these limited, approximate, prevalent rules and uniformities.[38]

Sorokin thus repudiates that formidable passion for facts that obscures rather than reveals the sociological ideas these facts exemplify; he recommends theories of intermediate range as guides to inquiry; and he continues to prefer, for himself, the quest for a system of general sociology.

REJECTION OF MIDDLE-RANGE THEORY

Since so much sociological ink has been spilled in the debate over theories of the middle range, it may be useful to examine the criticisms of them. Unlike single systems of sociological theory, it has been said, theories of the middle range call for low intellectual ambitions. Few have expressed this view with more eloquence than Robert Bierstedt, when he writes:

> We have even been invited to forego those larger problems of human society that occupied our ancestors in the history of social thought and to seek instead what T. H. Marshall called, in his inaugural lecture at the University of Lon-

38. Sorokin, *Sociological Theories of Today*, 106, 127, 645, 375. In his typically vigorous and forthright fashion, Sorokin taxes me with ambivalence toward "grand systems of sociology" and "theories of the middle range" and with other ambivalences as well. But an effort at rebuttal here, although ego-salving, would be irrelevant to the subject at hand. What remains most significant is that though Sorokin continues to be personally committed to the quest for developing a complete system of sociological theory, he nonetheless moves toward the position taken in this discussion.

don, 'stepping stones in the middle distance,' and other sociologists since, 'theories of the middle range.' But what an anemic ambition this is! Shall we strive for half a victory? Where are the visions that enticed us into the world of learning in the first place? I had always thought that sociologists too knew how to dream and that they believed with Browning that a man's reach should exceed his grasp.[39]

One might infer from this quotation that Bierstedt would prefer to hold fast the sanguine ambition of developing an all-encompassing general theory rather than accept the "anemic ambition" of middle-range theory. Or that he considers sociological solutions to the large and urgent "problems of human society" the theoretically significant touchstone in sociology. But both inferences would evidently be mistaken. For middle-range theory is often accepted by those who ostensibly dispute it. Thus, Bierstedt goes on to say that "in my own opinion one of the greatest pieces of sociological research ever conducted by anyone is Max Weber's *The Protestant Ethic and the Spirit of Capitalism.*" I do not question this appraisal of Weber's monograph—though I would nominate Durkheim's *Suicide* for that lofty position—for, like many other sociologists familiar with the library of criticism that has accumulated around Weber's work, I continue to regard it as a major contribution.[40] But I find it hard to reconcile Bierstedt's appraisal of Weber's monograph with the rhetoric that would banish theories of the middle range as sickly pale and singularly unambitious. For surely this monograph is a prime example of theorizing in the middle range; it deals with a severely delimited problem —one that happens to be exemplified in a particular historical epoch with implications for other societies and other times; it employs a limited theory about the ways in which religious commitment and economic behavior are connected; and it contributes to a somewhat more general theory of the modes of interdependence between social institutions. Is Weber to be indicted for anemic ambition or emulated in his effort to develop an empirically grounded theory of delimited scope?

Bierstedt rejects such theory, I suspect, for two reasons: first, his

39. Robert Bierstedt, "Sociology and humane learning," *American Sociological Review,* 1960, 25, 3-9, at 6.

40. I have even followed up some of the implications of Weber's special theory of the interdependence of social institutions in a monograph, covering much the same period as Weber's, that examines the functional interdependence between science conceived as a social institution, and contemporary economic and religious institutions. See *Science, Technology and Society in Seventeenth-Century England* in *Osiris: Studies on the History and Philosophy of Science, and on the History of Learning and Culture,* ed. by George Sarton (Bruges, Belgium: St. Catherine Press, Ltd., 1938); reprinted with a new introduction (New York: Howard Fertig, Inc. 1970; Harper & Row, 1970). Though Weber had only a few sentences on the interdependence of Puritanism and science, once I began my investigation, these took on special relevance. This is precisely the point of cumulative work in middle-range theory; one takes off from antecedent theory and inquiry and tries to extend the theory into new empirical areas.

observation that theories of the middle range are remote from the aspirations of our intellectual ancestors more than hints that this concept is comparatively new and thus alien to us. However, as I have noted earlier in the chapter and elsewhere[41] the policy of middle-range theory has been repeatedly anticipated.

Second, Bierstedt seems to assume that middle-range theory completely excludes macrosociological inquiry in which a particular theory generates specific hypotheses to be examined in the light of systematically assembled data. As we have seen, this assumption is unfounded. Indeed, the main work in comparative macrosociology today is based largely on specific and delimited theories of the interrelations between the components of social structure that can be subjected to systematic empirical test using the same logic and much the same kinds of indicators as those employed in microsociological research.[42]

The tendency to polarize theoretical issues into all-or-none terms is expressed by another critic, who converts the position of the middle-range theorist into a claim to have found a panacea for contemporary sociological theory. After conceding that "most of the works of Marshall and Merton do display the kind of concern with *problems* which I am here advocating," Dahrendorf goes on to say:

> My objection to their formulations is therefore not directed against these works but against their explicit assumption [*sic*] that all [*sic*] that is wrong with recent theory is its generality and that by simply [*sic*] reducing the level of generality we can solve all [*sic*] problems.[43]

Yet it must be clear from what we have said that theorists of the middle range do not maintain that the deficiencies of sociological theory result solely from its being excessively general. Far from it. Actual theories of the middle range—dissonance theory, the theory of social differentiation, or the theory of reference groups—have great generality, extending beyond a particular historical epoch or culture.[44] But these theories are *not* derived from a unique and total system of theory. Within wide limits, they are consonant with a variety of theoretical orientations. They are confirmed by a variety of empirical data and if any general theory in effect asserts that such data cannot be, so much the worse for that theory.

Another criticism holds that theories of the middle range splinter the

41. Merton, "The role-set," *British Journal of Sociology*, June 1957, 108.
42. For an extensive résumé of these developments, see Robert M. Marsh, *Comparative Sociology: Toward a Codification of Cross-Societal Analysis* (New York: Harcourt, Brace & World, 1967).
43. Ralf Dahrendorf, "Out of Utopia: toward a reorientation of sociological analysis," *American Journal of Sociology*, 1958, 64 115-127, at 122-3.
44. William L. Kolb has seen this with great clarity, succinctly showing that theories of the middle range are not confined to specific historical societies. *American Journal of Sociology*, March 1958, 63, 544-5.

field of sociology into unrelated special theories.[45] Tendencies toward fragmentation in sociology have indeed developed. But this is scarcely a *result* of working toward theories of intermediate scope. On the contrary, theories of the middle range *consolidate*, not fragment, empirical findings. I have tried to show this, for example, with reference group theory, which draws together findings from such disparate fields of human behavior as military life, race and ethnic relations, social mobility, delinquency, politics, education, and revolutionary activity.[46]

These criticisms quite clearly represent efforts to locate middle-range theory in the contemporary scheme of sociology. But the process of polarization pushes criticism well beyond this point into distortion of readily available information. Otherwise, it would not seem possible that anyone could note Riesman's announced position in support of middle-range theory and still maintain that "the Middle Range strategies of exclusion" include a

> systematic attack levelled against those contemporary sociological craftsmen who attempt to work at the problems of the classical tradition. This attack usually takes the form of classifying such sociological work as 'speculative,' 'impressionistic,' or even as downright 'journalistic.' Thus the penetrating efforts at interpreting modern society made by such men as C. Wright Mills and David Riesman, which stand in an organic relationship to the classical tradition just because they dare to deal with the problems at the center of the tradition, are systematically downgraded within the profession.[47]

According to this claim, Riesman is being "systematically downgraded" by advocates of the very type of theory which he himself advocates. Similarly, although this statement suggests that it is a middle-range "strategy of exclusion" to "downgrade" the work of C. Wright Mills, it is a matter of record that one middle-range theorist gave strong endorsement to that part of Mills' work which provides systematic analyses of social structure and social psychology.[48]

---

45. E. K. Francis, *Wissenschaftliche Grundlagen Soziologischen Denkens* (Bern: Francke Verlag, 1957), 13.

46. *Social Theory and Social Structure*, 278-80, 97-98, 131-94.

47. Maurice R. Stein, "Psychoanalytic thought and sociological inquiry," *Psychoanalysis and the Psychoanalytic Review*, Summer 1962, 49, 21-9, at 23-4. Benjamin Nelson, the editor of this issue of the journal, goes on to observe: "Every subject matter hopeful of becoming a science engenders its 'middle range' approach. The animus expressed against this development seems to me in large part misdirected." "Sociology and psychoanalysis on trial: an epilogue," *ibid.*, 144-60, at 153.

48. I refer here to the significant theoretical work which Mills developed in collaboration with the initiating author, Hans Gerth: *Character and Social Structure: The Psychology of Social Institutions* (New York: Harcourt, Brace & Co., 1953). In its introduction, I describe that signal work as follows: "The authors lay no claim to having achieved a fully rounded synthesis which incorporates all the major conceptions of psychology and sociology that bear upon the formation of character and personality in the context of social structure. Such a goal, they make it clear, is still a distant objective rather than a currently possible achievement. Nevertheless, they have systematized a substantial part of the field and have provided perspectives

Recent Soviet sociologists have gone on to interpret "the notorious 'theory of the middle range'" as a positivist conception. According to G. M. Andreeva, such theory is conceived at

> the level of a relatively low order of abstraction, which on principle does not go beyond empirical data. 'Theoretical' knowledge on this level is again in the category of empirical knowledge, for theory itself is in essence reduced to the level of empirical generalizations . . .[49]

This misconception of middle-range theory requires little discussion here. After all, the chapter on "the bearing of sociological theory on empirical research" reprinted in this volume has been in print for nearly a quarter of a century. As long ago as that, I distinguished between a theory, a set of logically interrelated assumptions from which empirically testable hypotheses are derived, and an empirical generalization, an isolated proposition summarizing observed uniformities of relationships between two or more variables. Yet the Marxist scholars construe middle-range theory in terms that are expressly excluded by these formulations.

This misconception may be based on a commitment to a total sociological theory and a fear that this theory will be threatened by the role of theories of the middle range. It should be noted, however, that to the extent that the general theoretical orientation provided by Marxist thought becomes a guide to systematic empirical research, it must do so by developing intermediate special theories. Otherwise, as appears to have been the case with such studies as the Sverdlov investigation of workers' attitudes and behavior, this orientation will lead at best to a series of empirical generalizations (such as the relation of the level of education attained by workers to the number of their organizational affiliations, number of books read, and the like).

The preceding chapter suggested that sociologists who are persuaded that there is a total theory encompassing the full scope of sociological knowledge are apt to believe that sociology must be adequate here and now to all practical demands made of it. This outlook makes for rejection of middle-range theory, as in the following observation by Osipov and Yovchuk:

> Merton's view that sociology is not yet ripe for a comprehensive integral theory and that there are only a few theories available at an intermediate

---

from which to examine much of the rest." This kind of scholarly work in collaboration with Gerth is of quite a different character than other books by Mills, such as *Listen Yankee: The Revolution in Cuba* and *The Causes of World War Three.* These are not "downgraded" by others as "downright 'journalistic'"; they *are* journalistic. But this judgment scarcely derives from the orientation of middle-range theory.

49. These opinions are expressed by A. G. Zdravomyslov and V. A. Yadov, "On the programming of concrete social investigations," *Voprosy Filosofi*, 1963, 17, 81 and by G. M. Andreeva, "Bourgeois empirical sociology seeks a way out of its crisis," *Filosofskie Nauki*, 1962, 5, 39. Extracts from both papers are translated by George Fischer, *Science and Politics: The New Sociology in the Soviet Union* (Ithaca, New York: Cornell University, 1964).

level of abstraction whose significance is relative and temporary is well known. We feel justified in believing that this definition cannot be applied to Marxist scientific sociology. The materialistic comprehension of history, first described by Marx approximately 125 years ago, has been time-tested and has been proved by the entire process of historical development. The materialistic understanding of history is based on the concrete study of social life. The emergence of Marxism in the 1840s and its further development has been organically linked to and supported by research on specific social problems.[50]

This research on specific social problems—what the Soviet sociologists call "concrete sociological investigation"—is not logically derived from the general theoretical orientation of historical materialism. And when intermediate theories have not been developed, these investigations have tended toward "practical empiricism": the methodical collection of just enough information to be taken into account in making practical decisions. For example, there have been various time-budget studies of workers' behavior, not unlike the studies by Sorokin in the early 1930s. Workers were asked to record how they allocated their time among such categories as work-time, household duties, physiological needs, rest, time spent with children and "socially useful work" (including participation in civic councils, workers' courts, attending lectures or doing "mass cultural work"). The analysis of the time budgets has two principal aims. The first is to identify and then to eliminate problems in the efficient scheduling of time. For example, it was found that one obstacle to evening school education for workers was that the time schedule of examinations required more workers to be released from their jobs than could be spared. The second aim of time budgets is to guide plans to change the activities of the workers. For example, when time-budget data were linked with inquiry into workers' motivations, it was concluded that younger workers could be counted on to study more and to be "more active in raising the efficiency of labor." These examples demonstrate that it is practical empiricism, rather than theoretical formulations, that pervades such research. Its findings are on the same low level of abstraction as much of the market-research in other societies. They must be incorporated into more abstract theories of the middle range if the gap between the general orientation of Marxist thought and empirical generalizations is to be filled.[51]

---

50. G. Osipov and M. Yovchuk, "Some principles of theory, problems and methods of research in sociology in the USSR: a Soviet view," reprinted in Alex Simirenko, ed., *Soviet Sociology: Historical Antecedents and Current Appraisals* (Chicago: Quadrangle Books, 1966), 299.

51. This passage is based upon R. K. Merton and Henry W. Riecken, "Notes on Sociology in the USSR," *Current Problems in Social-Behavioral Research,* (Washington, D.C.: National Institute of Social and Behavioral Science, 1962), 7-14. For a summary of one such concrete sociological investigation, see A G. Zdravomyslov and V. A. Yadov, "Soviet workers' attitude toward work: an empirical study," in Simirenko, *op. cit.,* 347-66.

SUMMARY AND RETROSPECT

The foregoing overview of polarized *pros* and *cons* of the theories of the middle range is enough to assure us of one conclusion: each of us is perpetually vulnerable to pharisaism. We thank whatever powers may be that we are not like other sociologists who merely talk rather than observe, or merely observe rather than think, or merely think rather than put their thoughts to the test of systematic empirical investigation.

Given these polarized interpretations of sociological theory of the middle range, it may be helpful to reiterate the attributes of this theory:

1. Middle-range theories consist of limited sets of assumptions from which specific hypotheses are logically derived and confirmed by empirical investigation.

2. These theories do not remain separate but are consolidated into wider networks of theory, as illustrated by theories of level of aspiration, reference-group, and opportunity-structure.

3. These theories are sufficiently abstract to deal with differing spheres of social behavior and social structure, so that they transcend sheer description or empirical generalization. The theory of social conflict, for example, has been applied to ethnic and racial conflict, class conflict, and international conflict.

4. This type of theory cuts across the distinction between microsociological problems, as evidenced in small group research, and macrosociological problems, as evidenced in comparative studies of social mobility and formal organization, and the interdependence of social institutions.

5. Total sociological systems of theory—such as Marx's historical materialism, Parsons' theory of social systems and Sorokin's integral sociology—represent general theoretical orientations rather than the rigorous and tightknit systems envisaged in the search for a "unified theory" in physics.

6. As a result, many theories of the middle range are consonant with a variety of systems of sociological thought.

7. Theories of the middle range are typically in direct line of continuity with the work of classical theoretical formulations. We are all residuary legatees of Durkheim and Weber, whose works furnish ideas to be followed up, exemplify tactics of theorizing, provide models for the exercise of taste in the selection of problems, and instruct us in raising theoretical questions that develop out of theirs.

8. The middle-range orientation involves the specification of ignorance. Rather than pretend to knowledge where it is in fact absent, it expressly recognizes what must still be learned in order to lay the foundation for still more knowledge. It does not assume itself to be equal to the task of providing theoretical solutions to all the urgent practical problems

of the day but addresses itself to those problems that might now be clarified in the light of available knowledge.

PARADIGMS: THE CODIFICATION OF SOCIOLOGICAL THEORY

As noted earlier, a major concern of this book is the codification of substantive theory and of procedures of qualitative analysis in sociology. As construed here, codification is the orderly and compact arrangement of fruitful procedures of inquiry and the substantive findings that result from this use. This process entails identification and organization of what has been implicit in work of the past rather than the invention of new strategies of research.

The following chapter, dealing with functional analysis, sets forth a paradigm as a basis for codifying previous work in this field.[52] I believe that such paradigms have great propaedeutic value. For one thing, they bring out into the open the array of assumptions, concepts, and basic propositions employed in a sociological analysis. They thus reduce the inadvertent tendency to hide the hard core of analysis behind a veil of random, though possibly illuminating, comments and thoughts. Despite the appearance of propositional inventories, sociology still has few formulae—that is, highly abbreviated symbolic expressions of relationships between sociological variables. Consequently, sociological interpretations tend to be discursive. The logic of procedure, the key concepts, and the relationships between them often become lost in an avalanche of words. When this happens, the critical reader must laboriously glean for himself the implicit assumptions of the author. The paradigm reduces this tendency for the theorist to employ tacit concepts and assumptions.

Contributing to the tendency for sociological exposition to become lengthy rather than lucid is the tradition—inherited slightly from philosophy, substantially from history, and greatly from literature—of writing sociological accounts vividly and intensely to convey all the rich fullness of the human scene. The sociologist who does not disavow this handsome but alien heritage becomes intent on searching for the exceptional constellation of words that will best express the *particularity* of the sociological case in hand, rather than on seeking out the objective, generalizable concepts and relationships it exemplifies—the core of a science, as distinct

---

52. I have elsewhere set forth other paradigms on deviant social behavior in Chapter IV of *Social Theory and Social Structure;* on the sociology of knowledge in Chapter XII of that book; on racial intermarriage in "Intermarriage and the social structure," *Psychiatry,* 1941, 4, 361-74; on racial prejudice and discrimination in "Discrimination and the American creed," in *Discrimination and National Welfare,* R. M. MacIver, ed. (New York: Harper & Brothers, 1948). It should be noted that the use of the term *paradigm* by T. S. Kuhn in his recent work on the history and philosophy of science is much more extended, referring to the basic set of assumptions adopted by a scientific discipline in a particular historical phase; see *The Structure of Scientific Revolutions, op. cit.*

from the arts. Too often, this misplaced use of genuine artistic skills is encouraged by the plaudits of a lay public, gratefully assuring the sociologist that he writes like a novelist and not like an overly-domesticated and academically-henpecked Ph.D. Not infrequently, he pays for this popular applause, for the closer he approaches eloquence, the farther he retreats from methodical sense. It must be acknowledged, however, as St. Augustine suggested in mild rebuttal long ago, that ". . . a thing is not necessarily true because badly uttered, nor false because spoken magnificently."

Nonetheless, ostensibly scientific reports often become obscured by irrelevancies. In extreme cases, the hard skeleton of fact, inference and theoretical conclusion becomes overlaid with the soft flesh of stylistic ornamentation. Yet other scientific disciplines—physics and chemistry as much as biology, geology and statistics—have escaped this misplaced concern with the literary graces. Anchored to the purposes of science, these disciplines prefer brevity, precision and objectivity to exquisitely rhythmic patterns of language, richness of connotation, and sensitive verbal imagery. But even if one disagrees that sociology must hew to the line laid down by chemistry, physics or biology, one need not argue that it must emulate history, discursive philosophy, or literature. Each to his last, and the last of the sociologist is that of lucidly presenting claims to logically interconnected and empirically confirmed propositions about the structure of society and its changes, the behavior of man within that structure and the consequences of that behavior. Paradigms for sociological analysis are intended to help the sociologist work at his trade.

Since sound sociological interpretation inevitably implies some theoretical paradigm, it seems the better part of wisdom to bring it out into the open. If true art consists in concealing all signs of art, true science consists in revealing its scaffolding as well as its finished structure.

Without pretending that this tells the whole story, I suggest that paradigms for qualitative analysis in sociology have at least five closely related functions.[53]

First, paradigms have a notational function. They provide a compact arrangement of the central concepts and their interrelations that are utilized for description and analysis. Setting out concepts in sufficiently small compass to allow their *simultaneous* inspection is an important aid in the self-correction of one's successive interpretations—a goal hard to achieve when the concepts are scattered throughout discursive exposition. (As the work of Cajori indicates, this appears to be one of the important functions of mathematical symbols: they provide for the simultaneous inspection of all terms entering into the analysis.)

Second, paradigms lessen the likelihood of inadvertently introducing

---

53. For a critical appraisal of this discussion, see Don Martindale, "Sociological theory and the ideal type," in Llewellyn Gross, ed., *Symposium on Sociological Theory* (Evanston: Row, Peterson, 1959), 57-91, at 77-80.

hidden assumptions and concepts, for each new assumption and each new concept must be either logically derived from previous components of the paradigm or explicitly introduced into it. The paradigm thus provides a guide for avoiding *ad hoc* (i.e. logically irresponsible) hypotheses.

Third, paradigms advance the cumulation of theoretical interpretation. In effect, the paradigm is the foundation upon which the house of interpretations is built. If a new story cannot be built directly upon this foundation, then it must be treated as a new wing of the total structure, and the foundation of concepts and assumptions must be extended to support this wing. Moreover, each new story that *can* be built upon the original foundation strengthens our confidence in its substantial quality just as every new extension, precisely because it requires an additional foundation, leads us to suspect the soundness of the original substructure. A paradigm worthy of great confidence will in due course support an interpretative structure of skyscraper dimensions, with each successive story testifying to the well-laid quality of the original foundation, while a defective paradigm will support only a rambling one-story structure, in which each new set of uniformities requires a new foundation to be laid, since the original cannot bear the weight of additional stories.

Fourth, paradigms, by their very arrangement, suggest the systematic cross-tabulation of significant concepts and can thus sensitize the analyst to empirical and theoretical problems which he might otherwise overlook.[54] Paradigms promote analysis rather than the description of concrete details. They direct our attention, for example, to the components of social behavior, to possible strains and tensions among these components, and thereby to sources of departures from the behavior which is normatively prescribed.

Fifth, paradigms make for the codification of qualitative analysis in a way that approximates the logical if not the empirical rigor of quantitative analysis. The procedures for computing statistical measures and their mathematical bases are codified as a matter of course; their assumptions and procedures are open to critical scrutiny by all. By contrast, the sociological analysis of qualitative data often resides in a private world of penetrating but unfathomable insights and ineffable understandings. Indeed, discursive expositions not based upon paradigms often include perceptive interpretations. As the cant phrase has it, they are rich in "illuminating insights." But it is not always clear just which operations on which analytic concepts were involved in these insights. In some quarters, even the suggestion that these intensely private experiences must be reshaped into publicly certifiable procedures if they are to be

54. Although they express doubts about the uses of systematic theory, Joseph Bensman and Arthur Vidich have admirably exhibited this heuristic function of paradigms in their instructive paper, "Social theory in field research," *American Journal of Sociology*, May 1960, 65, 577-84.

incorporated into the science of society is taken as a sign of blind impiety. Yet the concepts and procedures of even the most perceptive of sociologists must be reproducible and the results of their insights testable by others. Science, and this includes sociological science, is public, not private. It is not that we ordinary sociologists wish to cut all talents to our own small stature; it is only that the contributions of the great and small alike must be codified if they are to advance the development of sociology.

All virtues can easily become vices merely by being carried to excess, and this applies to the sociological paradigm. It is a temptation to mental indolence. Equipped with his paradigm, the sociologist may shut his eyes to strategic data not expressly called for by the paradigm. Thus it can be turned from a sociological field-glass into a sociological blinder. Misuse results from absolutizing the paradigm rather than using it as a tentative point of departure. But if they are recognized as provisional and changing, destined to be modified in the immediate future as they have been in the recent past, these paradigms are preferable to sets of tacit assumptions.

III MANIFEST AND LATENT FUNCTIONS

TOWARD THE CODIFICATION OF FUNCTIONAL ANALYSIS IN SOCIOLOGY

FUNCTIONAL ANALYSIS is at once the most promising and possibly the least codified of contemporary orientations to problems of sociological interpretation. Having developed on many intellectual fronts at the same time, it has grown in shreds and patches rather than in depth. The accomplishments of functional analysis are sufficient to suggest that its large promise will progressively be fulfilled, just as its current deficiencies testify to the need for periodically overhauling the past the better to build for the future. At the very least, occasional re-assessments bring into open discussion many of the difficulties which otherwise remain tacit and unspoken.

Like all interpretative schemes, functional analysis depends upon a triple alliance between theory, method and data. Of the three allies, method is by all odds the weakest. Many of the major practitioners of functional analysis have been devoted to theoretic formulations and to the clearing up of concepts; some have steeped themselves in data directly relevant to a functional frame of reference; but few have broken the prevailing silence regarding how one goes about the business of functional analysis. Yet the plenty and variety of functional analyses force the conclusion that *some* methods have been employed and awaken the hope that much may be learned from their inspection.

Although methods can be profitably examined without reference to theory or substantive data—methodology or the logic of procedure of course has precisely that as its assignment—empirically oriented disciplines are more fully served by inquiry into procedures if this takes due account of their theoretic problems and substantive findings. For the use of "method" involves not only logic but, unfortunately perhaps for those who must struggle with the difficulties of research, also the practical problems of aligning data with the requirements of theory. At least, that is our premise. Accordingly, we shall interweave our account with a systematic review of some of the chief conceptions of functional theory.

THE VOCABULARIES OF FUNCTIONAL ANALYSIS

From its very beginnings, the functional approach in sociology has been caught up in terminological confusion. *Too often, a single term has been used to symbolize different concepts, just as the same concept has been symbolized by different terms.* Clarity of analysis and adequacy of communication are both victims of this frivolous use of words. At times, the analysis suffers from the unwitting shift in the conceptual content of a given term, and communication with others breaks down when the essentially same content is obscured by a battery of diverse terms. We have only to follow, for a short distance, the vagaries of the concept of 'function' to discover how conceptual clarity is effectively marred and communication defeated by competing vocabularies of functional analysis.

Single Term, Diverse Concepts

The word "function" has been pre-empted by several disciplines and by popular speech with the not unexpected result that its connotation often becomes obscure in sociology proper. By confining ourselves to only five connotations commonly assigned to this one word, we neglect numerous others. There is first, popular usage, according to which function refers to some public gathering or festive occasion, usually conducted with ceremonial overtones. It is in this connection, one must assume, that a newspaper headline asserts: "Mayor Tobin Not Backing Social Function," for the news account goes on to explain that "Mayor Tobin announced today that he is not interested in any social function, nor has he authorized anyone to sell tickets or sell advertising for any affair." Common as this usage is, it enters into the academic literature too seldom to contribute any great share to the prevailing chaos of terminology. Clearly, *this* connotation of the word is wholly alien to functional analysis in sociology.

A second usage makes the term function virtually equivalent to the term occupation. Max Weber, for example, defines occupation as "the mode of specialization, specification and combination of the functions of an individual so far as it constitutes for him the basis of a continual opportunity for income or for profit."[1] This is a frequent, indeed almost a typical, usage of the term by some economists who refer to the "functional analysis of a group" when they report the distribution of occupations in that group. Since this is the case, it may be expedient to follow the suggestion of Sargant Florence,[2] that the more nearly descriptive phrase "occupational analysis" be adopted for such inquiries.

1. Max Weber, *Theory of Social and Economic Organization* (edited by Talcott Parsons), (London: William Hodge and Co., 1947), 230.

2. P. Sargent Florence, *Statistical Method in Economics,* (New York: Harcourt, Brace and Co., 1929), 357-58n.

A third usage, representing a special instance of the preceding one, is found both in popular speech and in political science. Function is often used to refer to the activities assigned to the incumbent of a social status, and more particularly, to the occupant of an office or political position. This gives rise to the term functionary, or official. Although function in this sense overlaps the broader meaning assigned the term in sociology and anthropology, it had best be excluded since it diverts attention from the fact that functions are performed not only by the occupants of designated positions, but by a wide range of standardized activities, social processes, culture patterns and belief-systems found in a society.

Since it was first introduced by Leibniz, the word function has its most precise significance in mathematics, where it refers to a variable considered in relation to one or more other variables in terms of which it may be expressed or on the value of which its own value depends. This conception, in a more extended (and often more imprecise) sense, is expressed by such phrases as "functional interdependence" and "functional relations," so often adopted by social scientists.[3] When Mannheim observes that "every social fact is a function of the time and place in which it occurs," or when a demographer states that "birth-rates are a function of economic status," they are manifestly making use of the mathematical connotation, though the first is not reported in the form of equations and the second is. The context generally makes it clear that the term function is being used in this mathematical sense, but social scientists not infrequently shuttle back and forth between this and another related, though distinct, connotation, which also involves the notion of "interdependence," "reciprocal relation" or "mutually dependent variations."

It is this fifth connotation which is central to functional analysis as this has been practiced in sociology and social anthropology. Stemming in part from the native mathematical sense of the term, this usage is more often explicitly adopted from the biological sciences, where the term function is understood to refer to the "vital or organic processes considered in the respects in which they contribute to the maintenance of the organism."[4] With modifications appropriate to the study of human

3. Thus, Alexander Lesser: "In its logical essentials, what is a functional relation? Is it any different in kind from functional relations in other fields of science? I think not. A genuinely functional relation is one which is established between two or more terms or variables such that it can be asserted that under certain defined conditions (which form one term of the relation) certain determined expressions of those conditions (which is the other term of the relation) are observed. The functional relation or relations asserted of any delimited aspect of culture must be such as to explain the nature and character of the delimited aspect under defined conditions." "Functionalism in social anthropology," *American Anthropologist,* N.S. 37 (1935), 386-93, at 392.

4. See for example, Ludwig von Bertalanffy, *Modern Theories of Development,* (New York: Oxford University Press, 1933), 9 ff., 184 ff.; W. M. Bayliss, *Principles of General Physiology* (London, 1915), 706, where he reports his researches on the functions of the hormone discovered by Starling and himself; W. B. Cannon, *Bodily Changes in Pain, Hunger, Fear and Rage* (New York: Appleton & Co., 1929), 222, describing the "emergency functions of the sympathetico-adrenal system."

society, this corresponds rather closely to the key concept of function as adopted by the anthropological functionalists, pure or tempered.[5]

Radcliffe-Brown is the most often explicit in tracing his working conception of social function to the analogical model found in the biological sciences. After the fashion of Durkheim, he asserts that "the function of a recurrent physiological process is thus a correspondence between it and the needs (*i.e.*, the necessary conditions of existence) of the organism." And in the social sphere where individual human beings, "the essential units," are connected by networks of social relations into an integrated whole, "the function of any recurrent activity, such as the punishment of a crime, or a funeral ceremony, is the part it plays in the social life as a whole and therefore the contribution it makes to the maintenance of the structural continuity."[6]

Though Malinowski differs in several respects from the formulations of Radcliffe-Brown, he joins him in making the core of functional analysis the study of "the part which [social or cultural items] play in the society." "This type of theory," Malinowski explains in one of his early declarations of purpose, "aims at the explanation of anthropological facts at all levels of development by *their function, by the part which they play within the integral system of culture, by the manner in which they are related to each other within the system. . . .*"[7]

As we shall presently see in some detail, such recurrent phrases as "the part played in the social or cultural system" tend to blur the important distinction between the concept of function as "interdependence" and as "process." Nor need we pause here to observe that the postulate which holds that every item of culture has *some* enduring relations with other items, that it has *some* distinctive place in the total culture scarcely equips the field-observer or the analyst with a specific guide to procedure. All this had better wait. At the moment, we need only recognize that more recent formulations have clarified and extended this concept of function through progressive specifications. Thus, Kluckhohn: ". . . a given bit of culture is 'functional' insofar as it defines a mode of response

5. Lowie makes a distinction between the "pure functionalism" of a Malinowski and the "tempered functionalism" of a Thurnwald. Sound as the distinction is, it will soon become apparent that it is not pertinent for our purposes. R. H. Lowie, *The History of Ethnological Theory* (New York: Farrar & Rinehart, 1937), Chapter 13.

6. A. R. Radcliffe-Brown, "On the concept of function in social science," *American Anthropologist*, 1935, 37, 395-6. See also his later presidential address before the Royal Anthropological Institute, where he states: ". . . I would define the social function of a socially standardized mode of activity, or mode of thought, as its relation to the social structure to the existence and continuity of which it makes some contribution. Analogously, in a living organism, the physiological function of the beating of the heart, or the secretion of gastric juices, is its relation to the organic structure. . . ." "On social structure," *The Journal of the Royal Anthropological Institute of Great Britain and Ireland*, 1940, 70, Pt. I, 9-10.

7. B. Malinowski, "Anthropology," *Encyclopaedia Britannica*, First Supplementary Volume, (London and New York, 1926), 132-133 [italics supplied].

which is adaptive from the standpoint of the society and adjustive from the standpoint of the individual."[8]

From these connotations of the term "function," and we have touched upon only a few drawn from a more varied array, it is plain that many concepts are caught up in the same word. This invites confusion. And when many different words are held to express the same concept, there develops confusion worse confounded.

Single Concept, Diverse Terms

The large assembly of terms used indifferently and almost synonymously with "function" presently includes use, utility, purpose, motive, intention, aim, consequences. Were these and similar terms put to use to refer to the same strictly defined concept, there would of course be little point in noticing their numerous variety. But the fact is that the undisciplined use of these terms, with their ostensibly similar conceptual reference, leads to successively greater departures from tight-knit and rigorous functional analysis. The connotations of each term which differ from rather than agree with the connotation that they have in common are made the (unwitting) basis for inferences which become increasingly dubious as they become progressively remote from the central concept of function. One or two illustrations will bear out the point that a shifting vocabulary makes for the multiplication of misunderstandings.

In the following passage drawn from one of the most sensible of treatises on the sociology of crime, one can detect the shifts in meaning of nominally synonymous terms and the questionable inferences which depend upon these shifts. (The key terms are italicized to help in picking one's way through the argument.)

> *Purpose* of Punishment. Attempts are being made to determine the *purpose or function* of punishment in different groups at different times. Many investigators have insisted that some one *motive* was *the motive* in punishment. On the other hand, the *function* of punishment in restoring the solidarity of the group which has been weakened by the crime is emphasized. Thomas and Znaniecki have indicated that among the Polish peasants the punishment of crime is *designed primarily* to restore the situation which existed before the crime and renew the solidarity of the group, and that revenge is *a secondary consideration.* From this point of view punishment *is concerned primarily* with the group and only *secondarily* with the offender. On the other hand, expiation, deterrence, retribution, reformation, income for the state, and other things have been posited as *the function* of punishment. In the past as at present it is not clear that any one of these is *the motive;* punishments seem to grow from *many motives* and to perform *many functions.* This is true both of the individual victims of crimes and of the state. Certainly the laws of the present

8. Clyde Kluckhohn, *Navaho Witchcraft,* Papers of the Peabody Museum of American Archaeology and Ethnology, Harvard University, (Cambridge: Peabody Museum, 1944), XXII, No. 2, 47a.

day are not consistent in *aims or motives;* probably the same condition existed in earlier societies.[9]

We should attend first to the list of terms ostensibly referring to the same concept: purpose, function, motive, designed, secondary consideration, primary concern, aim. Through inspection, it becomes clear that *these terms group into quite distinct conceptual frames of reference.* At times, some of these terms—motive, design, aim and purpose—clearly refer to the *explicit ends-in-view of the representatives of the state.* Others —motive, secondary consideration—refer to the *ends-in-view of the victim of the crime.* And both of these sets of terms are alike in referring to the *subjective anticipations of the results of punishment.* But the concept of function involves the standpoint of *the observer,* not necessarily that of the participant. Social function refers to *observable objective consequences,* and not to *subjective dispositions* (aims, motives, purposes). And the failure to distinguish between the objective sociological consequences and the subjective dispositions inevitably leads to confusion of functional analysis, as can be seen from the following excerpt (in which the key terms are again italicized):

> The extreme of unreality is attained in the discussion of the so-called "functions" of the family. The family, we hear, performs important *functions* in society; it provides for the perpetuation of the species and the training of the young; it performs economic and religious functions, and so on. Almost we are encouraged to believe that *people marry and have children because* they are eager to perform these needed societal functions. In fact, people marry *because* they are in love, or for other less romantic but no less personal reasons. The *function* of the family, *from the viewpoint of individuals,* is to satisfy their wishes. The *function* of the family or any other social institution is *merely what people use it for.* Social "*functions*" are mostly *rationalizations of established practices; we* act first, explain afterwards; *we* act for *personal reasons,* and justify *our* behavior by social and ethical *principles.* Insofar as these *functions* of institutions have any real basis, it must be stated in terms of the social processes in which people engage *in the attempt* to satisfy their wishes. Functions arise from the inter-action of concrete human beings and concrete *purposes.*[10]

This passage is an interesting medley of small islets of clarity in the midst of vast confusion. Whenever it mistakenly identifies (subjective) motives with (objective) functions, it abandons a lucid functional approach. For it need not be assumed, as we shall presently see, that the *motives* for entering into marriage ("love," "personal reasons") are identical with the *functions* served by families (socialization of the child). Again, it need not be assumed that the *reasons* advanced by people for their behavior ("*we* act for personal reasons") are one and

9. Edwin H. Sutherland, *Principles of Criminology,* third edition, (Philadelphia: J. B. Lippincott, 1939), 349-350.

10. Willard Waller, *The Family,* (New York: Cordon Company, 1938), 26.

the same as the observed consequences of these patterns of behavior. The subjective disposition may coincide with the objective consequence, but again, it may not. The two vary independently. When, however, it is said that people are motivated to engage in behavior which may give rise to (not necessarily intended) functions, there is offered escape from the troubled sea of confusion.[11]

This brief review of competing terminologies and their unfortunate consequences may be something of a guide to later efforts at codification of the concepts of functional analysis. There will plainly be occasion to limit the use of the sociological concept of function, and there will be need to distinguish clearly between subjective categories of disposition and objective categories of observed consequences. Else the substance of the functional orientation may become lost in a cloud of hazy definitions.

PREVAILING POSTULATES IN FUNCTIONAL ANALYSIS

Chiefly but not solely in anthropology, functional analysts have commonly adopted three interconnected postulates which, it will now be suggested, have proved to be debatable and unnecessary to the functional orientation.

Substantially, these postulates hold first, that standardized social activities or cultural items are functional for the *entire* social or cultural system; second, that *all* such social and cultural items fulfill sociological functions; and third, that these items are consequently *indispensable*. Although these three articles of faith are ordinarily seen only in one another's company, they had best be examined separately, since each gives rise to its own distinctive difficulties.

Postulate of the Functional Unity of Society

It is Radcliffe-Brown who characteristically puts this postulate in explicit terms:

> The function of a particular social usage is the contribution it makes to the *total social life* as the functioning of the *total social system*. Such a view implies that a social system (*the total social structure* of a society together with the totality of social usages, in which that structure appears and on which it depends for its continued existence) has a certain kind of unity, which we

11. These two instances of confusion between motive and function are drawn from an easily available storehouse of additional materials of the same kind. Even Radcliffe-Brown, who ordinarily avoids this practice, occasionally fails to make the distinction. For example: ". . . the exchange of presents did not serve the same *purpose* as trade and barter in more developed communities. The *purpose* that it did serve is a moral one. The *object* of the exchange was to produce a friendly feeling between the two persons concerned, and unless it did this it failed of its *purpose*." Is the "object" of the transaction seen from the standpoint of the observer, the participant, or both? See A. R. Radcliffe-Brown, *The Andaman Islanders,* (Glencoe, Illinois: The Free Press, 1948), 84 [italics supplied].

may speak of as a functional unity. We may define it as a condition in which all parts of the social system work together with a sufficient degree of harmony or internal consistency, *i.e.*, without producing persistent conflicts which can neither be resolved nor regulated.[12]

It is important to note, however, that he goes on to describe this notion of functional unity as a hypothesis which requires further test.

It would at first appear that Malinowski was questioning the empirical acceptability of this postulate when he notes that "the sociological school" (into which he thrusts Radcliffe-Brown) "exaggerated the social solidarity of primitive man" and "neglected the individual."[13] But it is soon apparent that Malinowski does not so much abandon this dubious assumption as he succeeds in adding another to it. He continues to speak of standardized practices and beliefs as functional "for culture as a whole," and goes on to assume that they are *also* functional for every member of the society. Thus, referring to primitive beliefs in the supernatural, he writes:

Here the functional view is put to its acid test. . . . It is bound to show in what way belief and ritual work for social integration, technical and economic efficiency, for *culture as a whole*—indirectly therefore for the biological and mental welfare *of each individual member*.[14]

If the one unqualified assumption is questionable, this twin assumption is doubly so. Whether cultural items do uniformly fulfill functions for the society viewed as a system and for all members of the society is presumably an empirical question of fact, rather than an axiom.

Kluckhohn evidently perceives the problem inasmuch as he extends the alternatives to include the possibility that cultural forms "are adjustive or adaptive . . . for the members of the society *or* for the society considered as a perduring unit."[15] This is a necessary first step in allowing for variation in the *unit* which is subserved by the imputed function. Compelled by the force of empirical observation, we shall have occasion to widen the range of variation in this unit even further.

It seems reasonably clear that the notion of functional unity is *not* a postulate beyond the reach of empirical test; quite the contrary. The

---

12. Radcliffe-Brown, "On the concept of function," *op. cit.*, 397 [italics supplied].

13. See Malinowski, "Anthropology," *op. cit.*, 132 and "The group and the individual in functional analysis," *American Journal of Sociology*, 1939, 44, 938-64, at 939.

14. Malinowski, "Anthropology," *op. cit.*, 135, Malinowski maintained this view, without essential change, in his later writings. Among these, consult, for example, "The group and the individual in functional analysis," *op. cit.*, at 962-3: ". . . we see that every institution contributes, on the one hand, toward the integral working of *the community as a whole*, but it also satisfies the derived and basic needs of the individual . . . everyone of the benefits just listed is enjoyed *by every individual member*." [italics supplied].

15. Kluckhohn, *Navaho Witchcraft*, 46b [italics supplied].

degree of integration is an empirical variable,[16] changing for the same society from time to time and differing among various societies. That all human societies must have *some* degree of integration is a matter of definition—and begs the question. But not all societies have that *high* degree of integration in which *every* culturally standardized activity or belief is functional for the society as a whole and uniformly functional for the people living in it. Radcliffe-Brown need in fact have looked no further than to his favored realm of analogy in order to suspect the adequacy of his assumption of functional unity. For we find significant variations in the degree of integration even among individual biological organisms, although the commonsense assumption would tell us that here, surely, all the parts of the organism work toward a "unified" end. Consider only this:

> One can readily see that there are *highly integrated organisms* under close control of the nervous system or of hormones, the loss of any major part of which will strongly affect the whole system, and frequently will cause death, but, on the other hand, there are the lower *organisms much more loosely correlated,* where the loss of even a major part of the body causes only temporary inconvenience pending the regeneration of replacement tissues. Many of these more loosely organized animals are *so poorly integrated that different parts may be in active opposition to each other.* Thus, when an ordinary starfish is placed on its back, part of the arms may attempt to turn the animal in one direction, while others work to turn it in the opposite way. . . . On account of its *loose integration,* the sea anemone may move off and leave a portion of its foot clinging tightly to a rock, so that the animal suffers serious rupture.[17]

If this is true of single organisms, it would seem *a fortiori* the case with complex social systems.

One need not go far afield to show that the assumption of the complete functional unity of human society is repeatedly contrary to fact. Social usages or sentiments may be functional for some groups and dysfunctional for others in the same society. Anthropologists often cite "increased solidarity of the community" and "increased family pride" as instances of functionally adaptive sentiments. Yet, as Bateson[18] among others has indicated, an increase of pride among individual families may often serve to disrupt the solidarity of a small local community. Not only is the postulate of functional unity often contrary to fact, but it has little heuristic value, since it diverts the analyst's attention from possible disparate consequences of a given social or cultural item (usage, belief,

16. It is the merit of Sorokin's early review of theories of social integration that he did not lose sight of this important fact. *Cf.* P. A. Sorokin, "Forms and problems of culture-integration," *Rural Sociology,* 1936, 1, 121-41; 344-74.

17. G. H. Parker, *The Elementary Nervous System,* quoted by W. C. Allee, *Animal Aggregation,* (University of Chicago Prses, 1931), 81-82.

18. Gregory Bateson, *Naven,* (Cambridge [England] University Press, 1936), 31-32.

behavior pattern, institution) for diverse social groups and for the individual members of these groups.

If the body of observation and fact which negates the assumption of functional unity is as large and easily accessible as we have suggested, it is interesting to ask how it happens that Radcliffe-Brown and others who follow his lead have continued to abide by this assumption. A possible clue is provided by the fact that this conception, in its recent formulations, was developed by social *anthropologists,* that is, by men primarily concerned with the study of non-literate societies. In view of what Radin has described as "the highly integrated nature of the majority of aboriginal civilizations," this assumption may be tolerably suitable for some, if not all, non-literate societies. But one pays an excessive intellectual penalty for moving this possibly useful assumption from the realm of small non-literate societies to the realm of large, complex and highly differentiated literate societies. In no field, perhaps, do the dangers of such a transfer of assumption become more visible than in the functional analysis of religion. This deserves brief review, if only because it exhibits in bold relief the fallacies one falls heir to by sympathetically adopting this assumption without a thorough screening.

The Functional Interpretation of Religion. In examining the price paid for the transfer of this tacit assumption of functional unity from the field of relatively small and relatively tightknit non-literate groups to the field of more highly differentiated and perhaps more loosely integrated societies, it is useful to consider the work of sociologists, particularly of sociologists who are ordinarily sensitized to the assumptions on which they work. This has passing interest for its bearing on the more general question of seeking, without appropriate modification, to apply to the study of literate societies conceptions developed and matured in the study of non-literate societies. (Much the same question holds for the transfer of research procedures and techniques, but this is not at issue here.)

The large, spaceless and timeless generalizations about "the integrative functions of religion" are largely, though not of course wholly, derived from observations in non-literate societies. Not infrequently, the social scientist implicitly adopts the findings regarding such societies and goes on to expatiate upon the integrative functions of religion *generally*. From this, it is a short step to statements such as the following:

> *The reason why religion is necessary* is apparently to be found in the fact that human society *achieves its unity* primarily through the possession by its members of certain ultimate values and ends in common. Although these values and ends are subjective, they influence behavior, and their integration enables this society to operate as a system.[19]

19. Kingsley Davis and Wilbert E. Moore, "Some principles of stratification," *American Sociological Review*, April 1945, 10, 242-49, at 244. [italics supplied].

> In an extremely advanced society built on scientific technology, the priesthood tends to lose status, because sacred tradition and supernaturalism drop into the background . . . [but] *No society* has become so completely secularized as to liquidate *entirely* the belief in transcendental ends and supernatural entities. Even in a secularized society *some system* must exist for the integration of ultimate values, for their ritualistic expression, and for the emotional adjustments required by disappointment, death, and disaster.[20]

Deriving from the Durkheim orientation which was based largely upon the study of non-literate societies, these authors tend to single out *only* the apparently integrative consequences of religion and to neglect its possibly disintegrative consequences *in certain types of social structure.* Yet consider the following very well-known facts and queries. (1) When different religions co-exist in the same society, there often occurs deep conflict between the several religious groups (consider only the enormous literature on inter-religious conflict in European societies). In what sense, then, does religion make for integration of "the" society in the numerous multi-religion societies? (2) It is clearly the case that "human society achieves its unity [insofar as it exhibits such unity] primarily through the possession by its members of certain ultimate values and ends in common." But what is the evidence indicating that "non-religious" people, say, in our own society less often subscribe to certain common "values and ends" than those devoted to religious doctrines? (3) In what sense does religion make for integration of the larger society, if the content of its doctrine and values is at odds with the content of other, non-religious values held by many people in the same society? (Consider, for example, the conflict between the opposition of the Catholic Church to child-labor legislation and the secular values of preventing "exploitation of youthful dependents." Or the contrasting evaluations of birth control by diverse religious groups in our society.)

This list of commonplace facts regarding the role of religion in contemporary literate societies could be greatly extended, and they are of course very well known to those functional anthropologists and sociologists who describe religion as integrative, without limiting the range of social structures in which this is indeed the case. It is at least conceivable that a theoretic orientation derived from research on non-literate societies has served to obscure otherwise conspicuous data on the functional role of religion in multi-religion societies. Perhaps it is the transfer of the assumption of functional unity which results in blotting out the entire history of religious wars, of the Inquisition (which drove a wedge into society after society), of internecine conflicts among religious groups. For the fact remains that all this abundantly known material is ignored in favor of illustrations drawn from the study of religion in non-literate society. And it is a further striking fact that the same paper, cited above,

---

20. *Ibid.*, 246. [italics supplied].

that goes on to speak of "religion, which provides integration in terms of sentiments, beliefs and rituals," does not make a single reference to the possibly divisive role of religion.

Such functional analyses may, of course, mean that religion provides integration of those who believe in the *same* religious values, but it is unlikely that this is meant, since it would merely assert that integration is provided by any consensus on any set of values.

Moreover, this again illustrates the danger of taking the assumption of functional unity, which *may* be a reasonable approximation for some non-literate societies, as part of an implicit model for *generalized* functional analysis. Typically, in non-literate societies, there is but one prevailing religious system so that, apart from individual deviants, the membership of the total society and the membership of the religious community are virtually co-extensive. Obviously, in this type of social structure, a common set of religious values may have as *one* of its consequences the reinforcement of common sentiments and of social integration. But this does not easily lend itself to defensible generalization about other types of society.

We shall have occasion to return to other theoretic implications of current functional analyses of religion but, for the moment, this may illustrate the dangers which one inherits in adopting the unqualified postulate of functional unity. This unity of the total society cannot be usefully posited in advance of observation. It is a question of fact, and not a matter of opinion. The theoretic framework of functional analysis must expressly require that there be *specification* of the *units* for which a given social or cultural item is functional. It must expressly allow for a given item having diverse consequences, functional and dysfunctional, for individuals, for subgroups, and for the more inclusive social structure and culture.

Postulate of Universal Functionalism

Most succinctly, this postulate holds that all standardized social or cultural forms have positive functions. As with other aspects of the functional conception, Malinowski advances this in its most extreme form:

> The functional view of culture *insists* therefore upon the principle that in *every type of civilization, every custom, material object, idea and belief fulfills some vital function. . . .*[21]

Although, as we have seen, Kluckhohn allows for variation in the unit subserved by a cultural form, he joins with Malinowski in postulating functional value for all surviving forms of culture. ("My basic postulate . . . is that *no* culture forms survive unless they constitute responses which

21. Malinowski, "Anthropology," *op. cit.*, 132 [The italics, though supplied, are perhaps superfluous in view of the forceful language of the original.]

are adjustive or adaptive, in some sense . . ."[22]) This universal functionalism may or may not be a heuristic postulate; that remains to be seen. But one should be prepared to find that it too diverts critical attention from a range of non-functional consequences of existing cultural forms.

In fact, when Kluckhohn seeks to illustrate his point by ascribing "functions" to seemingly functionless items, he falls back upon a type of function which would be found, *by definition* rather than by inquiry, served by all persisting items of culture. Thus, he suggests that

> The at present mechanically useless buttons on the sleeve of a European man's suit subserve the "function" of preserving the familiar, of maintaining a tradition. People are, in general, more comfortable if they feel a continuity of behavior, if they feel themselves as following out the orthodox and socially approved forms of behavior.[23]

This would appear to represent the marginal case in which the imputation of function adds little or nothing to the direct description of the culture pattern or behavior form. It may well be assumed that all *established* elements of culture (which are loosely describable as 'tradition') have the minimum, though not exclusive, function of "preserving the familiar, of maintaining a tradition." This is equivalent to saying that the 'function' of conformity to *any* established practice is to enable the conformist to avoid the sanctions otherwise incurred by deviating from the established practice. This is no doubt true but hardly illuminating. It serves, however, to remind us that we shall want to explore the *types of functions* which the sociologist imputes. At the moment, it suggests the provisional assumption that, although any item of culture or social structure *may* have functions, it is premature to hold unequivocally that every such item *must* be functional.

The postulate of universal functionalism is of course the historical product of the fierce, barren and protracted controversy over "survivals" which raged among the anthropologists during the early part of the century. The notion of a social survival, that is, in the words of Rivers, of "a custom . . . [which] cannot be explained by its present utility but only becomes intelligible through its past history,"[24] dates back at least to Thucydides. But when the evolutionary theories of culture became prominent, the concept of survival seemed all the more strategically important for reconstructing "stages of development" of cultures, particularly for non-literate societies which possessed no written record. For

22. Kluckhohn, *Navaho Witchcraft,* 46. [italics supplied].

23. *Ibid.*, 47.

24. W. H. R. Rivers, "Survival in sociology," *The Sociological Review,* 1913, 6, 293-305. See also E. B. Tylor, *Primitive Culture,* (New York, 1874), esp. I, 70-159; and for a more recent review of the matter, Lowie, *The History of Ethnological Theory,* 44 ff., 81 f. For a sensible and restrained account of the problem, see Emile Durkheim, *Rules of Sociological Method,* Chapter 5, esp. at 91.

the functionalists who wished to turn away from what they regarded as the usually fragmentary and often conjectural "history" of non-literate societies, the attack on the notion of survival took on all the symbolism of an attack on the entire and intellectually repugnant system of evolutionary thought. In consequence, perhaps, they over-reacted against this concept central to evolutionary theory and advanced an equally exaggerated "postulate" to the effect that "every custom [everywhere] . . . fulfills some vital function."

It would seem a pity to allow the polemics of the anthropological forefathers to create splendid exaggerations in the present. Once discovered, ticketed and studied, social survivals cannot be exorcized by a postulate. And if no specimens of these survivals can be produced, then the quarrel dwindles of its own accord. It can be said, furthermore, that even when such survivals are identified in contemporary literate societies, they seem to add little to our understanding of human behavior or the dynamics of social change. Not requiring their dubious role as poor substitutes for recorded history, the sociologist of literate societies may neglect survivals with no apparent loss. But he need not be driven, by an archaic and irrelevant controversy, to adopt the unqualified postulate that all culture items fulfill vital functions. For this, too, is a problem for investigation, not a conclusion in advance of investigation. Far more useful as a directive for research would seem the provisional assumption that persisting cultural forms have a *net balance of functional consequences* either for the society considered as a unit or for subgroups sufficiently powerful to retain these forms intact, by means of direct coercion or indirect persuasion. This formulation at once avoids the tendency of functional analysis to concentrate on positive functions and directs the attention of the research worker to other types of consequences as well.

Postulate of Indispensability

The last of this trio of postulates common among functional social scientists is, in some respects, the most ambiguous. The ambiguity becomes evident in the aforementioned manifesto by Malinowski to the effect that

> in every type of civilization, every custom, material object, idea and belief fulfills some *vital* function, has some task to accomplish, represents an *indispensable part* within a working whole.[25]

From this passage, it is not at all clear whether he asserts the indispensability of the *function*, or of the *item* (custom, object, idea, belief) fulfilling the function, or *both*.

This ambiguity is quite common in the literature. Thus, the previously cited Davis and Moore account of the role of religion seems at

25. Malinowski, "Anthropology," *op. cit.*, 132 [italics supplied].

first to maintain that it is the *institution* which is indispensable: "The reason why religion is necessary . . ."; ". . . religion . . . plays a unique and indispensable part in society."[26] But it soon appears that it is not so much the institution of religion which is regarded as indispensable but rather the functions which religion is taken typically to perform. For Davis and Moore regard religion as indispensable only insofar as it functions to make the members of a society adopt "certain ultimate values and ends in common." These values and ends, it is said,

> must . . . appear to the members of the society to have some reality, and it is the role of religious belief and ritual to supply and reinforce this appearance of reality. Through ritual and belief the common ends and values are connected with an imaginary world symbolized by concrete sacred objects, which world in turn is related in a meaningful way to the facts and trials of the individual's life. Through the worship of the sacred objects and the beings they symbolize, and the acceptance of *supernatural prescriptions* that are at the same time codes of behavior, a powerful control over human conduct is exercised, guiding it along lines sustaining the institutional structure and conforming to the ultimate ends and values.[27]

The alleged indispensability of religion, then, is based on the assumption of fact that it is through "worship" and "supernatural prescriptions" *alone* that the necessary minimum of "control over human conduct" and "integration in terms of sentiments and beliefs" can be achieved.

In short, the postulate of indispensability as it is ordinarily stated contains two related, but distinguishable, assertions. First, it is assumed that there are certain *functions* which are indispensable in the sense that, unless they are performed, the society (or group or individual) will not persist. This, then, sets forth a concept of *functional prerequisites,* or *preconditions functionally necessary* for a society, and we shall have occasion to examine this concept in some detail. Second, and this is quite another matter, it is assumed that *certain cultural or social forms* are indispensable for fulfilling each of these functions. This involves a concept of specialized and irreplaceable structures, and gives rise to all manner of theoretic difficulties. For not only can this be shown to be manifestly contrary to fact, but it entails several subsidiary assumptions which have plagued functional analysis from the very outset. It diverts attention from the fact that alternative social structures (and cultural forms) have served, under conditions to be examined, the functions necessary for the persistence of groups. Proceeding further, we must set forth a major theorem of functional analysis; *just as the same item may have multiple functions, so may the same function be diversely fulfilled*

26. Kingsley Davis and Wilbert E. Moore, *op. cit.*, 244, 246. See the more recent review of this matter by Davis in his Introduction to W. J. Goode, *Religion Among the Primitives* (Glencoe, Illinois: The Free Press, 1951) and the instructive functional interpretations of religion in that volume.

27. Ibid., 244-245. [italics supplied].

by alternative items. Functional needs are here taken to be permissive, rather than determinant, of specific social structures. Or, in other words, there is a range of variation in the structures which fulfill the function in question. (The limits upon this range of variation involve the concept of structural constraint, of which more presently).

In contrast to this implied concept of indispensable cultural forms (institutions, standardized practices, belief-systems, etc.), there is, then, the concept of *functional alternatives,* or *functional equivalents,* or *functional substitutes.* This concept is widely recognized and used, but it should be noted that it cannot rest comfortably in the same theoretical system which entails the postulate of indispensability of particular cultural forms. Thus, after reviewing Malinowski's theory of "the functional necessity for such mechanisms as magic," Parsons is careful to make the following statement:

> . . . wherever such uncertainty elements enter into the pursuit of emotionally important goals, if not magic, at least *functionally equivalent* phenomena could be expected to appear.[28]

This is a far cry from Malinowski's own insistence that

> Thus magic fulfills *an indispensable function* within culture. It satisfies a definite need *which cannot be satisfied by any other factors of primitive civilization.*[29]

This twin concept of the indispensable function and the irreplaceable belief-and-action pattern flatly excludes the concept of functional alternatives.

In point of fact, the concept of functional alternatives or equivalents has repeatedly emerged in every discipline which has adopted a functional framework of analysis. It is, for example, widely utilized in the psychological sciences, as a paper by English admirably indicates.[30] And in neurology, Lashley has pointed out on the basis of experimental and clinical evidence, the inadequacy of the "assumption that individual neurons are specialized for particular functions," maintaining instead that a particular function may be fulfilled by a range of alternative structures.[31]

Sociology and social anthropology have all the more occasion for avoiding the postulate of indispensability of given structures, and for systematically operating with the concept of functional alternatives and functional substitutes. For just as laymen have long erred in assuming

28. Talcott Parsons, *Essays in Sociological Theory, Pure and Applied,* (Glencoe, Illinois: The Free Press, 1949), 58.

29. Malinowski, "Anthropology," *op. cit.,* 136. [italics supplied].

30. Horace B. English, "Symbolic versus functional equivalents in the neuroses of deprivation," *Journal of Abnormal and Social Psychology,* 1937, 32, 392-94.

31. K. S. Lashley, "Basic neural mechanisms in behavior," *Psychological Review,* 1930, 37, 1-24.

that the "strange" customs and beliefs of other societies were "mere superstitions," so functional social scientists run the risk of erring in the other extreme, first, by being quick to find functional or adaptive value in these practices and beliefs, and second, by failing to see which alternative modes of action are ruled out by cleaving to these ostensibly functional practices. Thus, there is not seldom a readiness among some functionalists to conclude that magic or certain religious rites and beliefs are functional, because of their effect upon the state of mind or self-confidence of the believer. Yet it may well be in some instances, that these magical practices obscure and take the place of accessible secular and more adaptive practices. As F. L. Wells has observed,

> To nail a horseshoe over the door in a smallpox epidemic may bolster the morale of the household but it will not keep out the smallpox; such beliefs and practices will not stand the secular tests to which they are susceptible, and the sense of security they give is preserved only while the real tests are evaded.[32]

Those functionalists who are constrained by their theory to attend to the effects of such symbolic practices *only* upon the individual's state of mind and who therefore conclude that the magical practice is functional, neglect the fact that these very practices may on occasion take the place of more effective alternatives.[33] And those theorists who refer to the indispensability of standardized practices or prevailing institutions because of their observed function in reinforcing common sentiments must look

---

32. F. L. Wells, "Social maladjustments: adaptive regression," in Carl A. Murchison, ed., *Handbook of Social Psychology,* (Clark University Press, 1935), 880. Wells's observation is far from being antiquarian. As late as the 1930's, smallpox was not "being kept out" in such states as Idaho, Wyoming, and Montana which, lacking compulsory vaccination laws, could boast some 4,300 cases of smallpox in a five-year period at the same time that the more populous states of Massachusetts, Pennsylvania and Rhode Island, states with compulsory vaccination laws, had no cases of smallpox at all. On the shortcomings of 'common sense' in such matters, see Hugh Cabot, *The Patient's Dilemma* (New York: Reynal & Hitchcock, 1940), 166-167.

33. It should perhaps be noted that this statement is made with full cognizance of Malinowski's observation that the Trobrianders did not *substitute* their magical beliefs and practices for the application of rational technology. The problem remains of assessing the degree to which technological development is slackened by the semi-dependence on magic for dealing with the "range of uncertainty." This area of uncertainty is presumably not fixed, but is itself related to the available technology. Rituals designed to regulate the weather, for example, might readily absorb the energies of men who might otherwise be reducing that "area of uncertainty" by attending to the advancement of meteorological knowledge. Each case must be judged on its merits. We refer here only to the increasing tendency among social anthropologists and sociologists to confine themselves to the observed "morale" effects of rationally and empirically ungrounded practices, and to forego analysis of the alternatives which would be available in a given situation, did not the orientation toward "the transcendental" and "the symbolic" focus attention on other matters. Finally, it is to be hoped that all this will not be mistaken for a re-statement of the sometimes naive rationalism of the Age of Enlightenment.

first to functional substitutes before arriving at a conclusion, more often premature than confirmed.

Upon review of this trinity of functional postulates, several basic considerations emerge which must be caught up in our effort to codify this mode of analysis. In scrutinizing, first, *the postulate of functional unity,* we found that one cannot assume full integration of all societies, but that this is an empirical question of fact in which we should be prepared to find a range of degrees of integration. And in examining the special case of functional interpretations of religion, we were alerted to the possibility that, though human nature may be of a piece, it does not follow that the structure of non-literate societies is uniformly like that of highly differentiated, "literate" societies. A difference in degree between the two—say, the existence of several disparate religions in the one and not in the other—may make hazardous the passage between them. From critical scrutiny of this postulate, it developed that a theory of functional analysis must call for *specification* of the social units subserved by given social functions, and that items of culture must be recognized to have multiple consequences, some of them functional and others, perhaps, dysfunctional.

Review of the second *postulate of universal functionalism,* which holds that all persisting forms of culture are inevitably functional, resulted in other considerations which must be met by a codified approach to functional interpretation. It appeared not only that we must be prepared to find dysfunctional as well as functional consequences of these forms but that the theorist will ultimately be confronted with the difficult problem of developing an organon for assessing the net balance of consequences if his research is to have bearing on social technology. Clearly, expert advice based only on the appraisal of a limited, and perhaps arbitrarily selected, range of consequences to be expected as a result of contemplated action, will be subject to frequent error and will be properly judged as having small merit.

The postulate of indispensability, we found, entailed two distinct propositions: the one alleging the indispensability of certain functions, and this gives rise to the concept of *functional necessity* or *functional prerequisites;* the other alleging the indispensability of existing social institutions, culture forms, or the like, and this when suitably questioned, gives rise to the concept of *functional alternatives, equivalents or substitutes.*

Moreover, the currency of these three postulates, singly and in concert, is the source of the common charge that functional analysis inevitably involves certain ideological commitments. Since this is a question which will repeatedly come to mind as one examines the further conceptions of functional analysis, it had best be considered now, if our attention is not to be repeatedly drawn away from the analytical problems in hand by the spectre of a social science tainted with ideology.

FUNCTIONAL ANALYSIS AS IDEOLOGY

Functional Analysis as Conservative

In many quarters and with rising insistence, it has been charged that, whatever the intellectual worth of functional analysis, it is inevitably committed to a "conservative" (even a "reactionary") perspective. For some of these critics, functional analysis is little more than a latter-day version of the eighteenth century doctrine of a basic and invariable identity of public and private interests. It is viewed as a secularized version of the doctrine set forth by Adam Smith, for example, when in his *Theory of Moral Sentiments,* he wrote of the "harmonious order of nature, under divine guidance, which promotes the welfare of man through the operation of his individual propensities."[34] Thus, say these critics, functional theory is merely the orientation of the conservative social scientist who would defend the present order of things, just as it is, and who would attack the advisability of change, however moderate. On this view, the functional analyst systematically ignores Tocqueville's warning not to confound the familiar with the necessary: ". . . what we call necessary institutions are often no more than institutions to which we have grown accustomed. . . ." It remains yet to be shown that functional analysis inevitably falls prey to this engaging fallacy but, having reviewed the postulate of indispensability, we can well appreciate that *this* postulate, if adopted, might easily give rise to this ideological charge. Myrdal is one of the most recent and not the least typical among the critics who argue the inevitability of a conservative bias in functional analysis:

> . . . if a thing has a "function" it is good or at least essential.* The term "function" can have a meaning *only* in terms of an assumed *purpose***; if that purpose is left undefined or implied to be the "interest of society" which is not further defined,*** a considerable leeway for arbitrariness in practical implication is allowed but the main direction is given: *a description of social institutions in terms of their functions must lead to a conservative teleology.*[35]

Myrdal's remarks are instructive less for their conclusion than for their premises. For, as we have noted, he draws upon two of the postu-

34. Jacob Viner, "Adam Smith and Laissez Faire," *Journal of Political Economy,* 1937, 35, 206.

35. Gunnar Myrdal, *An American Dilemma* (New York: Harper and Brothers, 1944) II, 1056 [italics and parenthetical remarks supplied].

* Here, be it noted, Myrdal gratuitously *accepts* the doctrine of indispensability as intrinsic to any functional analysis.

** This, as we have seen, is not only gratuitous, but false.

*** Here, Myrdal properly notes the dubious and vague postulate of functional unity.

lates so often adopted by functional analysts to reach the unqualified charge that he who describes institutions in terms of functions is unavoidably committed to "a conservative teleology." But nowhere does Myrdal challenge the inevitability of the postulates themselves. It will be interesting to ask how ineluctable the commitment when one has escaped from the premises.

In point of fact, if functional analysis in sociology were committed to teleology, let alone a conservative teleology, it would soon be subjected, and properly so, to even more harsh indictments than these. As has so often happened with teleology in the history of human thought, it would be subjected to a *reductio ad absurdum*. The functional analyst might then meet the fate of Socrates (though not for the same reason) who suggested that God put our mouth just under our nose so that we might enjoy the smell of our food.[36] Or, like the Christian theologians devoted to the argument from design, he might be cozened by a Ben Franklin who demonstrated that God clearly "wants us to tipple, because He has made the joints of the arm just the right length to carry a glass to the mouth, without falling short of or overshooting the mark: 'Let us adore, then, glass in hand, this benevolent wisdom; let us adore and drink.' "[37] Or, he might find himself given to more serious utterances, like Michelet who remarked "how beautifully everything is arranged by nature. As soon as the child comes into the world, it finds a mother who is ready to care for it."[38] Like any other system of thought which borders on teleology, though it seeks to avoid crossing the frontier into that alien and unproductive territory, functional analysis in sociology is threatened with a reduction to absurdity, once it adopts the postulate of all existing social structures as indispensable for the fulfillment of salient functional needs.

Functional Analysis as Radical

Interestingly enough, others have reached a conclusion precisely opposed to this charge that functional analysis is intrinsically committed to the view that whatever is, is right or that this is, indeed, the best of all possible worlds. These observers, LaPiere for example, suggest that functional analysis is an approach inherently critical in outlook and pragmatic in judgment:

> There is . . . a deeper significance than might at first appear in the shift from structural description to functional analysis in the social sciences. This shift represents a break with the social absolutism and moralism of Christian

36. Farrington has some further interesting observations on pseudo-teleology in his *Science in Antiquity* (London: T. Butterworth, 1936), 160.

37. This, in a letter by Franklin to the Abbé Morellet, quoted from the latter's *mémoires* by Dixon Wecter, *The Hero in America*, (New York: Scribner, 1941), 53-54.

38. It is Sigmund Freud who picked up this remark in Michelet's *The Woman.*

theology. If the important aspect of any social structure is its functions, it follows that no structure can be judged in terms of structure alone. In practice this means, for example, that the patriarchal family system is collectively valuable *only if and to the extent that* it functions to the satisfaction of collective ends. As a social structure, *it has no inherent value,* since its functional value will vary from time to time and from place to place.

The functional approach to collective behavior will, undoubtedly, *affront all those who believe that specific sociopsychological structures have inherent values.* Thus, to those who believe that a church service is good because it is a church service, the statement that some church services are formal motions which are devoid of religious significance, that others are functionally comparable to theatrical performances, and that still others are a form of revelry and are therefore comparable to a drunken spree will be an affront to common sense, an attack upon the integrity of decent people, or, at the least, the ravings of a poor fool.[39]

The fact that functional analysis can be seen by some as inherently conservative and by others as inherently radical suggests that it may be *inherently* neither one nor the other. It suggests that functional analysis may involve no *intrinsic* ideological commitment although, like other forms of sociological analysis, it can be infused with any one of a wide range of ideological values. Now, this is not the first time that a theoretic orientation in social science or social philosophy has been assigned diametrically opposed ideological implications. It may be helpful, therefore, to examine one of the most notable prior instances in which a sociological and methodological conception has been the object of the most varied ideological imputations, and to compare this instance, so far as possible, with the case of functional analysis. The comparable case is that of dialectical materialism; the spokesmen for dialectical materialism are the nineteenth century economic historian, social philosopher and professional revolutionary, Karl Marx, and his close aide and collaborator, Friedrich Engels.

The Ideological Orientations of Dialectical Materialism	*Comparative Ideological Orientations of Functional Analysis*
1. "The mystification which dialectic suffers at Hegel's hands by no means prevents him from being the first to present *its general form* of working in a comprehensive and conscious manner. With him it is standing on its head. It must be turned right side up again if you would discover the *rational kernel* within the *mystical shell.*	1. *Some* functional analysts have gratuitously *assumed* that *all* existing social structures fulfill indispensable social functions. This is sheer faith, mysticism, if you will, rather than the final product of sustained and systematic inquiry. The postulate must be earned, not inherited, if it is to gain the acceptance of men of social science.
2. "*In its mystified form* dialectic became the fashion in Germany, *because it seemed to transfigure and to glorify the existing state of things.*	2. The three postulates of functional unity, universality and indispensability comprise a system of premises which must inevitably lead to a glorification of the existing state of things.

39. Richard LaPiere, *Collective Behavior,* (New York: McGraw-Hill, 1938) 55-56 [italics supplied].

The Ideological Orientations of Dialectical Materialism	*Comparative Ideological Orientations of Functional Analysis*
3. "*In its rational form* it is a scandal and an abomination to bourgeoisdom and its doctrinaire professors, because *it includes in its comprehensive and affirmative recognition of the existing state of things,* at the same time also, *the recognition of the negation of* that state [of affairs], of its inevitable breaking up;	3. In its more empirically oriented and analytically precise forms, functional analysis is often regarded with suspicion by those who consider an existing social structure as eternally fixed and beyond change. This more exacting form of functional analysis includes, not only a study of the *functions* of existing social structures, but also a study of their *dysfunctions* for diversely situated individuals, subgroups or social strata, and the more inclusive society. It provisionally assumes, as we shall see, that when *the net balance of the aggregate of consequences* of an existing social structure is clearly dysfunctional, there develops a strong and insistent pressure for change. It is possible, though this remains to be established, that beyond a given point, this pressure will inevitably result in more or less predetermined directions of social change.
4. "because it regards *every historically developed form* as in fluid movement, and therefore takes into account *its transient nature* not less than *its momentary existence;* because it lets nothing impose upon it, and is *in its essence* critical and revolutionary."[40]	4. Though functional analysis has often focused on the *statics* of social structure rather than the *dynamics* of social change, this is not intrinsic to that system of analysis. By focusing on dysfunctions as well as on functions, this mode of analysis can assess not only the bases of social stability but the potential sources of social change. The phrase "historically developed forms" may be a useful reminder that social structures are typically undergoing discernible change. It remains to discover the pressures making for various types of change. To the extent that functional analysis focuses wholly on functional consequences, it leans toward an ultraconservative ideology; to the extent that it focuses wholly on dysfunctional consequences, it leans toward an ultra-radical utopia. "In its essence," it is neither one nor the other.
5. ". . . all successive historical situations are *only transitory stages* in the endless course of development of human society from the lower to the higher. *Each stage is necessary, therefore justi-*	5. Recognizing, as they must, that social structures are forever changing, functional analysts must nevertheless explore the interdependent and often mutually supporting elements of social

40. The passage to this point is quoted, without deletion or addition but only with the introduction of italics for appropriate emphasis, from that fount of dialectical materialism, Karl Marx, *Capital,* (Chicago: C. H. Kerr, 1906), I, 25-26.

The Ideological Orientations of Dialectical Materialism

fied for the time and conditions to which it owes its origin.

6. "But in the newer and higher conditions which *gradually develop in its own bosom, each loses its validity and justification.* It must give way to a higher form which will also in its turn decay and perish . . .

7. "It [dialectical materialism] reveals the transitory character of everything and in everything; nothing can endure before it except the uninterrupted process of becoming and of passing away . . . *It [dialectic] has, of course, also a conservative side: it recognizes that definite stages of knowledge and society are justified for their time and circumstances; but only so far. The conservatism of this mode of outlook is relative; its revolutionary character is absolute—the only absolute it admits.*"[41]

Comparative Ideological Orientations of Functional Analysis

structure. In general, it seems that most societies are integrated to the extent that many, if not all, of their several elements are reciprocally adjusted. Social structures do not have a random assortment of attributes, but these are variously interconnected and often mutually sustaining. To recognize this, is not to adopt an uncritical affirmation of every *status quo;* to fail to recognize this, is to succumb to the temptations of radical utopianism.

6. The strains and stresses in a social structure which accumulate as dysfunctional consequences of existing elements are not cabin'd, cribb'd and confined by appropriate social planning and will in due course lead to institutional breakdown and basic social change. When this change has passed beyond a given and not easily identifiable point, it is customary to say that a new social system has emerged.

7. But again, it must be reiterated: neither change alone nor fixity alone can be the proper object of study by the functional analyst. As we survey the course of history, it seems reasonably clear that all major social structures have in due course been cumulatively modified or abruptly terminated. In either event, they have not been eternally fixed and unyielding to change. But, at a given moment of observation, any such social structure may be tolerably well accommodated both to the subjective values of many or most of the population, and to the objective conditions with which it is confronted. To recognize this is to be true to the facts, not faithful to a preestablished ideology. And by the same token, when the structure is observed to be out of joint with the wants of the people or with the equally solid conditions of action, this too must be recognized. Who dares do all that, may become a functional analyst, who dares do less is none.[42]

41. Similarly, the subsequent passage is quoted, with deletion only of irrelevant material and again with italics supplied, from Friedrich Engels, in *Karl Marx, Selected Works,* (Moscow: Cooperative Publishing Society, 1935), I, 422.

42. It is recognized that this paraphrase does violence to the original intent of the bard, but it is hoped that the occasion justifies the offense.

This systematic comparison may be enough to suggest that functional analysis does not, any more than the dialectic, *necessarily* entail a specific ideological commitment. This is not to say that such commitments are not often implicit in the works of functional analysts. But this seems extraneous rather than intrinsic to functional theory. Here, as in other departments of intellectual activity, abuse does not gainsay the possibility of use. *Critically* revised, functional analysis is neutral to the major ideological systems. To this extent, and only in this limited sense,[43] it is like those theories or instruments of the physical sciences which lend themselves indifferently to use by opposed groups for purposes which are often no part of the scientists' intent.

Ideology and the Functional Analysis of Religion

Again, it is instructive to turn, however briefly, to discussions of the functions of religion to show how the *logic* of functional analysis is adopted by people otherwise opposed in their ideological stance.

The social role of religion has of course been repeatedly observed and interpreted over the long span of many centuries. The hard core of continuity in these observations consists in an emphasis on religion as an institutional means of social control, whether this be in Plato's concept of "noble lies," or in Aristotle's opinion that it operates "with a view to the persuasion of the multitude" or in the comparable judgment by Polybius that "the masses . . . can be controlled only by mysterious terrors and tragic fears." If Montesquieu remarks of the Roman lawmakers that they sought "to inspire a people that feared nothing with fear of the gods, and to use that fear to lead it whithersoever they pleased," then Jawaharlal Nehru observes, on the basis of his own experience, that "the only books that British officials heartily recommended [to political prisoners in India] were religious books or novels. It is wonderful how dear to the heart of the British Government is the subject of religion and how impartially it encourages all brands of it."[44] It would appear that there is an ancient and abiding tradition holding, in one form or another, that religion has served to control the masses. It appears, also, that the language in which this proposition is couched usually gives a clue to the ideological commitment of the author.

How is it, then, with some of the current functional analyses of religion? In his critical consolidation of several major theories in the sociology of religion, Parsons summarizes some of the basic conclusions

43. This should not be taken to deny the important fact that the values, implicit and openly acknowledged, of the social scientist may help fix his choice of problems for investigation, his formulation of these problems and, consequently, the utility of his findings for certain purposes, and not for others. The statement intends only what it affirms: functional analysis had no *intrinsic* commitment to any ideological camp, as the foregoing discussion at least illustrates.

44. Jawaharlal Nehru, *Toward Freedom*, (New York: John Day, 1941), 7.

which have emerged regarding the "functional significance of religion":

> . . . if moral norms and the sentiments supporting them are of such primary importance, what are the mechanisms by which they are maintained *other than external processes of enforcement?* It was Durkheim's view that religious ritual was of primary significance as a mechanism for *expressing and reinforcing* the *sentiments* most essential to the *institutional integration* of the society. It can readily be seen that this is clearly linked to Malinowski's views of the significance of funeral ceremonies as *a mechanism for reasserting the solidarity of the group* on the occasion of severe emotional strain. Thus Durkheim worked out certain aspects of the specific relations between *religion and social structure* more sharply than did Malinowski, and in addition put the problem in a different functional perspective in that he applied it to the society as a whole in abstraction from particular situations of tension and strain for the individual.[45]

And again, summarizing an essential finding of the major comparative study in the sociology of religion, Parsons observes that "perhaps the most striking feature of Weber's analysis is the demonstration of the extent to which precisely the variations in socially sanctioned values and goals in secular life correspond to the variations in the dominant religious philosophy of the great civilizations."[46]

Similarly, in exploring the role of religion among racial and ethnic subgroups in the United States, Donald Young in effect remarks the close correspondence between their "socially sanctioned values and goals in secular life" and their "dominant religious philosophy":

> One function which a minority religion may serve is that of *reconciliation with inferior status and its discriminatory consequences.* Evidence of religious service of this function may be found among all American minority peoples. On the other hand, religious institutions may also develop in such a way as to be *an incitement and support of revolt against inferior status.* Thus, the Christianized Indian, with due allowance for exceptions, has tended to be *more submissive* than the pagan. Special cults such as those associated with the use of peyote, the Indian Shaker Church, and the Ghost Dance, all three containing both Christian and native elements, were foredoomed attempts to develop *modes of religious expression adapted to individual and group circumstances.* The latter, with its emphasis on an assured millennium of freedom from the white man, encouraged forceful revolt. The Christianity of the Negro, in spite of appreciable encouragement of verbal criticism of the existing order, *has emphasized acceptance of present troubles in the knowledge of better times to come in the life hereafter.* The numerous varieties of Christianity and the Judaism brought by immigrants from Europe and Mexico, in spite of common nationalistic elements, also *stressed later rewards rather than immediate direct action.*[47]

---

45. Talcott Parsons, *Essays in Sociological Theory,* 61 [italics supplied].

46. *Ibid.,* 63.

47. Donald Young, *American Minority Peoples,* (New York: Harper, 1937), 204 [italics supplied]. For a functional analysis of the Negro church in the United States, see George Eaton Simpson and J. Milton Yinger, *Racial and Cultural Minorities* (New York: Harper & Brothers, 1953), 522-530.

These diverse and scattered observations, with their notably varied ideological provenience, exhibit some basic similarities. First, they are all given over to the consequences of specific religious systems for prevailing sentiments, definitions of situations and action. These consequences are rather consistently observed to be those of reinforcement of prevailing moral norms, docile acceptance of these norms, postponement of ambitions and gratifications (if the religious doctrine so demands), and the like. However, as Young observes, religions have also served, under determinate conditions, to provoke rebellion, or as Weber has shown, religions have served to motivate or to canalize the behavior of great numbers of men and women toward the modification of social structures. It would seem premature, therefore, to conclude that all religion everywhere has only the one consequence of making for mass apathy.

Second, the Marxist view implicitly and the functionalist view explicitly affirm the central point that systems of religion *do affect behavior,* that they are *not merely* epiphenomena but partially independent determinants of behavior. For presumably, it makes a difference if "the masses" do or do not accept a particular religion just as it makes a difference if an individual does or does not take opium.

Third, the more ancient as well as the Marxist theories deal with the *differential* consequences of religious beliefs and rituals for various subgroups and strata in the society—*e.g.*, "the masses"—as, for that matter, does the non-Marxist Donald Young. The functionalist is not confined, as we have seen, to exploring the consequences of religion for "society as a whole."

Fourth, the suspicion begins to emerge that the functionalists, with their emphasis on religion as a *social mechanism* for "reinforcing the sentiments most essential to the institutional integration of the society," may not differ materially in their *analytical framework* from the Marxists who, if their metaphor of "opium of the masses" is converted into a neutral statement of social fact, also assert that religion operates as a social mechanism for reinforcing certain secular as well as sacred sentiments among its believers.

The point of difference appears only when *evaluations* of this commonly accepted fact come into question. Insofar as the functionalists refer only to "institutional integration" without exploring the diverse consequences of integration about very different types of values and interests, they confine themselves to purely *formal* interpretation. For integration is a plainly formal concept. A society may be integrated around norms of strict caste, regimentation, and docility of subordinated social strata, just as it may be integrated around norms of open mobility, wide areas of self-expression and independence of judgment among temporarily lower strata. And insofar as the Marxists assert, without qualification, that all religion everywhere, whatever its doctrinal content and its organizational form, involves "an opiate" for the masses, they too shift to purely formal interpretations, without allowing, as the excerpt from Young shows to be the case, for particular religions in particular social structures serving to activate rather than to lethargize mass action. It is in the *evaluation* of these functions of religion, rather than in the logic of analysis, then, that the functionalists and the Marxists part company. And it is the *evaluations* which permit the pouring of ideological content into the bottles of *functionalism*.[48] The bottles themselves are

---

48. This type of talking-past-each-other is perhaps more common than one is wont to suspect. Often, the basic agreement in the *analysis* of a situation is plentifully obscured by the basic disagreement in the *evaluation* of that situation. As a result, it is erroneously assumed that the opponents differ in their cognitive procedures and findings, whereas they differ only in their sets of values. Consider, for example, the recent striking case of the public debates and conflicts between Winston Churchill and Harold Laski, where it was generally assumed, among others by Churchill himself, that the two disagreed on the substantive premise that social change is more readily accepted in time of war than in time of peace. Yet compare the following excerpts from the writings of the two men.

"The former peace-time structure of society had for more than four years been superseded and life had been raised to a strange intensity by the war spell. Under that mysterious influence, men and women had been appreciably exalted above death and pain and toil. *Unities and comradeships had become possible* between men and classes and nations and grown stronger *while the hostile pressure and the common cause endured.* But now the spell was broken: too late for some purposes, too soon for others, and too suddenly for all! *Every victorious country subsided to its old levels and its previous arrangements;* but these latter were found to have fallen into much disrepair, their fabric was weakened and disjointed, they seemed narrow and out of date."

"*With the passing of the spell there passed also,* just as the new difficulties were at their height, *much of the exceptional powers of guidance and control.* . . . To the faithful, toil-burdened masses the victory was so complete that no further effort seemed required. . . . *A vast fatigue dominated collective action.* Though every subversive element endeavored to assert itself, *revolutionary rage like every other form of psychic energy burnt low.*"

"The atmosphere of war permits, and even compels, innovations and experiments that are not possible when peace returns. The invasion of our wonted routine of life accustoms us to what William James called the vital habit of breaking habits. . . . *We find ourselves stimulated to exertions, even sacrifices,* we did not know we had it in us to make. *Common danger builds a basis for a new fellowship* the future of which is dependent wholly upon whether its foundations are temporary or permanent. If they are temporary, then the end of the war sees the resumption of all our previous differences exacerbated tenfold by the grave problems it will have left." "I am, therefore, arguing that the changes which we require we can make by consent in a period in which, as now, conditions make men remember their identities and not their differences."

"We can begin those changes now because the atmosphere is prepared for their reception. It is highly *doubtful whether we can make them by consent when that atmosphere is absent.* It is the more doubtful because the effort the war requires will induce in many, above all in those who have agreed to the suspension of privilege, *a fatigue, a hunger for the ancient ways, which it will be difficult to resist.*"

neutral to their contents, and may serve equally well as containers for ideological poison or for ideological nectar.

THE LOGIC OF PROCEDURE

Prevalence of the Functional Orientation

The functional orientation is of course neither new nor confined to the social sciences. It came, in fact, relatively late on the sociological scene, if one may judge by its earlier and extended use in a great variety of other disciplines.[49] The central orientation of functionalism—expressed

---

"The intensity of the exertions evoked by the national danger far exceeded the ordinary capacities of human beings. All were geared up to an abnormal pitch. *Once the supreme incentive had disappeared, everyone became conscious of the severity of the strain. A vast and general relaxation and descent to the standards of ordinary life was imminent.* No community could have gone on using up treasure and life energy at such a pace. *Most of all was the strain apparent in the higher ranks of the brain workers.* They had carried on uplifted by the psychological stimulus which was now to be removed. 'I can work until I drop' was sufficient while the cannon thundered and armies marched. *But now it was peace: and on every side exhaustion,* nervous and physical, unfelt or unheeded before, became evident."

"In all revolutions there comes a period of inertia when *the fatigue of the effort compels a pause in the process of innovation.* That period is bound to come with the cessation of hostilities. *After a life on the heights the human constitution seems to demand tranquility and relaxation.* To insist, in the period of pause, that we gird up our loins for a new and difficult journey, above all for a journey into the unknown, is to ask the impossible. . . . When hostilities against Nazism cease, *men will want, more than anything, a routine of thought and habit which does not compel the painful adaptation of their minds to disturbing excitement.*"

The Gibbonesque passages in the first column are, of course, by Churchill, the Winston Churchill between the Great Wars, writing in retrospect about the aftermath of the first of these: *The World Crisis:* Volume 4, *The Aftermath,* (London: Thornton Butterworth, 1928), 30, 31, 33. The observations in the second column are those of Harold Laski, writing during the Second Great War to say that it is the policy of Mr. Churchill to make "the conscious postponement of any issue deemed 'controversial' until the victory is won [and] this means . . . that the relations of production are to remain unchanged until peace comes, and that, accordingly, none of the instruments for social change on a large scale, will be at the national disposal for agreed purposes." *Revolution of Our Time,* (New York: Viking Press, 1943), 185, 187, 193, 227-8, 309. Unless Churchill had forgotten his analysis of the aftermath of the first war, it is plain that he and Laski were *agreed on the diagnosis* that significant and deliberately enacted social change was unlikely in the immediate post-war era. The difference clearly lay in the appraisal of the desirability of instituting designated changes at all. (The italics in both columns were by neither author.)

It may be noted, in passing, that the very expectation on which both Churchill and Laski were *agreed—i.e.* that the post-war period in England would be one of mass lethargy and indifference to planned institutional change—was not altogether borne out by the actual course of events. England after the second great war did not exactly repudiate the notion of planned change.

---

49. The currency of a functionalist outlook has been repeatedly noted. For example: "The fact that in all fields of thinking the same tendency is noticeable, proves that there is now a general trend toward interpreting the world in terms of interconnection of operation rather than in terms of separate substantial units. Albert

in the practice of interpreting data by establishing their consequences for larger structures in which they are implicated—has been found in virtually all the sciences of man—biology and physiology, psychology, economics and law, anthropology and sociology.[50] The prevalence of the

---

Einstein in physics, Claude Bernard in physiology, Alexis Carrel in biology, Frank Lloyd Wright in architecture, A. N. Whitehead in philosophy, W. Koehler in psychology, Theodor Litt in sociology, Hermann Heller in political science, B. Cardozo in law: these are men representing different cultures, different countries, different aspects of human life and the human spirit, and yet all approaching their problems with a sense of 'reality' which is looking not to material substance but to functional interaction for a comprehension of phenomena." G. Niemeyer, *Law Without Force,* (Princeton University Press, 1941), 300. This motley company suggests anew that agreement on the functional outlook need not imply identity of political or social philosophy.

50. The literature commenting on the trend toward functionalism is almost as large and considerably more sprawling than the diverse scientific literatures exemplifying the trend. Limitations of space and concern for immediate relevance limit the number of such references which must here take the place of an extended review and discussion of these collateral developments in scientific thought.

For *biology,* a general, now classical, source is J. H. Woodger, *Biological Principles: A Critical Study,* (New York: Harcourt Brace and Co., 1929), esp. 327 ff. For correlative materials, at least the following are indicated: Bertalanffy, *Modern Theories of Development, op. cit.,* particularly 1-46, 64 ff., 179 ff.; E. S. Russell, *The Interpretation of Development and Heredity: A Study in Biological Method,* (Oxford: Clarendon Press, 1930), esp. 166-280. Foreshadowing discussions will be found in the less instructive writings of W. E. Ritter, E. B. Wilson, E. Ungerer, J. Schaxel, J. von Uexküll, etc. The papers of J. Needham—*e.g.,* "Thoughts on the problem of biological organization," *Scientia,* August 1932, 84-92—can be consulted with profit.

For *physiology,* consider the writings of C. S. Sherrington, W. B. Cannon, G. E. Coghill, Joseph Barcroft, and especially the following: C. S. Sherrington, *The Integrative Action of the Nervous System,* (New Haven: Yale University Press, 1923); W. B. Cannon, *Bodily Changes in Pain, Hunger, Fear and Rage,* chapter 12, and *The Wisdom of the Body,* (New York: W. W. Norton, 1932), all but the unhappy epilogue on "social homeostasis"; G. E. Coghill, *Anatomy and the Problem of Behavior,* (Cambridge University Press, 1929); Joseph Barcroft, *Features in the Architecture of Physiological Function,* (Cambridge University Press, 1934).

For *psychology,* virtually any of the basic contributions to dynamic psychology are in point. It would not only be low wit but entirely true to say that Freudian conceptions are instinct with functionalism, since the major concepts are invariably referred to a functional (or dysfunctional) framework. For a different order of conception, see Harvey Carr, "Functionalism," in Carl Murchison, ed. *Psychologies of 1930,* (Clark University Press, 1930); and as one among many articles dealing with substantially this set of conceptions, see J. M. Fletcher, "Homeostasis as an explanatory principle in psychology," *Psychological Review,* 1942, 49, 80-87. For a statement of application of the functional approach to personality, see chapter I in Clyde Kluckhohn and Henry A. Murray, ed. *Personality in Nature, Society and Culture,* (New York: A. A. Knopf, 1948), 3-32. The important respects in which the Lewin group is oriented toward functionalism have been widely recognized.

For *law,* see the critical paper by Felix S. Cohen, "Transcendental nonsense and the functional approach," *Columbia Law Review,* 1935, XXXV, 809-849, and the numerous annotated references therein.

For *sociology and anthropology,* see the brief sampling of references throughout this chapter. The volume edited by Robert Redfield provides a useful bridge across the chasm too often separating the biological from the social sciences. Levels of Integration in Biological and Social Systems, *Biological Symposia,* 1943, VIII. For an important effort to set out the conceptual framework of functional analysis, see Talcott Parsons, *The Social System,* (Glencoe, Illinois: Free Press, 1951).

functional outlook is in itself no warrant for its scientific value, but it does suggest that cumulative experience has forced this orientation upon the disciplined observers of man as biological organism, psychological actor, member of society and bearer of culture.

More immediately relevant is the possibility that prior experience in other disciplines may provide useful methodological models for functional analysis in sociology. To learn from the canons of analytical procedure in these often more exacting disciplines is not, however, to adopt their specific conceptions and techniques, lock, stock and barrel. To profit from the logic of procedure successfully employed in the biological sciences, for example, is not to backslide into accepting the largely irrelevant analogies and homologies which have so long fascinated the devotees of organismic sociology. To examine the *methodological* framework of biological researches is not to adopt their *substantive* concepts.

The *logical structure* of experiment, for example, does not differ in physics, or chemistry or psychology, although the substantive hypotheses, the technical tools, the basic concepts and the practical difficulties may differ enormously. Nor do the near-substitutes for experiment—controlled observation, comparative study and the method of 'discerning'—differ in their *logical structure* in anthropology, sociology or biology.

In turning briefly to Cannon's logic of procedure in physiology, then, we are looking for a methodological model which might possibly be derived for sociology, without adopting Cannon's unfortunate homologies between the structure of biological organisms and of society.[51] His procedures shape up somewhat as follows. Adopting the orientatior of Claude Bernard, Cannon first indicates that the organism *requires* a relatively constant and stable state. One task of the physiologist, then, is to provide "a concrete and detailed account of the modes of assuring steady states." In reviewing the numerous "concrete and detailed" accounts provided by Cannon, we find that the *general mode of formulation* is invariable, irrespective of the specific problem in hand. A typical formulation is as follows: "*In order that* the blood shall . . . serve as a circulating medium, fulfilling the various *functions* of a common carrier of nutriment and waste . . ., *there must be* provision for holding it back whenever there is danger of escape." Or, to take another statement: "*If* the life of the cell is to continue . . ., the blood . . . *must* flow with sufficient speed to deliver to the living cells the (necessary) supply of oxygen."

51. As previously implied, Cannon's epilogue to his *Wisdom of the Body* remains unexcelled as an example of the fruitless extremes to which even a distinguished mind is driven once he sets about to draw *substantive* analogies and homologies between biological organisms and social systems. Consider, for example, his comparison between the fluid matrix of the body and the canals, rivers and railroads on which "the products of farm and factory, of mine and forest, are borne to and fro." This kind of analogy, earlier developed in copious volumes by René Worms, Schaeffle, Vincent, Small, and Spencer among others, does *not* represent the distinctive value of Cannon's writings for the sociologist.

Having established the *requirements* of the organic system, Cannon then proceeds to describe *in detail* the various *mechanisms* which operate to meet these requirements (*e.g.*, the complicated changes which lead to clotting, the local contraction of injured blood vessels that lessen the severity of bleeding; accelerated clot formation through the secretion of adrenin and the action of adrenin upon the liver, *etc.*). Or again, he describes the various biochemical arrangements which ensure a proper supply of oxygen to the normal organism and the compensating changes which occur when some of these arrangements do not operate adequately.

If the logic of this approach is stated in its more general terms, the following interrelated sequence of steps becomes evident. First of all, certain functional requirements of the organisms are established, requirements which must be satisfied if the organism is to survive, or to operate with some degree of effectiveness. Second, there is a concrete and detailed description of the arrangements (structures and processes) through which these requirements are typically met in "normal" cases Third, if some of the typical mechanisms for meeting these requirements are destroyed, or are found to be functioning inadequately, the observer is sensitized to the need for detecting compensating mechanisms (if any) which fulfill the necessary function. Fourth, and implicit in all that precedes, there is a detailed account of the structure *for which* the functional requirements hold, as well as a detailed account of the arrangements *through which* the function is fulfilled.

So well established is the logic of functional analysis in the biological sciences that these requirements for an adequate analysis come to be met almost as a matter of course. Not so with sociology. Here, we find extraordinarily varied conceptions of the appropriate design of studies in functional analysis. For some, it consists largely (or even exclusively) in establishing empirical interrelations between "parts" of a social system; for others, it consists in showing the "value for society" of a socially standardized practice or a social organization; for still others, it consists in elaborate accounts of the purposes of formal social organizations.

As one examines the varied array of functional analyses in sociology, it becomes evident that sociologists in contrast, say, to physiologists, do not typically carry through operationally intelligible procedures, do not systematically assemble needed types of data, do not employ a common body of concepts and do not utilize the same criteria of validity. In other words, we find in physiology, a body of standard concepts, procedures and design of analysis and in sociology, a variegated selection of concepts, procedures and designs, depending, it would seem, on the interests and tastes of the individual sociologist. To be sure, this difference between the two disciplines has *something*—perhaps, a good deal—to do with differences in the character of the data examined by the physiologist and the sociologist. The relatively large opportunities for experimental work in physiology are, to be trite about it, scarcely matched in sociology. But this scarcely accounts for the systematic ordering of procedure and concepts in the one instance and the disparate, often uncoordinated and not infrequently defective character of procedure and concepts in functional sociology.

A PARADIGM FOR FUNCTIONAL ANALYSIS IN SOCIOLOGY

As an initial and admittedly tentative step in the direction of codifying functional analysis in sociology, we set forth a paradigm of the concepts and problems central to this approach. It will soon become evident that the chief components of this paradigm have progressively emerged in the foregoing pages as we have critically examined the vocabularies, postulates, concepts and ideological imputations now current in the field. The paradigm brings these together in compact form, thus permitting simultaneous inspection of the major requirements of functional analysis and serving as an aid to self-correction of provisional interpretations, a result difficult to achieve when concepts are scattered and hidden in page after page of discursive exposition.[52] The paradigm presents the hard core of concept, procedure and inference in functional analysis.

Above all, it should be noted that the paradigm does not represent a set of categories introduced *de novo,* but rather a *codification* of those concepts and problems which have been forced upon our attention by critical scrutiny of current research and theory in functional analysis. (Reference to the preceding sections of this chapter will show that the groundwork has been prepared for every one of the categories embodied in the paradigm.)

1. *The item(s) to which functions are imputed*

The entire range of sociological data can be, and much of it has been, subjected to functional analysis. The basic requirement is that the object of analysis represent a *standardized* (*i.e.* patterned and repetitive) item, such as social roles, institutional patterns, social processes, cultural pattern, culturally patterned emotions, social norms, group organization, social structure, devices for social control, *etc.*

BASIC QUERY: What must enter into the protocol of observation of the given item if it is to be amenable to systematic functional analysis?

2. *Concepts of subjective dispositions* (*motives, purposes*)

At some point, functional analysis invariably assumes or explicitly operates with some conception of the motivation of individuals involved in a social system. As the foregoing discussion has shown, these concepts of subjective disposition are often and erroneously merged with the related, but different, concepts of objective consequences of attitude, belief and behavior.

---

52. For a brief statement of the purpose of analytical paradigms such as this, see the note on paradigms elsewhere in this volume.

BASIC QUERY: In which types of analysis is it sufficient to take observed motivations as *data*, as given, and in which are they properly considered as *problematical*, as derivable from other data?

3. *Concepts of objective consequences* (*functions, dysfunctions*)

We have observed two prevailing types of confusion enveloping the several current conceptions of "function":

(1) The tendency to confine sociological observations to the *positive* contributions of a sociological item to the social or cultural system in which it is implicated; and

(2) The tendency to confuse the subjective category of *motive* with the objective category of *function.*

Appropriate conceptual distinctions are required to eliminate these confusions.

The first problem calls for a concept of *multiple consequences* and *a net balance of an aggregate of consequences.*

Functions are those observed consequences which make for the adaptation or adjustment of a given system; and *dysfunctions,* those observed consequences which lessen the adaptation or adjustment of the system. There is also the empirical possibility of *nonfunctional* consequences, which are simply irrelevant to the system under consideration.

In any given instance, an item may have both functional and dysfunctional consequences, giving rise to the difficult and important problem of evolving canons for assessing the net balance of the aggregate of consequences. (This is, of course, most important in the use of functional analysis for guiding the formation and enactment of policy.)

The second problem (arising from the easy confusion of motives and functions) requires us to introduce a conceptual distinction between the cases in which the subjective aim-in-view coincides with the objective consequence, and the cases in which they diverge.

Manifest functions are those objective consequences contributing to the adjustment or adaptation of the system which are intended and recognized by participants in the system;

Latent functions, correlatively, being those which are neither intended nor recognized.*

BASIC QUERY: What are the effects of the transformation of a previously latent function into a manifest function (involving the problem of the role of knowledge in human behavior and the problems of "manipulation" of human behavior)?

---

* The relations between the "unanticipated consequences" of action and "latent functions" can be clearly defined, since they are implicit in the foregoing section of the paradigm. The unintended consequences of action are of three types:

(1) those which are functional for a designated system, and these comprise the latent functions;

(2) those which are dysfunctional for a designated system, and these comprise the latent dysfunctions; and

(3) those which are irrelevant to the system which they affect neither functionally nor dysfunctionally, *i.e.*, the pragmatically unimportant class of non-functional consequences.

For a preliminary statement, see R. K. Merton, "The unanticipated consequences of purposive social action," *American Sociological Review* 1936, 1, 894-904; for a tabulation of these types of consequences see Goode, *Religion Among the Primitives,* 32-33.

4. *Concepts of the unit subserved by the function*

We have observed the difficulties entailed in *confining* analysis to functions fulfilled for "the society," since items may be functional for some individuals and subgroups and dysfunctional for others. It is necessary, therefore, to consider a *range* of units for which the item has designated consequences: individuals in diverse statuses, subgroups, the larger social system and culture systems. (Terminologically, this implies the concepts of psychological function, group function, societal function, cultural function, *etc.*)

5. *Concepts of functional requirements* (*needs, prerequisites*)

Embedded in every functional analysis is some conception, tacit or expressed, of the functional requirements of the system under observation. As noted elsewhere,[53] this remains one of the cloudiest and empirically most debatable concepts in functional theory. As utilized by sociologists, the concept of functional requirement tends to be tautological or *ex post facto;* it tends to be confined to the conditions of "survival" of a given system; it tends, as in the work of Malinowski, to include biological as well as social "needs."

This involves the difficult problem of establishing *types* of functional requirements (universal vs. specific); procedures for validating the assumption of these requirements; *etc.*

BASIC QUERY: What is required to establish the validity of such a variable as "functional requirement" in situations where rigorous experimentation is impracticable?

6. *Concepts of the mechanisms through which functions are fulfilled*

Functional analysis in sociology, as in other disciplines like physiology and psychology, calls for a "concrete and detailed" account of the mechanisms which operate to perform a designated function. This refers, not to psychological, but to social, mechanisms (*e.g.*, role-segmentation, insulation of institutional demands, hierarchic ordering of values, social division of labor, ritual and ceremonial enactments, *etc.*).

BASIC QUERY: What is the presently available inventory of social mechanisms corresponding, say, to the large inventory of psychological mechanisms? What methodological problems are entailed in discerning the operation of these social mechanisms?

7. *Concepts of functional alternatives* (*functional equivalents or substitutes*)

As we have seen, once we abandon the gratuitous assumption of the functional indispensability of particular social structures, we immediately require some concept of functional alternatives, equivalents, or substitutes. This focuses attention on the *range of possible variation* in the items which can, in the case under examination, subserve a functional requirement. It unfreezes the identity of the existent and the inevitable.

BASIC QUERY: Since scientific proof of the equivalence of an alleged functional alternative ideally requires rigorous experimentation, and since this is not often practicable in large-scale sociological situations, which practicable procedures of inquiry most nearly approximate the logic of experiment?

8. *Concepts of structural context* (*or structural constraint*)

The range of variation in the items which *can* fulfill designated functions in a social structure is not unlimited (and this has been repeatedly noted in our foregoing discussion). The interdependence of the elements of a social structure limits the effective possibilities of change or functional alternatives.

53. R. K. Merton, "Discussion of Parsons' 'Position of sociological theory,'" *American Sociological Review,* 1949, 13, 164-168.

The concept of structural constraint corresponds, in the area of social structure, to Goldenweiser's "principle of limited possibilities" in a broader sphere. Failure to recognize the relevance of interdependence and attendant structural restraints leads to utopian thought in which it is tacitly assumed that certain elements of a social system can be eliminated without affecting the rest of that system. This consideration is recognized by both Marxist social scientists (*e.g.* Karl Marx) and by non-Marxists (*e.g.* Malinowski).[54]

Basic Query: How narrowly does a given structural context limit the range of variation in the items which can effectively satisfy functional requirements? Do we find, under conditions yet to be determined, an area of indifference, in which any one of a wide range of alternatives may fulfill the function?

9. *Concepts of dynamics and change*

We have noted that functional analysts *tend* to focus on the statics of social structure and to neglect the study of structural change.

This emphasis upon statics is not, however, *inherent* in the theory of functional analysis. It is, rather, an adventitious emphasis stemming from the concern of early anthropological functionalists to counteract preceding tendencies to write conjectural histories of non-literate societies. This practice, useful at the time it was first introduced into anthropology, has disadvantageously persisted in the work of some functional sociologists.

The concept of dysfunction, which implies the concept of strain, stress and tension on the structural level, provides an analytical approach to the study of dynamics and change. How are observed dysfunctions contained within a particular structure, so that they do not produce instability? Does the accumulation of stresses and strains produce pressure for change in such directions as are likely to lead to their reduction?

Basic Query: Does the prevailing concern among functional analysts

---

54. Previously cited excerpts from Marx document this statement, but these are, of course, only a few out of many places in which Marx in effect stresses the importance of taking account of the structural context. In *A Contribution to the Critique of Political Economy* (appearing in 1859 and republished in Karl Marx, *Selected Works, op. cit.*, I, 354-371), he observes for example: "No social order ever disappears before all the productive forces for which there is room in it have been developed; and new higher relations of production never appear before the material conditions of their existence have matured in the womb of the old society itself. Therefore, mankind always sets itself only such tasks as it can solve; since, looking at the matter more closely, we will always find that the task itself arises only when the material conditions necessary for its solution already exist or are at least in the process of formation." (p. 357) Perhaps the most famous of his many references to the constraining influence of a given social structure is found in the second paragraph of *The Eighteenth Brumaire of Louis Napoleon:* "Man makes his own history, but he does not make it out of whole cloth: he does not make it out of conditions chosen by himself, but out of such conditions as he finds close at hand." (From the paraphrase of the original as published in Marx, *Selected Works,* II, 315.) To my knowledge, A. D. Lindsay is the most perceptive among the commentators who have noted the theoretic implications of statements such as these. See his little book, *Karl Marx's Capital: An Introductory Essay,* (Oxford University Press, 1931), esp. at 27-52.

And for other language with quite different ideological import and essentially similar theoretic implications, see B. Malinowski, "Given a definite cultural need, the means of its satisfaction are small in number, and therefore the cultural arrangement which comes into being in response to the need is determined within narrow limits." "Culture," *Encyclopedia of the Social Sciences, op. cit.*, 626.

with the concept of *social equilibrium* divert attention from the phenomena of *social disequilibrium*? Which available procedures will permit the sociologist most adequately to gauge the accumulation of stresses and strains in a social system? To what extent does knowledge of the structural context permit the sociologist to anticipate the most probable directions of social change?

10. *Problems of validation of functional analysis*

Throughout the paradigm, attention has been called repeatedly to the *specific* points at which assumptions, imputations and observations must be validated.[55] This requires, above all, a rigorous statement of the sociological procedures of analysis which most nearly approximate the *logic* of experimentation. It requires a systematic review of the possibilities and limitations of *comparative* (cross-cultural and cross-group) *analysis*.

Basic Query: To what extent is functional analysis limited by the difficulty of locating adequate *samples of social systems* which can be subjected to comparative (quasi-experimental) study?[56]

11. *Problems of the ideological implications of functional analysis*

It has been emphasized in a preceding section that functional analysis has no intrinsic commitment to an ideological position. This does not gainsay the fact that *particular* functional analyses and *particular* hypotheses advanced by functionalists may have an identifiable ideological role. This, then, becomes a specific problem for the sociology of knowledge: to what extent does the social position of the functional sociologist (*e.g.*, *vis-a-vis* a particular "client" who has authorized a given research) evoke one rather than another formulation of a problem, affect his assumptions and concepts, and limit the range of inferences drawn from his data?

Basic Query: How does one detect the ideological tinge of a functional analysis and to what degree does a particular ideology stem from the basic assumptions adopted by the sociologist? Is the incidence of these assumptions related to the status and research role of the sociologist?

Before proceeding to a more intensive study of some parts of this paradigm, let us be clear about the uses to which it is supposed the paradigm can be put. After all, taxonomies of concepts may be multiplied endlessly without materially advancing the tasks of sociological analysis. What, then, are the purposes of the paradigm and how might it be used?

---

55. By this point, it is evident that we are considering functional analysis as a method for the *interpretation* of sociological data. This is not to gainsay the important role of the functional orientation in sensitizing sociologists to the *collection* of types of data which might otherwise be neglected. It is perhaps unnecessary to reiterate the axiom that one's concepts *do* determine the inclusion or exclusion of data, that, despite the etymology of the term, *data* are not "given" but are "contrived" with the inevitable help of concepts. In the process of evolving a functional interpretation, the sociological analyst invariably finds it necessary to obtain data other than those initially contemplated. Interpretation and the collection of data are thus inextricably bound up in the array of concepts and propositions relating these concepts. For an extension of these remarks, see Chapter II.

56. George P. Murdock's *Social Structure*, (New York: Macmillan, 1949), is enough to show that procedures such as those involved in the cross-cultural survey hold large promise for dealing with certain methodological problems of functional analysis. See also the procedures of functional analysis in George C. Homans and David M. Schneider, *Marriage, Authority, and Final Causes* (Glencoe: The Free Press, 1955)

Purposes of the Paradigm

The first and foremost purpose is to supply a provisional codified guide for adequate and fruitful functional analyses. This objective evidently implies that the paradigm contains the minimum set of concepts with which the sociologist must operate in order to carry through an adequate functional analysis and, as a corollary, that it can be used here and now as a guide for the critical study of existing analyses. It is thus intended as an all-too-compact and elliptical guide to the formulation of researches in functional analysis and as an aid in locating the distinctive contributions and deficiencies of earlier researches. Limitations of space will permit us to apply only limited sections of the paradigm to a critical appraisal of a selected list of cases in point.

Secondly, the paradigm is intended to lead directly to the postulates and (often tacit) assumptions underlying functional analysis. As we have found in earlier parts of this chapter, some of these assumptions are of central importance, others insignificant and dispensable, and still others, dubious and even misleading.

In the third place, the paradigm seeks to sensitize the sociologist not only to the narrowly scientific implications of various types of functional analysis, but also to their political and sometimes ideological implications. The points at which a functional analysis presupposes an implicit political outlook and the points at which it has bearing on "social engineering" are concerns which find an integral place in the paradigm.

It is obviously beyond the limits of this chapter to explore in detail the large and inclusive problems involved in the paradigm. This must await fuller exposition in a volume devoted to this purpose. We shall, therefore, confine the remainder of the present discussion to brief applications of only the first parts of the paradigm to a severely limited number of cases of functional analysis in sociology. And, from time to time, these few cases will be used as a springboard for discussion of special problems which are only imperfectly illustrated by the cases in hand.

ITEMS SUBJECTED TO FUNCTIONAL ANALYSIS

At first glance, it would appear that the sheer *description* of the item to be analyzed functionally entails few, if any, problems. Presumably, one should describe the item "as fully and as accurately" as possible. Yet, at second thought, it is evident that this maxim provides next to no guidance for the observer. Consider the plight of a functionally oriented neophyte armed only with this dictum as an aid to answering the question: *what* am I to observe, *what* am I to incorporate into my field notes, and *what* may I safely omit?

Without assuming that a detailed and circumstantial answer can now be supplied to the field worker, we can nevertheless note that the question itself is legitimate and that *implicit* answers have been partly developed. To tease out these implicit answers and to codify them, it is necessary to approach cases of functional analysis with the query: *what kinds of data have been consistently included, no matter what the item undergoing analysis, and why have these rather than other data been included?*

It soon becomes apparent that the functionalist orientation largely determines what is included in the description of the item to be interpreted. Thus, the description of a magical performance or a ceremonial is not confined to an account of the spell or formula, the rite and the performers. It includes a systematic account of the people participating and the onlookers, of the types and rates of interaction among performers and audience, of changes in these patterns of interaction in the course of the ceremonial. Thus, the description of Hopi rain ceremonials, for example, entails more than the actions seemingly oriented toward the intervention of the gods in meteorological phenomena. It involves a report of the persons *who* are variously involved in the pattern of behavior. And the description of the participants (and on-lookers) is in *structural terms,* that is, in terms of locating these people in their inter-connected social statuses.

Brief excerpts will illustrate how functional analyses begin with a systematic inclusion (and, preferably, charting) of the statuses and social interrelations of those engaging in the behavior under scrutiny.

> *Chiricahua puberty ceremonial for girls: the extended domestic family* (parents and relatives financially able to help) bear the expense of this four-day ceremony. The parents select the time and place for the ceremonial. "All the members of the *girl's encampment* attend and nearly all the *members of the local group.* A goodly sprinkling of visitors from *other local groups* and some *travelers from outside bands* are to be seen, and their numbers increase as the day wears on." The *leader of the local group* to which the girl's family belongs speaks, welcoming all visitors. In short, this account explicitly calls attention to the following statuses and groups variously involved in the ceremonial: the girl; her parents and immediate family; the local group, especially through its leader; the band represented by members of outside local groups, and the "tribe by members of other bands."[57]

As we shall see in due course, although it bears stating at this point, *the sheer description* of the ceremony in terms of the statuses and group affiliations of those variously involved *provides a major clue to the functions* performed by this ceremonial. In a word, we suggest that the structural description of participants in the activity under analysis provides hypotheses for subsequent functional interpretations.

---

57. Morris E. Opler, "An outline of Chiricahua Apache social organization," in Fred Eggan ed. *Social Anthropology of North American Tribes,* (Chicago: University of Chicago Press, 1937), 173-239, esp. at 226-230 [italics supplied].

Another illustration will again indicate the nature of such descriptions in terms of role, status, group affiliation and the interrelations among these.

Patterned responses to mirriri (hearing obscenity directed at one's sister) among the Australian Murngin. The standardized pattern must be all too briefly described: when a husband swears at his wife in the presence of her brother, the brother engages in the seemingly anomalous behavior of throwing spears at the wife (not the husband) and her sisters. The description of this pattern goes on to include status descriptions of the participants. The *sisters* are members of the brother's *clan;* the husband comes from another clan.

Note again that participants are *located* within social structures and this location is basic to the subsequent functional analysis of this behavior.[58]

Since these are cases drawn from non-literate society, it might be assumed that these requirements for description are peculiar to non-literate materials. Turning to other instances of functional analyses of patterns found in modern Western society, however, we can identify this same requirement as well as additional guides to "needed descriptive data."

The "romantic love complex" in American society: although all societies recognize "occasional violent emotional attachments," contemporary American society is among the few societies which capitalize upon romantic attachments and in popular belief, at least, make these the basis for choice of a marriage partner. This characteristic pattern of choice minimizes or eliminates the selection of one's mate by parents or the wider kinship group.[59]

Note that the emphasis upon one pattern of choice of mates thereby excludes alternative patterns of choice known to occur elsewhere.

This case suggests a *second* desideratum for a type of data to be included in the account of the item subjected to functional analysis. In describing the characteristic (modal) pattern for handling a standardized problem (choice of marriage-partner), the observer, wherever possible, indicates the principal alternatives which are thereby excluded. This, as we shall see, provides direct clues to the structural context of the pattern and, by suggesting pertinent comparative materials, points toward the validation of the functional analysis.

A *third* integral element of the description of the problematical item

58. W. L. Warner, *A Black Civilization—A Social Study of an Australian Tribe,* (New York: Harper & Bros., 1937), 112-113.

59. For various approaches to a functional analysis of the "romantic love complex," see Ralph Linton, *Study of Man,* (New York: D. Appleton-Century Co., 1936), 174-5; T. Parsons, "Age and sex in the social structure of the United States," *American Sociological Review,* Oct. 1942, 7, 604-616, esp. at 614-15; T. Parsons, "The kinship system of the contemporary United States," *American Anthropologist,* 1943, 45, 22-38, esp. at 31-32, 36-37, both reprinted in his *Essays in Sociological Theory, op. cit.;* T. Parsons, "The social structure of the family," in Ruth N. Anshen ed., *The Family: Its Function and Destiny,* (New York: Harper, 1949), 173-201; R. K. Merton, "Intermarriage and the social structure," *Psychiatry,* 1941, 4, 361-74, esp. at 367-8; and Isidor Thorner, "Sociological aspects of affectional frustration," *Psychiatry,* 1943, 6, 157-173, esp. at 169-172.

preparatory to the actual functional analysis—a further requirement for preparing the specimen for analysis, so to speak—is to include the "*meanings*" (or cognitive and affective significance) of the activity or pattern for members of the group. In fact, as will become evident, a fully circumstantial account of the meanings attached to the item goes far toward suggesting appropriate lines of functional analysis. A case drawn from Veblen's many functional analyses serves to illustrate the general thesis:

> *The cultural pattern of conspicuous consumption:* the conspicuous consumption of relatively expensive commodities "means" (symbolizes) the possession of sufficient wealth to "afford" such expenditures. Wealth, in turn, is honorific. Persons engaging in conspicuous consumption not only derive gratification from the direct consumption but also from the heightened status reflected in the attitudes and opinions of others who observe their consumption. This pattern is most notable among the leisure class, *i.e.*, those who can and largely do refrain from productive labor [this is the status or role component of the description]. However, it diffuses to other strata who seek to emulate the pattern and who likewise experience pride in "wasteful" expenditures. Finally, consumption in conspicuous terms tends to crowd out other criteria for consumption (*e.g.* "efficient" expenditure of funds). [This is an explicit reference to alternative modes of consumption obscured from view by the cultural emphasis on the pattern under scrutiny.][60]

As is well known, Veblen goes on to impute a variety of functions to the pattern of conspicuous consumption—functions of aggrandizement of status, of validation of status, of "good repute," of display of pecuniary strength (p. 84). These consequences, as experienced by participants in the patterned activity, are gratifying and go far toward explaining the continuance of the pattern. *The clues to the imputed functions are provided almost wholly by the description of the pattern itself* which includes explicit references to (1) the status of those differentially exhibiting the pattern, (2) known alternatives to the pattern of consuming in terms of display and "wastefulness" rather than in terms of private and "intrinsic" enjoyment of the item of consumption; and (3) the divers meanings culturally ascribed to the behavior of conspicuous consumption by participants in and observers of the pattern.

These three components of the description of the specimen to be analyzed are by no means exhaustive. A full descriptive protocol, adequate for subsequent functional analysis, will inevitably spill over into a range of immediate psychological and social consequences of the behavior. But these may be more profitably examined in connection with the concepts of function. It is here only necessary to repeat that the description of the item does not proceed according to whim or intuition, but must include at least these three characteristics of the item, if the descriptive protocol is to be of optimum value for functional analysis. Although much remains to be learned concerning desiderata for the de-

60. Thorstein Veblen, *The Theory of the Leisure Class,* (New York: Vanguard Press, 1928), esp. chapters 2-4.

scriptive phase of the total analysis, this brief presentation of models for descriptive content may serve to indicate that procedures for functional analysis *can* be codified—ultimately to the point where the sociological field worker will have a chart guiding observation.

Another case illustrates a further desideratum for the description of the item to be analyzed.

> *Taboo on out-marriage:* the greater the degree of group solidarity, the more marked the sentiment adverse to marriage with people outside the group. "It makes no difference what is the cause of the desire for group solidarity. . . ." Outmarriage *means* either losing one's group-member to another group or incorporation into one's own group of persons who have not been thoroughly socialized in the values, sentiments and practices of the in-group.[61]

This suggests a *fourth* type of datum to be included in the description of the social or cultural specimen, prior to functional analysis. Inevitably, participants in the practice under scrutiny have *some* array of motives for conformity or for deviation. *The descriptive account should, so far as possible, include an account of these motivations, but these motives must not be confused, as we have seen, with (a) the objective pattern of behavior or (b) with the social functions of that pattern.* Inclusion of motives in the descriptive account helps explain the *psychological* functions subserved by the pattern and often proves suggestive with respect to the social functions.

Thus far, we have been considering items which are clearly patterned practices or beliefs, patterns recognized as such by participants in the society. Thus, members of the given society can, in varying degrees, describe the contours of the Chiricahua puberty ceremony, the Murngin mirriri pattern, the choice of mates on the basis of romantic attachments, the concern with consuming conspicuously and the taboos on out-marriage. These are all parts of the overt culture and, as such, are more or less fully known to those who share in this culture. The social scientist, however, does not confine himself to these overt patterns. From time to time, he uncovers a covert cultural pattern, a set of practices or beliefs which is as consistently patterned as overt patterns, but which is not regarded as a normatively regulated pattern by the participants. Examples of this are plentiful. Thus, statistics show that in a quasi-caste situation such as that governing Negro-white relations in this country, the prevailing pattern of interracial marriage (when it occurs) is between white females and Negro males (rather than between Negro females and white males). Although this pattern, which we may call caste hypogamy, is not institutionalized, it is persistent and remarkably stable.[62]

---

61. Romanzo Adams, *Interracial Marriage in Hawaii,* esp. at 197-204; Merton, "Intermarriage . . .," *op. cit.,* esp. at 368-9; K. Davis "Intermarriage in caste societies," *American Anthropologist,* 1941, 43, 376-395.

62. *Cf.* Merton, "Intermarriage . . .," *op. cit.;* Otto Klineberg ed., *Characteristics of the American Negro,* (New York: Harper, 1943).

Or consider another instance of a fixed but apparently unrecognized pattern. Malinowski reports that Trobrianders cooperatively engaged in the technological task of building a canoe are engaged not only in that explicit technical task but also in establishing and reinforcing interpersonal relations among themselves in the process. Much of the recent data on those primary groups called "informal organizations" deals with these patterns of relations which are observed by the social scientist but are unrecognized, at least in their full implications, by the participants.[63]

All this points to a *fifth* desideratum for the descriptive protocol: regularities of behavior *associated* with the nominally central activity (although not part of the explicit culture pattern) should be included in the protocols of the field worker, since these *unwitting regularities* often provide basic clues to distinctive functions of the total pattern. As we shall see, the inclusion of these "unwitting" regularities in the descriptive protocol directs the investigator almost at once to analysis of the pattern in terms of what we have called latent functions.

In summary, then, the descriptive protocol should, so far as possible, include:

1) location of participants in the pattern within the social structure—differential participation;

2) consideration of alternative modes of behavior excluded by emphasis on the observed pattern (*i.e.* attention not only to what occurs but also to what is neglected by virtue of the existing pattern);

3) the emotive and cognitive meanings attached by participants to the pattern;

4) a distinction between the motivations for participating in the pattern and the objective behavior involved in the pattern;

5) regularities of behavior not recognized by participants but which are nonetheless associated with the central pattern of behavior.

That these desiderata for the observer's protocol are far from complete is altogether likely. But they do provide a tentative step in the direction of *specifying* points of observation which facilitate subsequent functional analysis. They are intended to be somewhat more specific than the suggestions ordinarily found in general statements of procedure, such as those advising the observer to be sensitive to the "context of situation."

MANIFEST AND LATENT FUNCTIONS

As has been implied in earlier sections, the distinction between manifest and latent functions was devised to preclude the inadvertent confusion, often found in the sociological literature, between conscious *motivations* for social behavior and its *objective consequences.* Our

63. The rediscovery of the primary group by those engaged in sociological studies of industry has been one of the chief fillips to the functional approach in recent sociological research. Reference is had here to the work of Elton Mayo, Roethlisberger and Dickson, William Whyte, and Burleigh Gardner, among many others. There remain, of course, the interesting differences in *interpretation* to which these data lend themselves

scrutiny of current vocabularies of functional analysis has shown how easily, and how unfortunately, the sociologist may identify *motives* with *functions*. It was further indicated that the motive and the function vary independently and that the failure to register this fact in an established terminology has contributed to the unwitting tendency among sociologists to confuse the subjective categories of motivation with the objective categories of function. This, then, is the central purpose of our succumbing to the not-always-commendable practice of introducing new terms into the rapidly growing tehnical vocabulary of sociology, a practice regarded by many laymen as an affront to their intelligence and an offense against common intelligibility.

As will be readily recognized, I have adapted the terms "manifest" and "latent" from their use in another context by Freud (although Francis Bacon had long ago spoken of "latent process" and "latent configuration" in connection with processes which are below the threshold of superficial observation).

The distinction itself has been repeatedly drawn by observers of human behavior at irregular intervals over a span of many centuries.[64] Indeed, it would be disconcerting to find that a distinction which we have come to regard as central to functional analysis had not been made by any of that numerous company who have in effect adopted a functional orientation. We need mention only a few of those who have, in recent decades, found it necessary to distinguish in their specific interpretations of behavior between the end-in-view and the functional consequences of action.

George H. Mead[65]: ". . . that attitude of hostility toward the law-breaker has the unique advantage [read: latent function] of uniting all members of the community in the emotional solidarity of aggression. While the most admirable of humanitarian efforts are sure to run counter to the individual interests of very many in the community, or fail to touch the interest and imagination of the multitude and to leave the community divided or indifferent, the cry of thief or murderer is attuned to profound complexes, lying below the surface of competing individual efforts, and citizens who have [been] separated by divergent interests stand together against the common enemy."

Emile Durkheim's[66] similar analysis of the social functions of punishment is also focused on its latent functions (consequences for the community) rather than confined to manifest functions (consequences for the criminal).

---

64. References to some of the more significant among these earlier appearances of the distinction will be found in Merton, "Unanticipated consequences . . .," *op. cit.*

65. George H. Mead, "The psychology of punitive justice," *American Journal of Sociology,* 1918, 23, 577-602, esp. 591.

66. As suggested earlier in this chapter, Durkheim adopted a functional orientation throughout his work, and he operates, albeit often without explicit notice, with concepts equivalent to that of latent function in all of his researches. The reference in the text at this point is to his "Deux lois de l'évolution penale," *L'année sociologique,* 1899-1900, 4, 55-95, as well as to his *Division of Labor in Society* (Glencoe, Illinois: The Free Press, 1947).

W. G. Sumner[67]: ". . . from the first acts by which men try to satisfy needs, each act stands by itself, and looks no further than the immediate satisfaction. From recurrent needs arise habits for the individual and customs for the group, but these results are consequences which were never conscious, and never foreseen or intended. They are not noticed until they have long existed, and it is still longer before they are appreciated." Although this fails to locate the latent functions of standardized social actions for a designated social structure, it plainly makes the basic distinction between ends-in-view and objective consequences.

R. M. MacIver[68]: In addition to the direct effects of institutions, "there are further effects by way of control which lie outside the direct purposes of men . . . this type of reactive form of control . . . may, though unintended, be of profound service to society."

W. I. Thomas and F. Znaniecki[69]: "Although all the new [Polish peasant cooperative] institutions are thus formed with the definite purpose of satisfying certain specific needs, their social function is by no means limited to their explicit and conscious purpose . . . every one of these institutions—commune or agricultural circle, loan and savings bank, or theater—is not merely a mechanism for the management of certain values but also an association of people, each member of which is supposed to participate in the common activities as a living, concrete individual. Whatever is the predominant, official common interest upon which the institution is founded, the association as a concrete group of human personalities unofficially involves many other interests; the social contacts between its members are not limited to their common pursuit, though the latter, of course, constitutes both the main reason for which the association is formed and the most permanent bond which holds it together. Owing to this combination of an abstract political, economic, or rather rational mechanism for the satisfaction of specific needs with the concrete unity of a social group, the new institution is also the best intermediary link between the peasant primary-group and the secondary national system."

These and numerous other sociological observers have, then, from time to time distinguished between categories of subjective disposition ("needs, interests, purposes") and categories of generally unrecognized but objective functional consequences ("unique advantages," "never conscious" consequences, "unintended . . . service to society," "function not limited to conscious and explicit purpose").

---

67. This one of his many such observations is of course from W. G. Sumner's *Folkways,* (Boston: Ginn & Co., 1906), 3. His collaborator, Albert G. Keller retained the distinction in his own writings; see, for example, his *Social Evolution,* (New York: Macmillan, 1927), at 93-95.

68. This is advisedly drawn from one of MacIver's earlier works, *Community,* (London: Macmillan, 1915). The distinction takes on greater importance in his later writings, becoming a major element in his *Social Causation,* (Boston: Ginn & Co., 1942), esp. at 314-321, and informs the greater part of his *The More Perfect Union,* (New York: Macmillan, 1948).

69. The single excerpt quoted in the text is one of scores which have led to *The Polish Peasant in Europe and America* being deservedly described as a "sociological classic." See pages 1426-7 and 1523 ff. As will be noted later in this chapter, the insights and conceptual distinctions contained in this one passage, and there are many others like it in point of richness of content, were forgotten or never noticed by those industrial sociologists who recently came to develop the notion of "informal organization" in industry.

Since the occasion for making the distinction arises with great frequency, and since the purpose of a conceptual scheme is to direct observations toward salient elements of a situation and to prevent the inadvertent oversight of these elements, it would seem justifiable to designate this distinction by an appropriate set of terms. This is the rationale for the distinction between manifest functions and latent functions; the first referring to those objective consequences for a specified unit (person, subgroup, social or cultural system) which contribute to its adjustment or adaptation and were so intended; the second referring to unintended and unrecognized consequences of the same order.

There are some indications that the christening of this distinction may serve a heuristic purpose by becoming incorporated into an explicit conceptual apparatus, thus aiding both systematic observation and later analysis. In recent years, for example, the distinction between manifest and latent functions has been utilized in analyses of racial intermarriage,[70] social stratification,[71] affective frustration,[72] Veblen's sociological theories,[73] prevailing American orientations toward Russia,[74] propaganda as a means of social control,[75] Malinowski's anthropological theory,[76] Navajo witchcraft,[77] problems in the sociology of knowledge,[78] fashion,[79] the dynamics of personality,[80] national security measures,[81] the internal social dynamics of bureaucracy,[82] and a great variety of other sociological problems.

The very diversity of these subject-matters suggests that the theoretic

70. Merton, "Intermarriage and the social structure," *op. cit.*

71. Kingsley Davis, "A conceptual analysis of stratification," *American Sociological Review,* 1942, 7, 309-321.

72. Thorner, *op. cit.*, esp. at 165.

73. A. K. Davis, *Thorstein Veblen's Social Theory,* Harvard Ph.D. dissertation, 1941 and "Veblen on the decline of the Protestant Ethic," *Social Forces,* 1944, 22, 282-86; Louis Schneider, *The Freudian Psychology and Veblen's Social Theory,* New York: King's Crown Press, 1948), esp. Chapter 2.

74. A. K. Davis, "Some sources of American hostility to Russia," *American Journal of Sociology,* 1947, 53, 174-183.

75. Talcott Parsons, "Propaganda and social control," in his *Essays in Sociological Theory.*

76. Clyde Kluckhohn, "Bronislaw Malinowski, 1884-1942," *Journal of American Folklore,* 1943, 56, 208-219.

77. Clyde Kluckhohn, *Navaho Witchcraft, op. cit.*, esp. at 46-47 and ff.

78. Merton, Chapter XII of this volume.

79. Bernard Barber and L. S. Lobel, "'Fashion' in women's clothes and the American social system," *Social Forces,* 1952, 31, 124-131.

80. O. H. Mowrer and C. Kluckhohn, "Dynamic theory of personality," in J. M. Hunt, ed., *Personality and the Behavior Disorders,* (New York: Ronald Press, 1944), 1, 69-135, esp. at 72.

81. Marie Jahoda and S. W. Cook, "Security measures and freedom of thought: an exploratory study of the impact of loyalty and security programs," *Yale Law Journal,* 1952, 61, 296-333.

82. Philip Selznick, *TVA and the Grass Roots* (University of California Press, 1949); A. W. Gouldner, *Patterns of Industrial Bureaucracy* (Glencoe, Illinois: The Free Press, 1954); P. M. Blau, *The Dynamics of Bureaucracy* (University of Chicago Press, 1955); A. K. Davis, "Bureaucratic patterns in Navy officer corps," *Social Forces* 1948, 27, 142-153.

distinction between manifest and latent functions is not bound up with a limited and particular range of human behavior. But there still remains the large task of ferreting out the specific uses to which this distinction can be put, and it is to this large task that we devote the remaining pages of this chapter.

Heuristic Purposes of the Distinction

Clarifies the analysis of seemingly irrational social patterns. In the first place, the distinction aids the sociological interpretation of many social practices which persist even though their manifest purpose is clearly not achieved. The time-worn procedure in such instances has been for diverse, particularly lay, observers to refer to these practices as "superstitions," irrationalities," "mere inertia of tradition," *etc.* In other words, when group behavior does not—and, indeed, often cannot—attain its ostensible purpose there is an inclination to attribute its occurrence to lack of intelligence, sheer ignorance, survivals, or so-called inertia. Thus, the Hopi ceremonials designed to produce abundant rainfall may be labelled a superstitious practice of primitive folk and that is assumed to conclude the matter. It should be noted that this in no sense accounts for the group behavior. It is simply a case of name-calling; it substitutes the epithet "superstition" for an analysis of the actual role of this behavior in the life of the group. Given the concept of latent function, however, we are reminded that this behavior *may* perform a function for the group, although this function may be quite remote from the avowed purpose of the behavior.

The concept of latent function extends the observer's attention beyond the question of whether or not the behavior attains its avowed purpose. Temporarily ignoring these explicit purposes, it directs attention *toward* another range of consequences: those bearing, for example, upon the individual personalities of Hopi involved in the ceremony and upon the persistence and continuity of the larger group. Were one to confine himself to the problem of whether a manifest (purposed) function occurs, it becomes a problem, not for the sociologist, but for the meteorologist. And to be sure, our meteorologists agree that the rain ceremonial does not produce rain; but this is hardly to the point. It is merely to say that the ceremony does not have this technological use; that this purpose of the ceremony and its actual consequences do not coincide. But with the concept of latent function, we continue our inquiry, examining the consequences of the ceremony not for the rain gods or for meteorological phenomena, but for the groups which conduct the ceremony. And here it may be found, as many observers indicate, that the ceremonial does indeed have functions—but functions which are non-purposed or latent.

Ceremonials may fulfill the latent function of reinforcing the group identity by providing a periodic occasion on which the scattered members of a group assemble to engage in a common activity. As Durkheim among others long since indicated, such ceremonials are a means by which collective expression is afforded the sentiments which, in a further analysis, are found to be a basic source of group unity. Through the systematic application of the concept of latent function, therefore, *apparently* irrational behavior may *at times* be found to be positively functional for the group. Operating with the concept of latent function, we are not too quick to conclude that if an activity of a group does not achieve its nominal purpose, then its persistence can be described only as an instance of "inertia," "survival," or "manipulation by powerful subgroups in the society."

In point of fact, some conception like that of latent function has very often, almost invariably, been employed by social scientists observing *a standardized practice designed to achieve an objective which one knows from accredited physical science cannot be thus achieved.* This would plainly be the case, for example, with Pueblo rituals dealing with rain or fertility. *But with behavior which is not directed toward a clearly unattainable objective, sociological observers are less likely to examine the collateral or latent functions of the behavior.*

Directs attention to theoretically fruitful fields of inquiry. The distinction between manifest and latent functions serves further to direct the attention of the sociologist to precisely those realms of behavior, attitude and belief where he can most fruitfully apply his special skills. For what is his task if he confines himself to the study of manifest functions? He is then concerned very largely with determining whether a practice instituted for a particular purpose does, in fact, achieve this purpose. He will then inquire, for example, whether a new system of wage-payment achieves its avowed purpose of reducing labor turnover or of increasing output. He will ask whether a propaganda campaign has indeed gained its objective of increasing "willingness to fight" or "willingness to buy war bonds," or "tolerance toward other ethnic groups." Now, these are important, and complex, types of inquiry. But, so long as sociologists *confine* themselves to the study of manifest functions, their inquiry is set for them by practical men of affairs (whether a captain of industry, a trade union leader, or, conceivably, a Navaho chieftain, is for the moment immaterial), rather than by the theoretic problems which are at the core of the discipline. By dealing primarily with the realm of manifest functions, with the key problem of whether deliberately instituted practices or organizations succeed in achieving their objectives, the sociologist becomes converted into an industrious and skilled recorder of the altogether familiar pattern of behavior. *The terms of appraisal are fixed and limited by the question put to him by the non-theoretic men of affairs, e.g.,* has the new wage-payment program achieved such-and-such purposes?

But armed with the concept of latent function, the sociologist extends his inquiry in those very directions which promise most for the theoretic development of the discipline. He examines the familiar (or planned) social practice to ascertain the latent, and hence generally unrecognized, functions (as well, of course, as the manifest functions). He considers, for example, the consequences of the new wage plan for, say, the trade union in which the workers are organized or the consequences of a propaganda program, not only for increasing its avowed purpose of stirring up patriotic fervor, but also for making large numbers of people reluctant to speak their minds when they differ with official policies, *etc.* In short, it is suggested that the *distinctive* intellectual contributions of the sociologist are found primarily in the study of unintended consequences (among which are latent functions) of social practices, as well as in the study of anticipated consequences (among which are manifest functions).[83]

There is some evidence that it is precisely at the point where the research attention of sociologists has shifted from the plane of manifest to the plane of latent functions that they have made their *distinctive* and major contributions. This can be extensively documented but a few passing illustrations must suffice.

THE HAWTHORNE WESTERN ELECTRIC STUDIES:[84] As is well known, the early stages of this inquiry were concerned with the problem of the relations of "illumination to efficiency" of industrial workers. For some two and a half years, attention was focused on problems such as this: do variations in the intensity of lighting affect production? The initial results showed that within wide limits there was no uniform relation between illumination and output. Production output increased *both* in the experimental group where illumination was increased (or *decreased*) *and* in the control group where no changes in illumination were introduced. In short, the investigators confined themselves wholly to a search for the manifest functions. Lacking a concept of latent social function, no attention whatever was initially paid to the social consequences *of the experiment* for relations among members of the test and control groups or for relations between workers and the test room authorities. In other words, the investigators lacked a sociological frame of reference and

83. For a brief illustration of this general proposition, see Robert K. Merton, Marjorie Fiske and Alberta Curtis, *Mass Persuasion,* (New York: Harper, 1946), 185-189; Jahoda and Cook, *op. cit.*

84. This is cited as a case study of how *an elaborate research was wholly changed in theoretic orientation and in the character of its research findings by the introduction of a concept approximating the concept of latent function.* Selection of the case for this purpose does not, of course, imply full acceptance of the *interpretations* which the authors give their findings. Among the several volumes reporting the Western Electric research, see particularly F. J. Roethlisberger and W. J. Dickson, *Management and the Worker,* (Harvard University Press, 1939)

operated merely as "engineers" (just as a group of meteorologists might have explored the "effects" upon rainfall of the Hopi ceremonial).

Only after continued investigation, did it occur to the research group to explore the consequences of the new "experimental situation" for the self-images and self-conceptions of the workers taking part in the experiment, for the interpersonal relations among members of the group, for the coherence and unity of the group. As Elton Mayo reports it, "the illumination fiasco had made them alert to the need that very careful records should be kept of everything that happened in the room in addition to the obvious engineering and industrial devices. Their observations therefore included not only records of industrial and engineering changes but also records of physiological or medical changes, and, *in a sense,* of social and anthropological. This last took the form of a 'log' that gave as full an account as possible of the actual events of every day. . . ."[85] In short, it was only after a long series of experiments which wholly neglected the latent social functions of the experiment (as a contrived social situation) that this distinctly sociological framework was introduced. "With this realization," the authors write, "the inquiry changed its character. No longer were the investigators interested in testing for the effects of single variables. In the place of a controlled experiment, they substituted the notion of a social situation which needed to be described and understood as a system of interdependent elements." Thereafter, as is now widely known, inquiry was directed very largely toward ferreting out the latent functions of standardized practices among the workers, of informal organization developing among workers, of workers' games instituted by "wise administrators," of large programs of worker counselling and interviewing, *etc.* The new conceptual scheme entirely altered the range and types of data gathered in the ensuing research.

One has only to return to the previously quoted excerpt from Thomas and Znaniecki in their classical work of some thirty years ago, to recognize the correctness of Shils' remark:

> . . . indeed the history of the study of primary groups in American sociology is a supreme instance of the *discontinuities of the development of this discipline:* a problem is stressed by one who is an acknowledged founder of the discipline, the problem is left unstudied, then, some years later, it is taken up with enthusiasm as if no one had ever thought of it before.[86]

For Thomas and Znaniecki had repeatedly emphasized the sociological view that, whatever its major purpose, "the association as a concrete group of human personalities unofficially involves many other interests;

85. Elton Mayo, *The Social Problems of an Industrial Civilization,* (Harvard University Press, 1945), 70.

86. Edward Shils, *The Present State of American Sociology,* (Glencoe, Illinois The Free Press, 1948), 42 [italics supplied].

the social contacts between its members are not limited to their common pursuit. . . ." In effect, then, it had taken years of experimentation to turn the attention of the Western Electric research team to the latent social functions of primary groups emerging in industrial organizations. It should be made clear that this case is not cited here as an instance of defective experimental design; that is not our immediate concern. It is considered only as an illustration of the pertinence for *sociological* inquiry of the concept of latent function, and the associated concepts of functional analysis. It illustrates how the inclusion of this concept (whether the term is used or not is inconsequential) can sensitize sociological investigators to a range of significant social variables which are otherwise easily overlooked. The explicit ticketing of the concept may perhaps lessen the frequency of such occasions of discontinuity in future sociological research.

The discovery of latent functions represents significant increments in sociological knowledge. There is another respect in which inquiry into latent functions represents a distinctive contribution of the social scientist. It is precisely the latent functions of a practice or belief which are *not* common knowledge, for these are unintended and generally unrecognized social and psychological consequences. As a result, findings concerning latent functions represent a greater increment in knowledge than findings concerning manifest functions. They represent, also, greater departures from "common-sense" knowledge about social life. Inasmuch as the latent functions depart, more or less, from the avowed manifest functions, the research which uncovers latent functions very often produces "paradoxical" results. The seeming paradox arises from the sharp modification of a familiar popular preconception which regards a standardized practice or belief *only* in terms of its manifest functions by indicating some of its subsidiary or collateral latent functions. The introduction of the concept of latent function in social research leads to conclusions which show that "social life is not as simple as it first seems." For as long as people confine themselves to *certain* consequences (*e.g.* manifest consequences), it is comparatively simple for them to pass moral judgments upon the practice or belief in question. Moral evaluations, generally based on these manifest consequences, tend to be polarized in terms of black or white. But the perception of further (latent) consequences often complicates the picture. Problems of moral evaluation (which are not our immediate concern) and problems of social engineering (which are our concern[87]) both take on the additional complexities usually involved in responsible social decisions.

87. This is not to deny that social engineering has direct moral implications or that technique and morality are inescapably intertwined, but I do not intend to deal with this range of problems in the present chapter. For some discussion of these problems see chapters VI, XV and XVII; also Merton, Fiske and Curtis, *Mass Persuasion,* chapter 7.

An example of inquiry which implicitly uses the notion of latent function will illustrate the sense in which "paradox"—discrepancy between the apparent, merely manifest, function and the actual, which also includes latent functions—tends to occur as a result of including this concept. Thus, to revert to Veblen's well-known analysis of conspicuous consumption, it is no accident that he has been recognized as a social analyst gifted with an eye for the paradoxical, the ironic, the satiric. For these are frequent, if not inevitable, outcomes of applying the concept of latent function (or its equivalent).

THE PATTERN OF CONSPICUOUS CONSUMPTION. The manifest purpose of buying consumption goods is, of course, the satisfaction of the needs for which these goods are explicitly designed. Thus, automobiles are obviously intended to provide a certain kind of transportation; candles, to provide light; choice articles of food to provide sustenance; rare art products to provide aesthetic pleasure. Since these products *do* have these uses, it was largely assumed that these encompass the range of socially significant functions. Veblen indeed suggests that this was ordinarily the prevailing view (in the pre-Veblenian era, of course): "The end of acquisition and accumulation is conventionally held to be the consumption of the goods accumulated. . . . This is at least felt to be the economically legitimate end of acquisition, *which alone it is incumbent on the theory to take account of.*"[88]

However, says Veblen in effect, as sociologists we must go on to consider the latent functions of acquisition, accumulation and consumption, and these latent functions are remote indeed from the manifest functions. "But, it is only when taken in a sense far removed from its naive meaning [*i.e.* manifest function] that the consumption of goods can be said to afford the incentive from which accumulation invariably proceeds." And among these latent functions, which help explain the persistence and the social location of the pattern of conspicuous consumption, is its symbolization of "pecuniary strength and so of gaining or retaining a good name." The exercise of "punctilious discrimination" in the excellence of "food, drink, shelter, service, ornaments, apparel, amusements" results not merely in direct gratifications derived from the consumption of "superior" to "inferior" articles, but also, and Veblen argues, more importantly, it results in a *heightening or reaffirmation of social status.*

The Veblenian paradox is that people buy expensive goods not so much because they are superior but because they are expensive. For it is the latent equation ("costliness = mark of higher social status") which he singles out in his functional analysis, rather than the manifest equation ("costliness = excellence of the goods"). Not that he denies manifest functions *any* place in buttressing the pattern of conspicuous

88. Veblen, *Theory of Leisure Class, op. cit.*, p. 25.

consumption. These, too, are operative. "What has just been said must not be taken to mean that there are no other incentives to acquisition and accumulation than this desire to excel in pecuniary standing and so gain the esteem and envy of one's fellowmen. The desire for added comfort and security from want is present as a motive at every stage. . . ." Or again: "It would be hazardous to assert that a useful purpose is ever absent from the utility of any article or of any service, however obviously its prime purpose and chief element is conspicuous waste" and derived social esteem.[89] It is only that *these direct, manifest functions do not fully account for the prevailing patterns of consumption. Otherwise put, if the latent functions of status-enhancement or status-reaffirmation were removed from the patterns of conspicuous consumption, these patterns would undergo severe changes of a sort which the "conventional" economist could not foresee.*

In these respects, Veblen's analysis of latent functions departs from the common-sense notion that the end-product of consumption is "of course, the direct satisfaction which it provides": "People eat caviar because they're hungry; buy Cadillacs because they want the best car they can get; have dinner by candlelight because they like the peaceful atmosphere." The common-sense interpretation in terms of selected manifest motives gives way, in Veblen's analysis, to the collateral latent functions which are also, and perhaps more significantly, fulfilled by these practices. To be sure, the Veblenian analysis has, in the last decades, entered so fully into popular thought, that these latent functions are now widely recognized. [This raises the interesting problem of the changes occurring in a prevailing pattern of behavior when its *latent* functions become generally recognized (and are thus no longer latent). There will be no occasion for discussing this important problem in the present publication.]

The discovery of latent functions does not merely render conceptions of the functions served by certain social patterns more precise (as is the case also with studies of manifest functions), but introduces a *qualitatively different increment in the previous state of knowledge.*

Precludes the substitution of naive moral judgments for sociological

---

89. *Ibid.*, 32, 101. It will be noted throughout that Veblen is given to loose terminology. In the marked passages (and repeatedly elsewhere) he uses "incentive," "desire," "purpose," and "function" interchangeably. Since the context usually makes clear the denotation of these terms, no great harm is done. But it is clear that the expressed purposes of conformity to a culture pattern are by no means identical with the latent functions of the conformity. Veblen occasionally recognizes this. For example, "In strict accuracy nothing should be included under the head of conspicuous waste but such expenditure as is incurred on the ground of an invidious pecuniary comparison. But in order to bring any given item or element in under this head *it is not necessary that it should be recognized as waste in this sense by the person incurring the expenditure.*" (*Ibid.* 99; italics supplied). *Cf.* A. K. Davis, "Veblen on the decline of the Protestant Ethic," *op. cit.*

analysis. Since moral evaluations in a society tend to be largely in terms of the manifest consequences of a practice or code, we should be prepared to find that analysis in terms of latent functions at times runs counter to prevailing moral evaluations. For it does not follow that the latent functions will operate in the same fashion as the manifest consequences which are ordinarily the basis of these judgments. Thus, in large sectors of the American population, the political machine or the "political racket" are judged as unequivocally "bad" and "undesirable." The grounds for such moral judgment vary somewhat, but they consist substantially in pointing out that political machines violate moral codes: political patronage violates the code of selecting personnel on the basis of impersonal qualifications rather than on grounds of party loyalty or contributions to the party war-chest; bossism violates the code that votes should be based on individual appraisal of the qualifications of candidates and of political issues, and not on abiding loyalty to a feudal leader; bribery, and "honest graft" obviously offend the proprieties of property; "protection" for crime clearly violates the law and the mores; and so on.

In view of the manifold respects in which political machines, in varying degrees, run counter to the mores and at times to the law, it becomes pertinent to inquire how they manage to continue in operation. The familiar "explanations" for the continuance of the political machine are not here in point. To be sure, it may well be that if "respectable citizenry" would live up to their political obligations, if the electorate were to be alert and enlightened; if the number of elective officers were substantially reduced from the dozens, even hundreds, which the average voter is now expected to appraise in the course of town, county, state and national elections; if the electorate were activated by the "wealthy and educated classes without whose participation," as the not-always democratically oriented Bryce put it, "the best-framed government must speedily degenerate";—if these and a plethora of similar changes in political structure were introduced, perhaps the "evils" of the political machine would indeed be exorcized.[90] But it should be noted that these changes are often not introduced, that political machines have had the phoenix-like quality of arising strong and unspoiled from their ashes, that, in short, this structure has exhibited a notable vitality in many areas of American political life.

Proceeding from the functional view, therefore, that we should

90. These "explanations" are "causal" in design. They profess to indicate the social conditions under which political machines come into being. In so far as they are empirically confirmed, these explanations of course add to our knowledge concerning the problem: how is it that political machines operate in certain areas and not in others? How do they manage to continue? *But these causal accounts are not sufficient.* The functional consequences of the machine, as we shall see, go far toward supplementing the causal interpretation.

ordinarily (not invariably) expect persistent social patterns and social structures to perform positive functions *which are at the time not adequately fulfilled by other existing patterns and structures,* the thought occurs that perhaps this publicly maligned organization is, *under present conditions,* satisfying basic latent functions.[91] A brief examination of current analyses of this type of structure may also serve to illustrate additional problems of functional analysis.

SOME FUNCTIONS OF THE POLITICAL MACHINE. Without presuming to enter into the variations of detail marking different political machines—a Tweed, Vare, Crump, Flynn, Hague are by no means identical types of bosses—we can briefly examine the functions more or less common to the political machine, as a generic type of social organization. We neither attempt to itemize all the diverse functions of the political machine nor imply that all these functions are similarly fulfilled by each and every machine.

The key structural function of the Boss is to organize, centralize and maintain in good working condition "the scattered fragments of power" which are at present dispersed through our political organization. By this centralized organization of political power, the boss and his apparatus can satisfy the needs of diverse subgroups in the larger community which are not adequately satisfied by legally devised and culturally approved social structures.

To understand the role of bossism and the machine, therefore, we must look at two types of sociological variables: (1) the *structural context* which makes it difficult, if not impossible, for morally approved structures to fulfill essential social functions, thus leaving the door open for political machines (or their structural equivalents) to fulfill these functions and (2) the subgroups whose distinctive needs are left unsatisfied, except for the latent functions which the machine in fact fulfills.[92]

Structural Context: The constitutional framework of American political organization specifically precludes the legal possibility of highly centralized power and, it has been noted, thus "discourages the growth

---

91. I trust it is superfluous to add that this hypothesis is not "in support of the political machine." The question whether the dysfunctions of the machine outweigh its functions, the question whether alternative structures are not available which may fulfill its functions without necessarily entailing its social dysfunctions, still remain to be considered at an appropriate point. We are here concerned with documenting the statement that moral judgments based *entirely* on an appraisal of manifest functions of a social structure are "unrealistic" in the strict sense, *i.e.,* they do not take into account other actual consequences of that structure, consequences which may provide basic social support for the structure. As will be indicated later, "social reforms" or "social engineering" which ignore latent functions do so on pain of suffering acute disappointments and boomerang effects.

92. Again, as with preceding cases, we shall not consider the possible dysfunctions of the political machine.

of effective and responsible leadership. The framers of the Constitution, as Woodrow Wilson observed, set up the check and balance system 'to keep government at a sort of mechanical equipoise by means of a standing amicable contest among its several organic parts.' They distrusted power as dangerous to liberty: and therefore they spread it thin and erected barriers against its concentration." This dispersion of power is found not only at the national level but in local areas as well. "As a consequence," Sait goes on to observe, "when *the people or particular groups* among them demanded positive action, no one had adequate authority to act. The machine provided an antidote."[93]

The constitutional dispersion of power not only makes for difficulty of effective decision and action but when action does occur it is defined and hemmed in by legalistic considerations. In consequence, there developed "a much *more human system* of partisan government, whose chief object soon became the circumvention of government by law. . . . The lawlessness of the extra-official democracy was merely the counterpoise of the legalism of the official democracy. The lawyer having been permitted to subordinate democracy to the Law, the Boss had to be called in to extricate the victim, which he did after a fashion and for a consideration."[94]

Officially, political power is dispersed. Various well-known expedients were devised for this manifest objective. Not only was there the familiar separation of powers among the several branches of the government but, in some measure, tenure in each office was limited, rotation in office approved. And the scope of power inherent in each office was severely circumscribed. Yet, observes Sait in rigorously functional terms, "Leadership is necessary; and *since* it does not develop readily within the constitutional framework, the Boss provides it in a crude and irresponsible form from the outside."[95]

Put in more generalized terms, *the functional deficiencies of the official structure generate an alternative (unofficial) structure to fulfill existing needs somewhat more effectively*. Whatever its specific historical origins, the political machine persists as an apparatus for satisfying otherwise unfulfilled needs of diverse groups in the population. By turning to a few of these subgroups and their characteristic needs, we shall be led at once to a range of latent functions of the political machine.

Functions of the Political Machine for Diverse Subgroups. It is well known that one source of strength of the political machine derives from

93. Edward M. Sait, "Machine, Political," *Encyclopedia of the Social Sciences*, IX, 658 b [italics supplied]; *cf.* A. F. Bentley, *The Process of Government* (Chicago, 1908), Chap. 2.

94. Herbert Croly, *Progressive Democracy*, (New York, 1914), p. 254, cited by Sait, *op. cit.*, 658 b.

95. Sait, *op. cit.*, 659 a. [italics supplied].

its roots in the local community and the neighborhood. The political machine does not regard the electorate as an amorphous, undifferentiated mass of voters. With a keen sociological intuition, the machine recognizes that the voter is a person living in a specific neighborhood, with specific personal problems and personal wants. Public issues are abstract and remote; private problems are extremely concrete and immediate. It is not through the generalized appeal to large public concerns that the machine operates, but through the direct, quasi-feudal relationships between local representatives of the machine and voters in their neighborhood. Elections are won in the precinct.

The machine welds its link with ordinary men and women by elaborate networks of personal relations. Politics is transformed into personal ties. The precinct captain "must be a friend to every man, assuming if he does not feel sympathy with the unfortunate, and utilizing in his good works the resources which the boss puts at his disposal."[96] The precinct captain is forever a friend in need. In our prevailingly impersonal society, the machine, through its local agents, fulfills the important social *function of humanizing and personalizing all manner of assistance* to those in need. Foodbaskets and jobs, legal and extra-legal advice, setting to rights minor scrapes with the law, helping the bright poor boy to a political scholarship in a local college, looking after the bereaved—the whole range of crises when a feller needs a friend, and, above all, a friend who knows the score and who can do something about it,—all these find the ever-helpful precinct captain available in the pinch.

To assess this function of the political machine adequately, it is important to note not only that aid *is* provided but *the manner in which it is provided.* After all, other agencies do exist for dispensing such assistance. Welfare agencies, settlement houses, legal aid clinics, medical aid in free hospitals, public relief departments, immigration authorities—these and a multitude of other organizations are available to provide the most varied types of assistance. But in contrast to the professional techniques of the welfare worker which may typically represent in the mind of the recipient the cold, bureaucratic dispensation of limited aid following upon detailed investigation of *legal* claims to aid of the "client" are the unprofessional techniques of the precinct captain who asks no questions, exacts no compliance with legal rules of eligibility and does not "snoop" into private affairs.[97]

96. *Ibid.,* 659 a.

97. Much the same contrast with official welfare policy is found in Harry Hopkins' open-handed and non-political distribution of unemployment relief in New York State under the governorship of Franklin Delano Roosevelt. As Sherwood reports: "Hopkins was harshly criticized for these irregular activities by the established welfare agencies, which claimed it was 'unprofessional conduct' to hand out work tickets without thorough investigation of each applicant, his own or his family's financial resources and probably his religious affiliations. 'Harry told the agency to go to hell,' said [Hopkins' associate, Dr. Jacob A.] Goldberg." Robert E. Sherwood, *Roosevelt and Hopkins, An Intimate History,* (New York: Harper, 1948), 30.

For many, the loss of "self-respect" is too high a price for legalized assistance. In contrast to the gulf between the settlement house workers who so often come from a different social class, educational background and ethnic group, the precinct worker is "just one of us," who understands what it's all about. The condescending lady bountiful can hardly compete with the understanding friend in need. In *this struggle between alternative structures for fulfilling the nominally same function* of providing aid and support to those who need it, it is clearly the machine politician who is better integrated with the groups which he serves than the impersonal, professionalized, socially distant and legally constrained welfare worker. And since the politician can at times influence and manipulate the official organizations for the dispensation of assistance, whereas the welfare worker has practically no influence on the political machine, this only adds to his greater effectiveness. More colloquially and also, perhaps, more incisively, it was the Boston ward-leader, Martin Lomasny, who described this essential function to the curious Lincoln Steffens: "I think," said Lomasny, "that there's got to be in every ward somebody that any bloke can come to—no matter what he's done—and get help. *Help, you understand; none of your law and justice, but help.*"[98]

The "deprived classes," then, constitute one subgroup for whom the political machine satisfies wants not adequately satisfied in the same fashion by the legitimate social structure.

For a second subgroup, that of business (primarily "big" business but also "small"), the political boss serves the function of providing those political privileges which entail immediate economic gains. Business corporations, among which the public utilities (railroads, local transportation and electric light companies, communications corporations) are simply the most conspicuous in this regard, seek special political dispensations which will enable them to stabilize their situation and to near their objective of maximizing profits. Interestingly enough, corporations often want to avoid a chaos of uncontrolled competition. They want the greater security of an economic czar who controls, regulates and organizes competition, providing that this czar is not a public official with his decisions subject to public scrutiny and public control. (The latter would be "government control," and hence taboo.) The political boss fulfills these requirements admirably.

Examined for a moment apart from any moral considerations, the political apparatus operated by the Boss is effectively designed to perform these functions with a minimum of inefficiency. Holding the strings of diverse governmental divisions, bureaus and agencies in his competent hands, the Boss rationalizes the relations between public and

98. *The Autobiography of Lincoln Steffens,* (Chautauqua, New York: Chautauqua Press, 1931), 618. Deriving largely from Steffens, as he says, F. Stuart Chapin sets forth these functions of the political machine with great clarity. See his *Contemporary American Institutions,* (New York: Harper, 1934), 40-54.

private business. He serves as the business community's ambassador in the otherwise alien (and sometimes unfriendly) realm of government. And, in strict business-like terms, he is well-paid for his economic services to his respectable business clients. In an article entitled, "An Apology to Graft," Lincoln Steffens suggested that "Our economic system, which held up riches, power and acclaim as prizes to men bold enough and able enough to buy corruptly timber, mines, oil fields and franchises and 'get away with it,' was at fault."[99] And, in a conference with a hundred or so of Los Angeles business leaders, he described a fact well known to all of them: the Boss and his machine were an *integral part* of the organization of the economy. "You cannot build or operate a railroad, or a street railway, gas, water, or power company, develop and operate a mine, or get forests and cut timber on a large scale, or run any privileged business, without corrupting or joining in the corruption of the government. You tell me privately that you must, and here I am telling you semi-publicly that you must. And that is so all over the country. And that means that we have an organization of society in which, *for some reason,* you and your kind, the ablest, most intelligent, most imaginative, daring, and resourceful leaders of society, are and must be against society and its laws and its all-around growth."[100]

Since the demand for the services of special privileges are built into the structure of the society, the Boss fulfills diverse functions for this second subgroup of business-seeking-privilege. These "needs" of business, as presently constituted, are not adequately provided for by conventional and culturally approved social structures; consequently, the extra-legal but more-or-less efficient organization of the political machine comes to provide these services. To adopt an *exclusively* moral attitude toward the "corrupt political machine" is to lose sight of the very structural conditions which generate the "evil" that is so bitterly attacked. To adopt a functional outlook is to provide not an apologia for the political machine but a more solid basis for modifying or eliminating the machine, *providing* specific structural arrangements are introduced either for eliminating these effective demands of the business community or, if that is the objective, of satisfying these demands through alternative means.

A third set of distinctive functions fulfilled by the political machine for a special subgroup is that of providing alternative channels of social mobility for those otherwise excluded from the more conventional avenues for personal "advancement." Both the sources of this special

99. *Autobiography of Lincoln Steffens,* 570.

100. *Ibid.,* 572-3 [italics supplied]. This helps explain, as Steffens noted after Police Commissioner Theodore Roosevelt, "the prominence and respectability of the men and women who intercede for crooks" when these have been apprehended in a periodic effort to "clean up the political machine." *Cf.* Steffens, 371, and *passim.*

"need" (for social mobility) and the respect in which the political machine comes to help satisfy this need can be understood by examining the structure of the larger culture and society. As is well known, the American culture lays enormous emphasis on money and power as a "success" goal legitimate for all members of the society. By no means alone in our inventory of cultural goals, it still remains among the most heavily endowed with positive affect and value. However, certain subgroups and certain ecological areas are notable for the relative absence of opportunity for achieving these (monetary and power) types of success. They constitute, in short, sub-populations where "the cultural emphasis upon pecuniary success has been absorbed, but where there is *little access to conventional and legitimate* means for attaining such success. The conventional occupational opportunities of persons in (such areas) are almost completely limited to manual labor. Given our cultural stigmatization of manual labor,[101] and its correlate, the prestige of white-collar work, it is clear that the result is a tendency to achieve these culturally approved objectives *through whatever means are possible.* These people are on the one hand, "asked to orient their conduct toward the prospect of accumulating wealth [and power] and, on the other, they are largely denied effective opportunities to do so institutionally."

It is within this context of social structure that the political machine fulfills the basic function of providing avenues of social mobility for the otherwise disadvantaged. Within this context, even the corrupt political machine and the racket "represent the triumph of amoral intelligence over morally prescribed 'failure' when the channels of vertical mobility are closed or narrowed *in a society which places a high premium on economic affluence,* [*power*] *and social ascent for all its members.*"[102] As one sociologist has noted on the basis of several years of close observation in a slum area:

---

101. See the National Opinion Research Center survey of evaluation of occupations which firmly documents the general impression that the manual occupations rate very low indeed in the social scale of values, *even among those who are themselves engaged in manual labor.* Consider this latter point in its full implications. In effect, the cultural and social structure exacts the values of pecuniary and power success even among those who find themselves confined to the stigmatized manual occupations. Against this background, consider the powerful motivation for achieving this type of "success" by any means whatsoever. A garbage-collector who joins with other Americans in the view that the garbage-collector is "the lowest of the low" occupations can scarcely have a self-image which is pleasing to him; he is in a "pariah" occupation in the very society where he is assured that "all who have genuine merit can get ahead." Add to this, his occasional recognition that "he didn't have the same chance as others, no matter what they say," and one perceives the enormous psychological pressure upon him for "evening up the score" by finding some means, whether strictly legal or not, for moving ahead. All this provides the structural and derivatively psychological background for the "socially induced need" in *some* groups to find some accessible avenue for social mobility.

102. Merton, "Social structure and anomie," chapter IV of this volume.

The sociologist who dismisses racket and political organizations as deviations from desirable standards thereby neglects some of the major elements of slum life. . . . *He does not discover the functions they perform for the members* [of the groupings in the slum]. The Irish and later immigrant peoples have had the greatest difficulty in finding places for themselves in our urban social and economic structure. Does anyone believe that the immigrants and their children could have achieved their present degree of social mobility without gaining control of the political organization of some of our largest cities? The same is true of the racket organization. *Politics and the rackets have furnished an important means of social mobility for individuals, who, because of ethnic background and low class position,* are blocked from advancement in the "respectable" channels.[103]

This, then, represents a third type of function performed for a distinctive subgroup. This function, it may be noted in passing, is fulfilled by the *sheer* existence and operation of the political machine, for it is in the machine itself that these individuals and subgroups find their culturally induced needs more or less satisfied. It refers to the services which the political apparatus provides for its own personnel. But seen in the wider social context we have set forth, it no longer appears as *merely* a means of self-aggrandizement for profit-hungry and power-hungry *individuals,* but as an organized provision for *subgroups* otherwise excluded from or handicapped in the race for "getting ahead."

Just as the political machine performs services for "legitimate" business, so it operates to perform not dissimilar services for "illegitimate" business: vice, crime and rackets. Once again, the basic sociological role of the machine in this respect can be more fully appreciated only if one temporarily abandons attitudes of moral indignation, to examine in all moral innocence the actual workings of the organization. In this light, it at once appears that the subgroup of the professional criminal, racketeer or gambler has basic similarities of organization, demands and operation to the subgroup of the industrialist, man of business or speculator. If there is a Lumber King or an Oil King, there is also a Vice King or a Racket King. If expansive legitimate business organizes administra-

---

103. William F. Whyte, "Social organization in the slums," *American Sociological Review,* Feb. 1943, 8, 34-39 (italics supplied). Thus, the political machine and the racket represent a special case of the type of organizational adjustment to the conditions described in chapter IV. It represents, note, an *organizational* adjustment: definite structures arise and operate to reduce somewhat the acute tensions and problems of individuals caught up in the described conflict between the "cultural accent on success-for-all" and the "socially structured fact of unequal opportunities for success." As chapter IV indicates, other types of *individual* "adjustment" are possible: lone-wolf crime, psychopathological states, rebellion, retreat by abandoning the culturally approved goals, etc. Likewise, other types of *organizational adjustment* sometimes occur; the racket or the political machine are not *alone* available as organized means for meeting this socially induced problem. Participation in revolutionary organizations, for example, can be seen within this context, as an alternative mode of organizational adjustment. All this bears theoretic notice here, since we might otherwise overlook the basic functional concepts of functional substitutes and functional equivalents, which are to be discussed at length in a subsequent publication.

tive and financial syndicates to "rationalize" and to "integrate" diverse areas of production and business enterprise, so expansive rackets and crime organize syndicates to bring order to the otherwise chaotic areas of production of illicit goods and services. If legitimate business regards the proliferation of small business enterprises as wasteful and inefficient, substituting, for example, the giant chain stores for hundreds of corner groceries, so illegitimate business adopts the same businesslike attitude and syndicates crime and vice.

Finally, and in many respects, most important, is the basic similarity, if not near-identity, of the economic role of "legitimate" business and of "illegitimate" business. *Both are in some degree concerned with the provision of goods and services for which there is an economic demand.* Morals aside, they are both business, industrial and professional enterprises, dispensing goods and services which some people want, for which there is a market in which goods and services are transformed into commodities. And, in a prevalently market society, we should expect appropriate enterprises to arise whenever there is a market demand for certain goods or services.

As is well known, vice, crime and the rackets *are* "big business." Consider only that there have been estimated to be about 500,000 professional prostitutes in the United States of 1950, and compare this with the approximately 200,000 physicians and 350,000 professional registered nurses. It is difficult to estimate which have the larger clientele: the professional men and women of medicine or the professional men and women of vice. It is, of course, difficult to estimate the economic assets, income, profits and dividends of illicit gambling in this country and to compare it with the economic assets, income, profits and dividends of, say, the shoe industry, but it is altogether possible that the two industries are about on a par. No precise figures exist on the annual expenditures on illicit narcotics, and it is probable that these are less than the expenditures on candy, but it is also probable that they are larger than the expenditure on books.

It takes but a moment's thought to recognize that, *in strictly economic terms,* there is no relevant difference between the provision of licit and of illicit goods and services. The liquor traffic illustrates this perfectly. It would be peculiar to argue that prior to 1920 (when the 18th amendment became effective), the provision of liquor constituted an economic service, that from 1920 to 1933, its production and sale no longer constituted an economic service dispensed in a market, and that from 1934 to the present, it once again took on a serviceable aspect. Or, it would be *economically* (not morally) absurd to suggest that the sale of bootlegged liquor in the dry state of Kansas is less a response to a market demand than the sale of publicly manufactured liquor in the neighboring wet state of Missouri. Examples of this sort can of course be multiplied many times over. Can it be held that in European countries, with registered and legalized prostitution, the prostitute contributes an economic service, whereas in this country, lacking legal sanction, the prostitute provides no such service? Or that the professional abortionist is in the economic market where he has approved legal status and that he is out of the economic market where he is legally taboo? Or that gambling satisfies a specific demand for entertainment in Nevada, where it constitutes the largest business enterprise of the larger cities in the state, but that it differs essentially in this respect from motion pictures in the neighboring state of California?[104]

The failure to recognize that these businesses are only *morally* and not *economically* distinguishable from "legitimate" businesses has led to badly scrambled analysis. Once the economic identity of the two is recognized, we may anticipate that if the political machine performs functions for "legitimate big business" it will be all the more likely to perform not dissimilar functions for "illegitimate big business." And, of course, such is often the case.

The distinctive function of the political machine for their criminal, vice and racket clientele is to enable them to operate in satisfying the economic demands of a large market without due interference from the government. Just as big business may contribute funds to the political party war-chest to ensure a minimum of governmental interference, so with big rackets and big crime. In both instances, the political machine can, in varying degrees, provide "protection." In both instances, many features of the structural context are identical: (1) market demands for goods and services; (2) the operators' concern with maximizing gains from their enterprises; (3) the need for partial control of government which might otherwise interfere with these activities of businessmen; (4) the need for an efficient, powerful and centralized agency to provide an effective liaison of "business" with government.

Without assuming that the foregoing pages exhaust either the range of functions or the range of subgroups served by the political machine, we can at least see that *it presently fulfills some functions for these diverse subgroups which are not adequately fulfilled by culturally approved or more conventional structures.*

Several additional implications of the functional analysis of the political machine can be mentioned here only in passing, although they

104. Perhaps the most perceptive statement of this view has been made by Hawkins and Waller. "The prostitute, the pimp, the peddler of dope, the operator of the gambling hall, the vendor of obscene pictures, the bootlegger, the abortionist, all are productive, all produce services or goods which people desire and for which they are willing to pay. It happens that society has put these goods and services under the ban, but people go on producing them and people go on consuming them, and an act of the legislature does not make them any less a part of the economic system." "Critical notes on the cost of crime," *Journal of Criminal Law and Criminology*, 1936, 26, 679-94, at 684.

obviously require to be developed at length. First, the foregoing analysis has direct implications for *social engineering.* It helps explain why the periodic efforts at "political reform," "turning the rascals out" and "cleaning political house" are typically (though not necessarily) short-lived and ineffectual. It exemplifies a basic theorem: *any attempt to eliminate an existing social structure without providing adequate alternative structures for fulfilling the functions previously fulfilled by the abolished organization is doomed to failure.* (Needless to say, this theorem has much wider bearing than the one instance of the political machine.) When "political reform" confines itself to the manifest task of "turning the rascals out," it is engaging in little more than sociological magic. The reform may for a time bring new figures into the political limelight; it may serve the casual social function of re-assuring the electorate that the moral virtues remain intact and will ultimately triumph; it may actually effect a turnover in the personnel of the political machine; it may even, for a time, so curb the activities of the machine as to leave unsatisfied the many needs it has previously fulfilled. But, inevitably, unless the reform also involves a "re-forming" of the social and political structure such that the existing needs are satisfied by alternative structures or unless it involves a change which eliminates these needs altogether, the political machine will return to its integral place in the social scheme of things. *To seek social change, without due recognition of the manifest and latent functions performed by the social organization undergoing change, is to indulge in social ritual rather than social engineering.* The concepts of manifest and latent functions (or their equivalents) are indispensable elements in the theoretic repertoire of the social engineer. In this crucial sense, these concepts are not "merely" theoretical (in the abusive sense of the term), but are eminently practical. In the deliberate enactment of social change, they can be ignored only at the price of considerably heightening the risk of failure.

A second implication of this analysis of the political machine also has a bearing upon areas wider than the one we have considered. The paradox has often been noted that the supporters of the political machine include both the "respectable" business class elements who are, of course, opposed to the criminal or racketeer and the distinctly "unrespectable" elements of the underworld. And, at first appearance, this is cited as an instance of very strange bedfellows. The learned judge is not infrequently called upon to sentence the very racketeer beside whom he sat the night before at an informal dinner of the political bigwigs. The district attorney jostles the exonerated convict on his way to the back room where the Boss has called a meeting. The big business man may complain almost as bitterly as the big racketeer about the "extortionate" contributions to the party fund demanded by the Boss. Social opposites meet—in the smoke-filled room of the successful politician.

In the light of a functional analysis all this of course no longer seems paradoxical. Since the machine serves both the businessman and the criminal man, the two seemingly antipodal groups intersect. This points to a more general theorem: *the social functions of an organization help determine the structure (including the recruitment of personnel involved in the structure), just as the structure helps determine the effectiveness with which the functions are fulfilled.* In terms of social status, the business group and the criminal group are indeed poles apart. But status does not fully determine behavior and the inter-relations between groups. Functions modify these relations. Given their distinctive needs, the several subgroups in the large society are "integrated," whatever their personal desires or intentions, by the centralizing structure which serves these several needs. In a phrase with many implications which require further study, *structure affects function and function affects structure.*

CONCLUDING REMARKS

This review of some salient considerations in structural and functional analysis has done little more than indicate some of the principal problems and potentialities of this mode of sociological interpretation. Each of the items codified in the paradigm require sustained theoretic clarification and cumulative empirical research. But it is clear that in functional theory, stripped of those traditional postulates which have fenced it in and often made it little more than a latter-day rationalization of existing practices, sociology has one beginning of a systematic and empirically relevant mode of analysis. It is hoped that the direction here indicated will suggest the feasibility and the desirability of further codification of functional analysis. In due course each section of the paradigm will be elaborated into a documented, analyzed and codified chapter in the history of functional analysis.

BIBLIOGRAPHICAL POSTSCRIPT

When first written in 1948, the preceding paper constituted an effort to systematize the principal assumptions and conceptions of the then slowly evolving theory of functional analysis in sociology. The development of this sociological theory has since gained marked momentum. In preparing this edition, I have incorporated some of the intervening extensions and emendations of theory, but have postponed a detailed and extended formulation for a volume now in preparation. It might therefore be useful to list, at this juncture, some, though manifestly far from all, recent theoretical contributions to functional analysis in sociology.

The major contribution in recent years is, of course, that by Talcott Parsons in *The Social System* (Glencoe, Illinois: The Free Press, 1951), supplemented by further works by Parsons and his associates: T. Parsons, R. F. Bales and E. A. Shils, *Working Papers in the Theory of Action*

(Glencoe, Illinois: The Free Press, 1953); T. Parsons and E. A. Shils (editors), *Toward a General Theory of Action* (Cambridge: Harvard University Press, 1951). The salient contributions of so comprehensive and logically complex a work as *The Social System* cannot be readily distinguished from its more provisional and at times debatable conceptual developments; sociologists are only now engaged in working out the needed discriminations. But on the evidence, both of research stemming from Parsons' formulations and of critical theoretical review, it is plain that this represents a decisive step toward a methodical statement of current sociological theory.

M. J. Levy, Jr., *The Structure of Society* (Princeton University Press, 1953) derives largely, as the author says, from Parsons' conceptual scheme, and presents a logical multiplication of numerous categories and concepts. It remains to be seen whether such taxonomies of concepts will prove appropriate and useful in the analysis of sociological problems.

Less extensive but more incisive analyses of selected theoretical problems of functional analyses have been provided in a number of papers stemming from diverse 'cultural areas' of sociological theory, as can be seen from the following short bibliography. Perhaps the most penetrating and productive among these is the pair of related papers by Ralf Dahrendorf, "Struktur und Funktion," *Kölner Zeitschrift für Soziologie und Sozialpsychologie,* 1955, 7, 492-519 and by David Lockwood, "Some remarks on 'The Social System,'" *The British Journal of Sociology,* 1956, 7, 134-146. Both papers are exemplary instances of *systematic* theorizing, designed to indicate specific gaps in the present state of functional theory. A considered and unpolemical statement of the status of functional theory and of some of its key unsolved problems will be found in Bernard Barber, "Structural-functional analysis: some problems and misunderstandings," *American Sociological Review,* 1956, 21, 129-135. An effort to clarify the important problem of the logic of analysis involved in that part of functional sociology which is designed to interpret observed structural patterns in society has been made by Harry C. Bredemeier, "The methodology of functionalism," *American Sociological Review,* 1955, 20, 173-180. Although this paper questionably attributes certain assumptions to several functional analyses under review, it has the distinct merit of raising the important question of the appropriate logic of functional analysis.

For anthropologists' ordering of functional analysis in contemporary sociology (not in anthropology, merely), see the instructive paper by Melford E. Spiro, "A typology of functional analysis," *Explorations,* 1953, 1, 84-95 and the thorough-going critical examination by Raymond Firth, "Function," in *Current Anthropology,* (edited by William L. Thomas, Jr.) University of Chicago Press, 1956, 237-258.

The diffusion of functional theory as recently developed in the United States is manifested in a series of critical examinations of that theory in

Belgium, France, Italy and Brazil. Among the most significant of these are: Henri Janne, "Fonction et finalité en sociologie," *Cahiers Internationaux de Sociologie,* 1954, 16, 50-67 which attempts to link up current functional theory with the antecedent and contemporary theory of French and Belgian sociologists. A thorough-going critique of functional analysis in sociology is undertaken by Georges Gurvitch, "Le concept de structure sociale," *Cahiers Internationaux de Sociologie,* 1955, 19, 3-44. A comprehensive examination of functional theory in its bearings upon selected problems of sociological research will be found in Filippo Barbano, *Teoria e Ricerca nella Sociologia Contemporanea* (Milano: Dott. A. Giuffrè, 1955). Florestan Fernandes, *Ensaio sôbre o Método de Interpretação Funcionalista na Sociologia* (São Paulo: Universidade de São Paulo, Boletim No. 170, 1953) is an informative and systematic monograph which rewards even a plodding and fallible reading such as mine.

The paradigm developed in the preceding pages has been formalized in terms of an abstract set of notations designed to make explicit how its various parts are related to elements of the functional approach in biology. See "A formalization of functionalism, with special reference to its application in the social sciences," in the forthcoming collection of papers by Ernest Nagel, *Logic Without Metaphysics* (Glencoe: The Free Press, 1957). For detailed application of the paradigm, see Warren Breed, "Social control in the newsroom: a functional analysis," *Social Forces,* 1955, 33, 326-335; A. H. Leighton and C. C. Hughes, "Notes on Eskimo patterns of suicide," *Southwestern Journal of Anthropology,* 1955, 11, 327-338; Joan Chapman and Michael Eckstein, "A social-psychological study of the alleged visitation of the Virgin Mary in Puerto Rico," *Year Book of the American Philosophical Society,* 1954, 203-206; Dennis Chapman, *The Home and Social Status* (London: Routledge & Kegan Paul, 1955); Christian Bay, *The Freedom of Expression: A Study in Political Ideals and Socio-Psychological Realities* (forthcoming); Michael Eckstein, "Diverse action and response to crime," (forthcoming); Y. B. Damle, *Communication of Modern Ideas and Knowledge in Indian Villages* (Cambridge: Massachusetts Institute of Technology, Center for International Studies, 1955).

For an interesting discussion of manifest and latent consequences of action in relation to self-justifying and self-defeating images, see Chapter 8 of Kenneth Boulding, *The Image* (Ann Arbor: University of Michigan Press, 1956).

IV THE BEARING OF SOCIOLOGICAL THEORY ON EMPIRICAL RESEARCH

THE RECENT HISTORY of sociological theory can in large measure be written in terms of an alternation between two contrasting emphases. On the one hand, we observe those sociologists who seek above all to generalize, to find their way as rapidly as possible to the formulation of sociological laws. Tending to assess the significance of sociological work in terms of scope rather than the demonstrability of generalizations, they eschew the "triviality" of detailed, small-scale observation and seek the grandeur of global summaries. At the other extreme stands a hardy band who do not hunt too closely the implications of their research but who remain confident and assured that what they report is so. To be sure, their reports of facts are verifiable and often verified, but they are somewhat at a loss to relate these facts to one another or even to explain why these, rather than other, observations have been made. For the first group the identifying motto would at times seem to be: "We do not know whether what we say is true, but it is at least significant." And for the radical empiricist the motto may read: "This is demonstrably so, but we cannot indicate its significance."

Whatever the bases of adherence to the one or the other of these camps—different but not necessarily contradictory accountings would be provided by psychologists, sociologists of knowledge, and historians of science—it is abundantly clear that there is no logical basis for their being ranged *against* each other. Generalizations can be tempered, if not with mercy, at least with disciplined observation; close, detailed observations need not be rendered trivial by avoidance of their theoretical pertinence and implications.

With all this there will doubtless be widespread if, indeed, not unanimous agreement. But this very unanimity suggests that these remarks are platitudinous. If, however, one function of theory is to explore the implications of the seemingly self-evident, it may not be amiss to look into what is entailed by such programmatic statements about the relations of sociological theory and empirical research. In doing so, every effort should be made to avoid dwelling upon illustrations drawn from the "more mature" sciences—such as physics and biology—not because these do not exhibit the logical problems involved but because their very maturity permits these disciplines to deal *fruitfully* with abstractions of a high order to a degree which, it is submitted, is not yet the case with sociology. An indefinitely large number of discussions of scientific method have set forth the logical prerequisites of scientific theory, but, it would seem, they have often done so on such a high level of abstraction that the prospect of translating these precepts into current sociological research becomes utopian. Ultimately, sociological research must meet the canons of scientific method; immediately, the task is so to express these requirements that they may have more direct bearing on the analytical work which is at present feasible.

The term "sociological theory" has been widely used to refer to the products of several related but distinct activities carried on by members of a professional group called sociologists. But since these several types of activity have significantly different bearings upon empirical social research—since they differ in their scientific functions—they should be distinguished for purposes of discussion. Moreover, such discriminations provide a basis for assessing the contributions and limitations characteristic of each of the following six types of work which are often lumped together as comprising sociological theory: (1) methodology; (2) general sociological orientations; (3) analysis of sociological concepts; (4) *post factum* sociological interpretations; (5) empirical generalizations in sociology and (6) sociological theory.

METHODOLOGY

At the outset we should distinguish clearly between sociological theory, which has for its subject matter certain aspects and results of the interaction of men and is therefore substantive, and methodology, or the logic of scientific procedure. The problems of methodology transcend those found in any one discipline, dealing either with those common to groups of disciplines[1] or, in more generalized form, with those common to all scientific inquiry. Methodology is not peculiarly bound up with sociological problems, and, though there is a plenitude of methodological discussions in books and journals of sociology, they are not thereby rendered sociological in character. Sociologists, in company with all others who essay scientific work, must be methodologically wise; they must be

1. Consider several volumes which set forth methodological as distinct from procedural concerns of sociology: Florian Znaniecki, *The Method of Sociology* (New York: Farrar & Rinehart, 1934); R. M. MacIver, *Social Causation* (Boston: Ginn & Co., 1942); G. A. Lundberg, *Foundations of Sociology* (New York: Macmillan Co., 1939); Felix Kaufmann, *Methodology of the Social Sciences* (New York: Oxford University Press, 1944); P. F. Lazarsfeld and M. Rosenberg, (eds.) *The Language of Social Research,* (Glencoe: The Free Press, 1955), esp. the Introductions to sections.

aware of the design of investigation, the nature of inference, the requirements of a theoretic system. But such knowledge does not contain or imply the particular *content* of sociological theory. There is, in short, a clear and decisive difference between *knowing how to test* a battery of hypotheses and *knowing the theory* from which to derive hypotheses to be tested.[2] It is my impression that current sociological training is more largely designed to make students understand the first than the second.

As Poincaré observed a half-century ago, sociologists have long been hierophants of methodology, thus, perhaps, diverting talents and energies from the task of building substantive theory. This focus of attention upon the logics of procedure has its patent scientific function, since such inventories serve a critical purpose in guiding and assessing theoretical and empirical inquiries. It also reflects the growing-pains of an immature discipline. Just as the apprentice who acquires new skills self-consciously examines each element of these skills in contrast to the master who habitually practices them with seeming indifference to their explicit formulation, so the exponents of a discipline haltingly moving toward scientific status laboriously spell out the logical grounds of their procedure. The slim books on methodology which proliferate in the fields of sociology, economics, and psychology do not find many counterparts among the technical works in the sciences which have long since come of age. Whatever their intellectual function, these methodological writings imply the perspectives of a fledgling discipline, anxiously presenting its credentials for full status in the fraternity of the sciences. But, significantly enough, the instances of adequate scientific method utilized by sociologists for illustrative or expository purposes are usually drawn from disciplines other than sociology itself. Twentieth-century, not sixteenth-century, physics and chemistry are taken as methodological prototypes or exemplars for twentieth-century sociology, with little explicit recognition that between sociology and these other sciences is a difference of centuries of cumulating scientific research. These comparisons are inevitably programmatic rather than realistic. More appropriate methodological demands would result in a gap between methodological aspiration and actual sociological attainment at once less conspicuous and less invidious.

GENERAL SOCIOLOGICAL ORIENTATIONS

Much of what is described in textbooks as sociological theory consists of general orientations toward substantive materials. Such orienta-

2. However, it should be noted not only that instruments and procedures used in sociological (or other scientific) inquiry must meet methodological criteria but that they also logically presuppose substantive theories. As Pierre Duhem observed in this connection, the instrument as well as the experimental results obtained in science are shot through with specific assumptions and theories of a substantive order. *La théorie physique* (Paris: Chevalier et Rivière, 1906), 278.

tions involve broad postulates which indicate *types* of variables which are somehow to be taken into account rather than specifying determinate relationships between particular variables. Indispensable though these orientations are, they provide only the broadest framework for empirical inquiry. This is the case with Durkheim's generic hypothesis, which holds that the "determining cause of a social fact should be sought among the social facts preceding it" and identifies the "social" factor as institutional norms toward which behavior is oriented.[3] Or, again, it is said that "to a certain approximation it is useful to regard society as an integrated system of mutually interrelated and functionally interdependent parts."[4] So, too, the importance of the "humanistic coefficient" in cultural data as expounded by Znaniecki and Sorokin, among others, belongs to this category. Such general orientations may be paraphrased as saying in effect that the investigator ignores this *order of fact* at his peril. They do not set forth specific hypotheses.

The chief function of these orientations is to provide a general context for inquiry; they facilitate the process of arriving at determinate hypotheses. To take a case in point: Malinowski was led to re-examine the Freudian notion of the Oedipus complex on the basis of a general sociological orientation, which viewed sentiment formation as patterned by social structure. This generic view clearly underlay his exploration of a specific "psychological" complex in its relation to a system of status relationships in a society differing in structure from that of western Europe. The *specific* hypotheses which he utilized in this inquiry were all congruent with the generic orientation but were not prescribed by it. Otherwise put, the general orientation indicated the relevance of *some* structural variables, but there still remained the task of ferreting out the particular variables to be included.

Though such general theoretic outlooks have a more inclusive and profound effect on the development of scientific inquiry than do specific hypotheses—they constitute the matrix from which, in the words of Maurice Arthus, "new hypotheses follow one another in breathless succession and a harvest of facts follow closely the blossoming of these hypotheses"—though this is the case, they constitute only the point of departure for the theorist. It is his task to develop specific, interrelated hypotheses by reformulating empirical generalizations in the light of these generic orientations.

It should be noted, furthermore, that the growing contributions of sociological theory to its sister-disciplines lie more in the realm of general sociological orientations than in that of specific confirmed hypotheses.

---

3. Durkheim, *The Rules of Sociological Method*, 110; *L'Education morale* (Paris: Félix Alcan, 1925), 9-45, *passim*.

4. Conrad M. Arensberg and Solon Kimball, *Family and Community in Ireland* (Cambridge: Harvard University Press, 1940). xxvi.

The development of social history, of institutional economics, and the importation of sociological perspectives into psychoanalytic theory involve recognition of the sociological dimensions of the data rather than incorporation of specific confirmed theories. Social scientists have been led to detect sociological gaps in the application of their theory to concrete social behavior. They do not so often exhibit sociological naiveté in their interpretations. The economist, the political scientist, and the psychologist have increasingly come to recognize that what they have systematically taken as given, as data, may be sociologically problematical. But this receptivity to a sociological outlook is often dissipated by the paucity of adequately *tested specific theories* of, say, the determinants of human wants or of the social processes involved in the distribution and exercise of social power. Pressures deriving from the respective theoretic gaps of the several social sciences may serve, in time, to bring about an increasing formulation of specific and systematic sociological theories appropriate to the problems implied by these gaps. General orientations do not suffice. Presumably this is the context for the complaint voiced by an economist:

> [The economist always seeks to refer his analysis of a problem] back to some "datum," that is to say, to something which is extra-economic. This something may be apparently very remote from the problem which was first taken up, for the chains of economic causation are often very long. But he always wants to hand over the problem in the end to some sociologist or other—*if there is a sociologist waiting for him. Very often there isn't.*[5]

ANALYSIS OF SOCIOLOGICAL CONCEPTS

It is at times held that theory is comprised of concepts, an assertion which, being incomplete, is neither true nor false but vague. To be sure, conceptual analysis, which is confined to the specification and clarification of key concepts, is an indispensable phase of theoretic work. But an array of concepts—status, role, *Gemeinschaft*, social interaction, social distance, *anomie*—does not constitute theory, though it may enter into a theoretic system. It may be conjectured that, in so far as an antitheoretic bias occurs among sociologists, it is in protest against those who identify theory with clarification of definitions, who mistakenly take the part for the whole of theoretic analysis. It is only when such concepts are interrelated in the form of a scheme that a theory begins to emerge. Concepts, then, constitute the definitions (or prescriptions) of what is to be observed; they are the variables between which empirical relationships are to be sought. When propositions are logically interrelated, a theory has been instituted.

---

5. J. R. Hicks, "Economic theory and the social sciences," *The Social Sciences: Their Relations in Theory and in Teaching* (London: Le Play Press, 1936), p. 135. (Italics mine.)

The choice of concepts guiding the collection and analysis of data is, of course, crucial to empirical inquiry. For, to state an important truism, if concepts are selected such that no relationships between them obtain, the research will be sterile, no matter how meticulous the subsequent observations and inferences. The importance of this truism lies in its implication that truly trial-and-error procedures in empirical inquiry are likely to be comparatively unfruitful, since the number of variables which are not significantly connected is indefinitely large.

It is, then, one function of conceptual clarification to make explicit the character of data subsumed under a concept.[6] It thus serves to reduce the likelihood that spurious empirical findings will be couched in terms of given concepts. Thus, Sutherland's re-examination of the received concept of "crime" provides an instructive instance of how such clarification induces a revision of hypotheses concerning the data organized in terms of the concept.[7] He demonstrates an equivocation implicit in criminological theories which seek to account for the fact that there is a much higher rate of crime, as "officially measured," in the lower than in the upper social classes. These crime "data" (organized in terms of a particular operational concept or measure of crime) have led to a series of hypotheses which view poverty, slum conditions, feeble-mindedness, and other characteristics held to be highly associated with low-class status as the "causes" of criminal behavior. Once the concept of crime is clarified to refer to the violation of criminal law and is thus extended to include "white-collar criminality" in business and professions—violations which are less often reflected in official crime statistics than are lower-class violations—the presumptive high association between low social status and crime may no longer obtain. We need not pursue Sutherland's analysis further to detect the function of conceptual clarification in this instance. It provides for a *reconstruction of data* by indicating more precisely just what they include and what they exclude. In doing so, it leads to a liquidation of hypotheses set up to account for spurious data by questioning the assumptions on which the initial statistical data were based. By hanging a question mark on an implicit assumption under-

6. As Schumpeter remarks about the role of "analytic apparatus": "If we are to speak about price levels and to devise methods of measuring them, we must know what a price level is. If we are to observe demand, we must have a precise concept of its elasticity. If we speak about productivity of labor, we must know what propositions hold true about total product per man-hour and what other propositions hold true about the partial differential coefficient of total product with respect to man-hours. No hypotheses enter into such concepts, which simply embody methods of description and measurement, nor into the propositions defining their relation (so-called theorems), and yet their framing is the chief task of theory, in economics as elsewhere. This is what we mean by *tools of analysis*." Joseph A. Schumpeter, *Business Cycles* (New York: McGraw-Hill Book Co., 1939), I, 31.

7. Edwin H. Sutherland, "White-collar criminality," *American Sociological Review*, 1940, 5, 1-12.

lying the research definition of crime—the assumption that violations of the criminal code by members of the several social classes are representatively registered in the official statistics—this conceptual clarification had direct implications for a nucleus of theories.

In similar fashion, conceptual analysis may often resolve apparent antinomies in empirical findings by indicating that such contradictions are more apparent than real. This familiar phrase refers, in part, to the fact that initially crudely defined concepts have tacitly included significantly different elements so that data organized in terms of these concepts differ materially and thus exhibit apparently contradictory tendencies.[8] The function of conceptual analysis in this instance is to maximize the likelihood of the comparability, in significant respects, of data which are to be included in a research.

The instance drawn from Sutherland merely illustrates the more general fact that in research, as in less disciplined activities, our conceptual language tends to fix our perceptions and, derivatively, our thought and behavior. The concept defines the situation, and the research worker responds accordingly. Explicit conceptual analysis helps him recognize to what he is responding and which (possibly significant) elements he is ignoring. The findings of Whorf on this matter are, with appropriate modifications, applicable to empirical research.[9] He found that behavior was oriented toward linguistic or conceptual meanings connoted by the terms applied to a situation. Thus, in the presence of objects which are conceptually described as "gasoline drums," behavior will tend modally toward a particular type: great care will be exercised. But when people are confronted with what are called "*empty* gasoline drums," behavior is different: it is careless, with little control over smoking and the disposition of cigarette stubs. Yet the "empty" drums are the more hazardous, since they contain explosive vapor. Response is not to the physical but to the conceptualized situation. The concept "empty" is here used equivocally: as a synonym for "null and void, negative, inert," and as a term applied to physical situations without regard to such "irrelevancies" as vapor and liquid vestiges in the container. The situation is conceptualized in the second sense, and the concept is then responded to in the first sense, with the result that "empty" gasoline drums become the occasion for fires. Clarification of just what "empty" means in the universe of discourse would have a profound effect on behavior. This case may serve as a paradigm of the functional effect of conceptual

8. Elaborate formulations of this type of analysis are to be found in Corrado Gini, *Prime linee di patologia economica* (Milan: Giuffre, 1935); for a brief discussion see C. Gini, "Un tentativo di armonizarre teorie disparate e osservazioni contrastanti nel campo dei fenomeni sociali," *Rivista di politica economica*, 1935, 12, 1-24.

9. B. L. Whorf, "Relation of habitual thought and behavior to language," in L. Spier, A. I. Hallowell, and S. S. Newman (eds.), *Language, Culture, and Personality* (Menasha: Sapir Memorial Fund Publication, 1941), 75-93.

clarification upon research behavior: it makes clear just what the research worker is doing when he deals with conceptualized data. He draws different consequences for empirical research as his conceptual apparatus changes.

This is not to say, however, that the vocabulary of concepts fixes perceptions, thought and associated behavior once and for all. Even less is it to say that such instances of misleading terminology are embedded in one or another language (as Whorf tended to imply in this theory of linguistic behaviorism). Men are not permanently imprisoned in the framework of the (often inherited) concepts they use; they can not only break out of this framework but can create a new one, better suited to the needs of the occasion. Yet, at any particular time, one should be prepared to find that the governing concepts can, and often do, lag behind the behavioral requirements of the case. During these sometimes prolonged periods of lag, misapplied concepts do their damage. However, this very inaptness of concept to situation, recognized through painful experience, will often evoke self-correcting and more appropriate formulations. The job is to identify conceptual lag and to liberate ourselves from the patterns of cognitive misbehavior which it tends to produce.[9a]

A further task of conceptual analysis is to institute observable indices of the social data with which empirical research is concerned. Early efforts in this direction were manifest in the works of Durkheim (and constitute one of his most significant contributions to sociology). Though his formalized conceptions along these lines do not approach the sophistication of more recent formulations, he was patently utilizing "intervening variables," as lately described by Tolman and Hull, and seeking to establish indices for these variables.[10] The problem, as far as it need be stated

9a. For an extended discussion, see the posthumously published volume of selected writings by B. L. Whorf, *Language, Thought and Reality* (Cambridge: Technology Press of M.I.T., 1956). It is the extreme Whorfian position which Joshua Whatmough attacks in his *Language: A Modern Synthesis* (New York: St Martin's Press, 1956), 85, 186-7, 227-34. Yet Whatmough's well-placed salvoes do not entirely destroy Whorf's position but only compel a retreat to a more limited and defensible position. Socially entrenched concepts do affect perception, thought and behavior but the structure of language provides sufficient scope for inappropriate concepts to be replaced by more suitable concepts. An appreciative review of Whorf's ideas will be found in Franklin Fearing, "An examination of the conceptions of Benjamin Whorf in the light of theories of perception and cognition," Harry Hoijer, ed. *Language in Culture* (University of Chicago Press, 1954), 47-81.

10. Durkheim's basic formulation, variously repeated in each of his monographs, reads as follows: "It is necessary . . . to substitute for the internal fact which escapes us an external fact that symbolizes it and to study the former through the latter." See his *Rules of Sociological Method*, chap. ii; *Le Suicide* (Paris: F. Alcan, 1930), 22 ff. Most detailed consideration of Durkheim's views on social indices is provided by Harry Alpert, *Emile Durkheim and His Sociology* (New York: Columbia University Press, 1939), 120 ff. On the general problem see C. L. Hull, "The problem of Intervening Variables in molar behavior theory," *Psychological Review*, 1943, 50, 273-91.

for our immediate purposes, consists in devising indices of unobservables or symbolic constructs (*e.g.*, social cohesion)—indices which are theoretically supportable. Conceptual analysis thus enters as one basis for an initial and periodic critical appraisal of the extent to which assumed signs and symbols are an adequate index of the social substratum. Such analysis suggests clues for determining whether in fact the index (or measuring instrument) proves adequate to the occasion.[11]

POST FACTUM SOCIOLOGICAL INTERPRETATIONS

It is often the case in empirical social research that data are collected and only then subjected to interpretative comment. This procedure in which the observations are at hand and the interpretations are subsequently applied to the data has the logical structure of clinical inquiry. The observations may be case-history or statistical in character. The defining characteristic of this procedure is the introduction of an interpretation *after* the observations have been made rather than the empirical testing of a predesignated hypothesis. The implicit assumption is that a body of generalized propositions has been so fully established that it can be approximately applied to the data in hand.

Such *post factum* explanations, designed to "explain" observations, differ in logical function from speciously similar procedures where the observational materials are utilized in order to *derive* fresh hypotheses to be confirmed by *new* observations.

A disarming characteristic of the procedure is that the explanations are indeed consistent with the given set of observations. This is scarcely surprising, in as much as only those *post factum* hypotheses are selected which do accord with these observations. If the basic assumption holds—namely, that the *post factum* interpretation utilizes abundantly confirmed theories—then this type of explanation indeed "shoots arrowy light into the dark chaos of materials." But if, as is more often the case in sociological interpretation, the *post factum* hypotheses are also *ad hoc* or, at the least, have but a slight degree of prior confirmation, then such "precocious explanations," as H. S. Sullivan called them, produce a spurious sense of adequacy at the expense of instigating further inquiry.

Post factum explanations remain at the level of *plausibility* (low evidential value) rather than leading to "compelling evidence" (a high degree of confirmation). Plausibility, in distinction to compelling evi-

11. Among the many functions of conceptual analysis at this point is that of instituting inquiry into the question of whether or not the index is "neutral" to its environment. By searching out the assumptions underlying the selection (and validation for a given population) of observables as indices (e.g., religious affiliation, an attitude scale), conceptual analysis initiates appropriate tests of the possibility that the index has become dissociated from its substratum. For a clear statement of this point see Louis Guttman, "A basis for scaling qualitative data," *American Sociological Review*, 1944, 9, 139-50, esp. 149-50.

dence, is found when an interpretation is consistent with one set of data (which typically has, indeed, given rise to the decision to utilize one, rather than another, interpretation). It also implies that alternative interpretations equally consistent with these data have not been systematically explored and that inferences drawn from the interpretation have not been tested by new observations.

The logical fallacy underlying the *post factum* explanation rests in the fact that there is available a variety of crude hypotheses, each with some measure of confirmation but designed to account for quite contradictory sets of affairs. The method of *post factum* explanation does not lend itself to nullifiability, if only because it is so completely flexible. For example, it may be reported that "the unemployed tend to read fewer books than they did previously." This is "explained" by the hypothesis that anxiety increases as a consequence of unemployment and, therefore, that any activity requiring concentration, such as reading, becomes difficult. This type of accounting is plausible, since there is some evidence that increased anxiety *may* occur in such situations and since a state of morbid preoccupation does interfere with organized activity. If, however, it is now reported that the original data were erroneous and it is a fact that "the unemployed read more than previously" a new *post factum* explanation can at once be invoked. The explanation now holds that the unemployed have more leisure or that they engage in activity intended to increase their personal skills. Consequently, they read more than before. Thus, whatever the observations, a new interpretation can be found to "fit the facts."[12] This example may be sufficient to indicate that such reconstructions serve only as illustrations and not as tests. It is this logical inadequacy of the *post factum* construction that led Peirce to observe:

> It is of the essence of induction that the consequence of the theory should be drawn first in regard to the unknown, or virtually unknown, result of experiment; and that this should virtually be only ascertained afterward. For if we look over the phenomena to find agreements with the theory, it is a mere question of ingenuity and industry how many we shall find.[13]

These reconstructions typically by-pass an explicit formulation of the conditions under which the hypotheses will be found to hold true. In order to meet this logical requirement, such interpretations would necessarily be predictive rather than postdictive.

As a case in point, we may quote the frequency with which Blumer asserts that the Thomas-Znaniecki analyses of documents "merely seem

12. The pertinent data have not been assembled. But, on the plausibility of the second interpretation, see Douglas Waples, *People and Print: Social Aspects of Reading in the Depression* (Chicago: University of Chicago Press, 1937), 198.

13. Charles Sanders Peirce, *Collected Papers,* ed. Charles Hartshorne and Paul Weiss (Cambridge: Harvard University Press, 1932). II, 496.

to be plausible."[14] The basis for plausibility rests in the consistency between the interpretation and the data; the absence of compelling evidence stems from the failure to provide distinctive tests of the interpretations apart from their consistency with the initial observations. The analysis is fitted to the facts, and there is no indication of just which data would be taken to contravene the interpretations. As a consequence, the documentary evidence merely illustrates rather than tests the theory.[15]

EMPIRICAL GENERALIZATIONS IN SOCIOLOGY

Not infrequently it is said that the object of sociological theory is to arrive at statements of social uniformities. This is an elliptical assertion and hence requires clarification. For there are two types of statements of sociological uniformities which differ significantly in their bearing on theory. The first of these is the empirical generalization: an isolated proposition summarizing observed uniformities of relationships between two or more variables.[16] The sociological literature abounds with such generalizations which have not been assimilated to sociological theory. Thus, Engel's "laws" of consumption may be cited as examples. So, too, the Halbwachs finding that laborers spend more per adult unit for food than white-collar employees of the same income class.[17] Such generalizations may be of greater or less precision, but this does not affect their logical place in the structure of inquiry. The Groves-Ogburn finding, for a sample of American cities, that "cities with a larger percentage engaged in manufacturing also have, on the average, slightly larger percentages of young persons married" has been expressed in an equation indicating the degree of this relationship. Although propositions of this order are essential in empirical research, a miscellany of such propositions only provides the raw materials for sociology as a discipline. The theoretic task, and the orientation of empirical research toward theory, first begins when the bearing of such uniformities on a set of interrelated propositions is tentatively established. The notion of directed research implies

---

14. Herbert Blumer, *An Appraisal of Thomas and Znaniecki's "The Polish Peasant in Europe and America"* (New York: Social Science Research Council, 1939), 38, see also *ibid.*, 39, 44, 46, 49, 50, 75.

15. It is difficult to see on what grounds Blumer asserts that these interpretations cannot be mere cases of illustration of a theory. His comment that the materials "acquire significance and understanding that they did not have" would apply to *post factum* explanations generally.

16. This usage of the term "empirical" is common, as Dewey notes. In this context, "*empirical* means that the subject-matter of a given proposition which has existential inference, represents merely a set of uniform conjunctions of traits repeatedly observed to exist, without any understanding of *why* the conjunction occurs; without a theory which states its rationale." John Dewey, *Logic: The Theory of Inquiry* (New York: Henry Holt & Co., 1938), 305.

17. See a considerable collection of such uniformities summarized by C. C. Zimmerman, *Consumption and Standards of Living* (New York: D. Van Nostrand Co., 1936), 51 ff.

that, in part,[18] empirical inquiry is so organized that if and when empirical uniformities are discovered, they have direct consequences for a theoretic system. In so far as the research is directed, the rationale of findings is set forth before the findings are obtained.

SOCIOLOGICAL THEORY

The second type of sociological generalization, the so-called scientific law, differs from the foregoing in as much as it is a statement of invariance *derivable* from a theory. The paucity of such laws in the sociological field perhaps reflects the prevailing bifurcation of theory and empirical research. Despite the many volumes dealing with the history of sociological theory and despite the plethora of empirical investigations, sociologists (including the writer) may discuss the logical criteria of sociological laws without citing a single instance which fully satisfies these criteria.[19]

Approximations to these criteria are not entirely wanting. To exhibit the relations of empirical generalizations to theory and to set forth the functions of theory, it may be useful to examine a familiar case in which such generalizations were incorporated into a body of substantive theory. Thus, it has long been established as a statistical uniformity that in a variety of populations, Catholics have a lower suicide rate than Protestants.[20] In this form the uniformity posed a theoretical problem. It merely constituted an empirical regularity which would become significant for theory only if it could be derived from a set of other propositions, a task

18. "In part," if only because it stultifies the possibilities of obtaining fertile new findings to confine researches *wholly* to the test of predetermined hypotheses. Hunches originating in the course of the inquiry which may not have immediately obvious implications for a broader theoretic system may eventuate in the discovery of empirical uniformities which can later be incorporated into a theory. For example, in the sociology of political behavior, it has been recently established that the larger the number of social cross-pressures to which voters are subjected, the less interest they exhibit in a presidential election (P. F. Lazarsfeld, Bernard Berelson, and Hazel Gaudet, *The People's Choice* [New York: Duell, Sloan & Pearce, 1944], 56-64). This finding, which was wholly unanticipated when the research was first formulated, may well initiate new lines of systematic inquiry into political behavior, even though it is not yet integrated into a generalized theory. Fruitful empirical research not only tests theoretically derived hypotheses; it also originates new hypotheses. This might be termed the "serendipity" component of research, i.e., the discovery, by chance or sagacity, of valid results which were not sought for.

19. E.g., see the discussion by George A. Lundberg, "The concept of law in the social sciences," *Philosophy of Science*, 1938, 5, 189-203, which affirms the possibility of such laws without including any case in point. The book by K. D. Har, *Social Laws* (Chapel Hill: University of North Carolina Press, 1930), does not fulfil the promise implicit in the title. A panel of social scientists discussing the possibility of obtaining social laws finds it difficult to instance cases (Blumer, *op. cit.*, 142-50).

20. It need hardly be said that this statement assumes that education, income, nationality, rural-urban residence, and other factors which might render this finding spurious have been held constant.

which Durkheim set himself. If we restate his theoretic assumptions in formal fashion, the paradigm of his theoretic analysis becomes clear:

1. Social cohesion provides psychic support to group members subjected to acute stresses and anxieties.
2. Suicide rates are functions of *unrelieved* anxieties and stresses to which persons are subjected.
3. Catholics have greater social cohesion than Protestants.
4. Therefore, lower suicide rates should be anticipated among Catholics than among Protestants.[21]

This case serves to locate the place of empirical generalizations in relation to theory and to illustrate the several functions of theory.

1. It indicates that theoretic pertinence is not inherently present or absent in empirical generalizations but appears when the generalization is conceptualized in abstractions of higher order (Catholicism–social cohesion–relieved anxieties–suicide rate) which are embodied in more general statements of relationships.[22] What was initially taken as an isolated uniformity is restated as a relation, not between religious affiliation and behavior, but between groups with certain conceptualized attributes (social cohesion) and the behavior. The *scope* of the original empirical finding is considerably extended, and several seemingly disparate uniformities are seen to be interrelated (thus differentials in suicide rates between married and single persons can be derived from the same theory).

2. Once having established the theoretic pertinence of a uniformity by deriving it from a set of interrelated propositions, we provide for the *cumulation* both of theory and of research findings. The differentials-in-suicide-rate uniformities add confirmation to the set of propositions from which they—and other uniformities—have been derived. This is a major function of *systematic theory*.

3. Whereas the empirical uniformity did not lend itself to the drawing of diverse consequences, the reformulation gives rise to various consequences in fields of conduct quite remote from that of suicidal behavior. For example, inquiries into obsessive behavior, morbid pre-

---

21. We need not examine further aspects of this illustration, e.g., (1) the extent to which we have adequately stated the premises implicit in Durkheim's interpretation; (2) the supplementary theoretic analysis which would take these premises not as given but as problematic; (3) the grounds on which the potentially infinite regression of theoretic interpretations is halted at one rather than another point; (4) the problems involved in the introduction of such intervening variables as social cohesion which are not directly measured; (5) the extent to which the premises have been empirically confirmed; (6) the comparatively low order of abstraction represented by this illustration and (7) the fact that Durkheim derived several empirical generalizations from this same set of hypotheses.

22. Thorstein Veblen has put this with typical cogency: "All this may seem like taking pains about trivialities. But the data with which any scientific inquiry has to do are trivialities in some other bearing than that one in which they are of account." *The Place of Science in Modern Civilization* (New York: Viking Press, 1932), 42.

occupations, and other maladaptive behavior have found these also to be related to inadequacies of group cohesion.[23] The conversion of empirical uniformities into theoretic statements thus increases the *fruitfulness* of research through the successive exploration of implications.

4. By providing a rationale, the theory introduces a *ground for prediction* which is more secure than mere empirical extrapolation from previously observed trends. Thus, should independent measures indicate a decrease of social cohesion among Catholics, the theorist would predict a tendency toward increased rates of suicide in this group. The atheoretic empiricist would have no alternative, however, but to predict on the basis of extrapolation.

5. The foregoing list of functions presupposes one further attribute of theory which is not altogether true of the Durkheim formulation and which gives rise to a general problem that has peculiarly beset sociological theory, at least, up to the present. If theory is to be productive, it must be sufficiently *precise* to be *determinate*. Precision is an integral element of the criterion of *testability*. The prevailing pressure toward the utilization of statistical data in sociology, whenever possible, to control and test theoretic inferences has a justifiable basis, when we consider the logical place of precision in disciplined inquiry.

The more precise the inferences (predictions) which can be drawn from a theory, the less the likelihood of *alternative* hypotheses which will be adequate to these predictions. In other words, precise predictions and data serve to reduce the *empirical* bearing upon research of the *logical* fallacy of affirming the consequent.[24] It is well known that verified predictions derived from a theory do not prove or demonstrate that theory; they merely supply a measure of confirmation, for it is always possible that alternative hypotheses drawn from different theoretic systems can also account for the predicted phenomena.[25] But those theories which

23. See, e.g., Elton Mayo, *Human Problems of an Industrial Civilization* (New York: Macmillan Co., 1933), 113 *et passim*. The theoretical framework utilized in the studies of industrial morale by Whitehead, Roethlisberger, and Dickson stemmed appreciably from the Durkheim formulations, as the authors testify.

24. The paradigm of "proof through prediction" is, of course, logically fallacious:

If *A* (hypothesis), then *B* (prediction).
B is observed.
Therefore, *A* is true.

This is not overdisturbing for scientific research, in as much as other than formal criteria are involved.

25. As a case in point, consider that different theorists had predicted war and internecine conflict on a large scale at midcentury. Sorokin and some Marxists, for example, set forth this prediction on the basis of quite distinct theoretic systems. The actual outbreak of large-scale conflicts does not in itself enable us to choose between these schemes of analysis, if only because the observed fact is consistent with both. Only if the predictions had been so *specified*, had been so precise, that the actual occurrences coincided with the one prediction and not with the other, would a determinate test have been instituted.

admit of precise predictions confirmed by observation take on strategic importance since they provide an initial basis for choice between competing hypotheses. In other words, precision enhances the likelihood of approximating a "crucial" observation or experiment.

The internal coherence of a theory has much the same function, for if a variety of empirically confirmed consequences are drawn from one theoretic system, this reduces the likelihood that competing theories can adequately account for the same data. The integrated theory sustains a larger measure of confirmation than is the case with distinct and unrelated hypotheses, thus accumulating a greater weight of evidence.

Both pressures—toward precision and logical coherence—can lead to unproductive activity, particularly in the social scienes. Any procedure can be abused as well as used. A premature insistence on precision at all costs may sterilize imaginative hypotheses. It may lead to a reformulation of the scientific problem in order to permit measurement with, at times, the result that the subsequent materials do not bear on the initial problem in hand.[26] In the search for precision, care must be taken to see that significant problems are not thus inadvertently blotted from view. Similarly, the pressure for logical consistency has at times invited logomachy and sterile theorizing, in as much as the assumptions contained in the system of analysis are so far removed from empirical referents or involve such high abstractions as not to permit of empirical inquiry.[27] But the warrant for these criteria of inquiry is not vitiated by such abuses.

FORMAL DERIVATIONS AND CODIFICATION

This limited account has, at the very least, pointed to the need for a closer connection between theory and empirical research. The prevailing division of the two is manifested in marked *discontinuities* of empirical research, on the one hand, and systematic theorizing unsustained by empirical test, on the other.[27a] There are conspicuously few instances of consecutive research which have cumulatively investigated a succession of hypotheses derived from a given theory. Rather, there tends to be a marked dispersion of empirical inquiries, oriented toward a concrete field of human behavior, but lacking a central theoretic orientation. The plethora of discrete empirical generalizations and of *post factum* inter-

26. Stuart A. Rice comments on this tendency in public opinion research; see *Eleven Twenty-six: A Decade of Social Science Research,* ed. Louis Wirth (Chicago: University of Chicago Press, 1940), 167.

27. It is this practice to which E. Ronald Walker refers, in the field of economics, as "theoretic blight." *From Economic Theory to Policy* (Chicago: University of Chicago Press, 1943), chap. iv.

27a. See in this connection the dramatic example of such *discontinuity* cited in Chapter I (*i.e.,* the recent rediscovery of the primary group within formal associations some decades after this had been elaborately treated by Thomas and Znaniecki).

pretations reflect this pattern of research. The large bulk of general orientations and conceptual analyses, as distinct from sets of interrelated hypotheses, in turn reflect the tendency to separate theoretic activity from empirical research. It is a commonplace that continuity, rather than dispersion, can be achieved only if empirical studies are theory-oriented and if theory is empirically confirmable. However, it is possible to go beyond such affirmations and to suggest certain conventions for sociological research which might well facilitate this process. These conventions may be termed "formalized derivation" and "codification."[28]

Both in the design and in the reporting of empirical research, it might be made a definite convention that hypotheses and, whenever possible, the theoretic grounds (assumptions and postulates) of these hypotheses be explicitly set forth. The report of data would be in terms of their immediate pertinence for the hypotheses and, derivatively, the underlying theory. Attention should be called specifically to the introduction of interpretative variables other than those entailed in the original formulation of hypotheses and the bearing of these upon the theory should be indicated. *Post factum* interpretations which will inevitably arise when new and unexpected relationships are discovered should be so stated that the direction of further probative research becomes evident. The conclusions of the research might well include not only a statement of the findings with respect to the initial hypotheses but, when this is in point, an indication of the order of observations needed to test anew the further implications of the investigation. Formal derivation of this character has had a salutary effect in psychology and economics, leading, in the one case, to sequential experiments[29] and, in the other, to an articulated series of investigations. One consequence of such formalization is that it serves as a control over the introduction of unrelated, undisciplined, and diffuse interpretations. It does not impose upon the reader the task of ferreting out the relations between the interpretations embodied in the text.[30] Above all, it prepares the way for consecutive and cumulative research rather than a buckshot array of dispersed investigations.

28. To be sure, these conventions are deduction and induction, respectively. Our sole interest at this point is to translate these logical procedures into terms appropriate to current sociological theory and research.

29. The work of Clark Hull and associates is preeminent in this respect. See, e.g., Hull, *Principles of Behavior* (New York: D. Appleton-Century Co., 1943); also comparable efforts toward formalization in the writings of Kurt Lewin (e.g., Kurt Lewin, Ronald Lippitt, and S. K. Escalona, *Studies in Topological and Vector Psychology I* ["University of Iowa Studies in Child Welfare," Vol. XVI (Iowa City, 1940)], 9-42).

30. A book such as John Dollard's *Caste and Class in a Southern Town* teems with suggestiveness, but it is an enormous task for the reader to work out explicitly the theoretic problems which are being attacked, the interpretative variables, and the implicit assumptions of the interpretations. Yet all this needs to be done if a sequence of studies building upon Dollard's work is proposed.

The correlative process which seems called for is that which Lazarsfeld terms "codification." Whereas formal derivation focuses our attention upon the implications of a theory, codification seeks to systematize available empirical generalizations in *apparently different* spheres of behavior. Rather than permitting such separate empirical findings to lie fallow or to be referred to distinctive areas of behavior, the deliberate attempt to institute relevant provisional hypotheses promises to extend existing theory, subject to further empirical inquiry. Thus, an abundance of empirical findings in such fields as propaganda and public opinion, reactions to unemployment, and family responses to crises suggest that when persons are confronted with an "objective stimulus-pattern" which would be expected to elicit responses counter to their "initial predispositions," their actual behavior can be more successfully predicted on the basis of predispositions than of the stimulus-pattern. This is implied by "boomerang effects" in propaganda,[31] by findings on adjustive and maladjustive responses to unemployment,[32] and by research on the stability of families confronted with severe reductions in income.[33] A codified formulation, even as crude as this, gives rise to theoretic problems which would be readily overlooked if the several empirical findings were not re-examined within a single context. It is submitted that codification, as a procedure complementing the formal derivation of hypotheses to be tested, will facilitate the codevelopment of viable sociological theory and pertinent empirical research.

---

31. Paul F. Lazarsfeld and Robert K. Merton, "Studies in radio and film propaganda," *Transactions of the New York Academy of Sciences, Series II*, 1943, 6, 58-79.

32. O. M. Hall, "Attitudes and unemployment," *Archives of Psychology*, No. 165 (March, 1934); E. W. Bakke, *The Unemployed Worker* (New Haven: Yale University Press, 1940).

33. Mirra Komarovsky, *The Unemployed Man and His Family* (New York: Dryden Press, 1940); R. C. Angell, *The Family Encounters the Depression* (New York: Charles Scribner's Sons, 1936); E. W. Burgess, R. K. Merton, *et al.*, *Restudy of the Documents Analyzed by Angell in The Family Encounters the Depression* (New York: Social Science Research Council, 1942).

V THE BEARING OF EMPIRICAL RESEARCH ON SOCIOLOGICAL THEORY

HISTORY HAS A CERTAIN GIFT for outmoding stereotypes. This can be seen, for example, in the historical development of sociology. The steretotype of the social theorist high in the empyrean of pure ideas uncontaminated by mundane facts is fast becoming no less outmoded than the stereotype of the social researcher equipped with questionnaire and pencil and hot on the chase of the isolated and meaningless statistic. For in building the mansion of sociology during the last decades, theorist and empiricist have learned to work together. What is more, they have learned to talk to one another in the process. At times, this means only that a sociologist has learned to talk to himself since increasingly the same man has taken up both theory and research. Specialization and integration have developed hand in hand. All this has led not only to the realization that theory and empirical research *should* interact but to the result that they *do* interact.

As a consequence, there is decreasing need for accounts of the relations between theory and research to be wholly programmatic in character. A growing body of theoretically oriented research makes it progressively possible to discuss with profit the actual relations between the two. And, as we all know, there has been no scarcity of such discussions. Journals abound with them. They generally center on the role of theory in research, setting forth, often with admirable lucidity, the functions of theory in the initiation, design and prosecution of empirical inquiry. But since this is not a one-way relationship, since the two *interact,* it may be useful to examine the other direction of the relationship: the role of empirical research in the development of social theory. That is the purpose of this chapter.

THE THEORETIC FUNCTIONS OF RESEARCH

With a few conspicuous exceptions, recent sociological discussions have assigned but one major function to empirical research: the testing or verification of hypotheses. The model for the proper way of performing this function is as familiar as it is clear. The investigator begins with a hunch or hypothesis, from this he draws various inferences and these, in turn, are subjected to empirical test which confirms or refutes the hypothesis.[1] But this is a logical model, and so fails, of course, to describe much of what actually occurs in fruitful investigation. It presents a set of logical norms, not a description of the research experience. And, as logicians are well aware, in purifying the experience, the logical model may also distort it. Like other models, it abstracts from the temporal sequence of events. It exaggerates the creative role of explicit theory just as it minimizes the creative role of observation. For research is not merely logic tempered with observation. It has its psychological as well as its logical dimensions, although one would scarcely suspect this from the logically rigorous sequence in which research is usually reported.[2] It is both the psychological and logical pressures of research upon social theory which we seek to trace.

It is my central thesis that empirical research goes far beyond the passive role of verifying and testing theory: it does more than confirm or refute hypotheses. Research plays an active role: it performs at least four major functions which help shape the development of theory. It *initiates*, it *reformulates*, it *deflects* and it *clarifies* theory.[3]

1. THE SERENDIPITY PATTERN

(The Unanticipated, Anomalous and Strategic Datum Exerts Pressure for Initiating Theory)

Under certain conditions, a research finding gives rise to social theory. In a previous paper, this was all too briefly expressed as follows: "Fruitful empirical research not only tests theoretically derived hypotheses; it also originates new hypotheses. This might be termed the 'serendipity' component of research, *i.e.*, the discovery, by chance or sagacity, of valid results which were not sought for."[4]

---

1. See, for example, the procedural review of Stouffer's "Theory of intervening opportunities" by G. A. Lundberg, "What are sociological problems?", *American Sociological Review*, 1941, 6, 357-369.

2. See R. K. Merton, "Science, population and society," *The Scientific Monthly*, 1937, 44, 170-171; the apposite discussion by Jean Piaget, *Judgment and Reasoning in the Child*, (London, 1929), Chaps. V, IX, and the comment by William H. George, *The Scientist in Action*, (London, 1936), 153. "A piece of research does not progress in the way it is 'written up' for publication."

3. The fourth function, clarification, has been elaborated in publications by Paul F. Lazarsfeld.

4. R. K. Merton, "Sociological Theory," *American Journal of Sociology*, 1945, 50, 469n. Interestingly enough, the same outlandish term 'serendipity' which has had little currency since it was coined by Horace Walpole in 1754 has also been used to refer to this component of research by the physiologist Walter B. Cannon. See his *The Way of an Investigator*, (New York: W. W. Norton, 1945), Chap. VI, in which he sets forth numerous instances of serendipity in several fields of science.

The serendipity[4a] pattern refers to the fairly common experience of observing an *unanticipated, anomalous and strategic* datum which becomes the occasion for developing a new theory or for extending an existing theory. Each of these elements of the pattern can be readily described. The datum is, first of all, unanticipated. A research directed toward the test of one hypothesis yields a fortuitous by-product, an unexpected observation which bears upon theories not in question when the research was begun.

Secondly, the observation is anomalous, surprising,[5] either because it seems inconsistent with prevailing theory or with other established facts. In either case, the seeming inconsistency provokes curiosity; it stimulates the investigator to "make sense of the datum," to fit it into a

---

4a. Since the foregoing note was first written in 1946, the word *serendipity,* for all its etymological oddity, has diffused far beyond the limits of the academic community. The marked speed of its diffusion can be illustrated by its most recent movement among the pages of the *New York Times.* On May 22, 1949, Waldemar Kaempffert, science editor of the *Times,* had occasion to refer to serendipity in summarizing an article by the research scientist, Ellice McDonald—this, in an innermost page devoted to recent developments in science. Some three weeks later, on June 14, Orville Prescott, book reviewer of the daily *Times,* has evidently become captivated by the word, for in a review of a book in which the hero has a love of outlandish words, Prescott wonders if the hero knew the word serendipity. On Independence Day of 1949, serendipity wins full social acceptance. Stripped of qualifying inverted commas and no longer needing an appositive defining phrase, serendipity appears, without apology or adornment, on the front page of the *Times.* It achieves this prominence in a news dispatch from Oklahoma City, reporting an address by Sir Alexander Fleming, the discoverer of penicillin, at the dedication of the Oklahoma Medical Research Foundation. ("Sir Alexander's experience, which led to the development of modern disease-killing drugs," says the dispatch under the by-line of Robert K. Plumb, "is frequently cited as an outstanding example of the importance of serendipity in science. He found penicillin by chance, but had been trained to look for significance in scientific accidents.") In these travels from the esoteric page devoted to science to the less restricted columns of the book-review to the popular front-page, serendipity had become naturalized. Perhaps it would soon find its way into American abridged dictionaries.

This, then, is yet another instance in which a term, long unmet in common usage, has been recovered and put to fairly frequent use. (Compare note 6 in Chapter IV, referring to the similar history of the term, *anomie.*) And here again, one might ask: what accounts for the cultural resonance in recent years of this contrived, odd-sounding and useful word?

Questions of this order are being explored in a monographic study, by Elinor G. Barber and myself, of the sociological semantics involved in the cultural diffusion of the word *serendipity.* The study examines the social and cultural contexts of the coinage of the word in the eighteenth century; the climate of relevant opinion in which it first saw print in the nineteenth century; the patterned responses to the neologism when it was first encountered; the diverse social circles of littérateurs, physical and social scientists, engineers, lexicographers and historians in which it has diffused; the changes of meaning it has undergone in the course of diffusion and the ideological uses to which it has been variously put.

5. Charles Sanders Peirce had long before noticed the strategic role of the "surprising fact" in his account of what he called "abduction," that is, the initiation and entertaining of a hypothesis as a step in inference. See his *Collected Papers,* VI, 522-528.

broader frame of knowledge. He explores further. He makes fresh observations. He draws inferences from the observations, inferences depending largely, of course, upon his general theoretic orientation. The more he is steeped in the data, the greater the likelihood that he will hit upon a fruitful direction of inquiry. In the fortunate circumstance that his new hunch proves justified, the anomalous datum leads ultimately to a new or extended theory. The curiosity stimulated by the anomalous datum is temporarily appeased.

And thirdly, in noting that the unexpected fact must be strategic, *i.e.*, that it must permit of implications which bear upon generalized theory, we are, of course, referring rather to what the observer brings to the datum than to the datum itself. For it obviously requires a theoretically sensitized observer to detect the universal in the particular. After all, men had for centuries noticed such "trivial" occurrences as slips of the tongue, slips of the pen, typographical errors, and lapses of memory, but it required the theoretic sensitivity of a Freud to see these as strategic data through which he could extend his theory of repression and symptomatic acts.

The serendipity pattern, then, involves the unanticipated, anomalous and strategic datum which exerts pressure upon the investigator for a new direction of inquiry which extends theory. Instances of serendipity have occurred in many disciplines, but I should like to draw upon a recent sociological research for illustration. In the course of our research into the social organization of Craftown,[6] a suburban housing community of some 700 families, largely of working class status, we observed that a large proportion of residents were affiliated with more civic, political and other voluntary organizations than had been the case in their previous places of residence. Quite incidentally, we noted further that this increase in group participation had occurred also among the parents of infants and young children. This finding was rather inconsistent with common-sense knowledge. For it is well known that, particularly on the lower economic levels, youngsters usually tie parents down and preclude their taking active part in organized group life outside the home. But Craftown parents themselves readily explained their behavior. "Oh, there's no real problem about getting out in the evenings," said one mother who belonged to several organizations. "It's easy to find teenagers around here to take care of the kids. There are so many more teen-agers around here than where I used to live."

The explanation appears adequate enough and would have quieted the investigator's curiosity, had it not been for one disturbing datum: like most new housing communities, Craftown actually has a very small proportion of adolescents—only 3.7 per cent for example, in the 15-19

6. Drawn from continuing studies in the Sociology and Social Psychology of Housing, under a grant from the Lavanburg Foundation.

year age group. What is more, the majority of the adults, 63 per cent, are under 34 years of age, so that their children include an exceptionally large proportion of infants and youngsters. Thus, far from their being many adolescents to look after the younger children in Craftown, quite the contrary is true: the ratio of adolescents to children under ten years of age is 1:10, whereas in the communities of origin, the ratio hovers about 1:1.5.[7]

We were at once confronted, then, by an anomalous fact which was certainly no part of our original program of observation. We manifestly did not enter and indeed could not have entered the field of research in Craftown with a hypothesis bearing upon an illusory belief in the abundance of teen-age supervisors of children. Here was an observation both unanticipated and anomalous. Was it also strategic? We did not prejudge its "intrinsic" importance. It seemed no more and no less trivial than Freud's observation during the last war (in which he had two sons at the front) that he had mis-read a newspaper headline, "Die *Feinde* vor Görz" (The *Enemy* before Görz), as "Der *Friede* von Görz" (The *Peace* of Görz). Freud took a trivial incident and converted it into a strategic fact. Unless the observed discrepancy between the subjective impressions of Craftown residents and the objective facts could undergo a somewhat similar transformation it had best be ignored, for it plainly had little "social significance."

What first made this illusion a peculiarly intriguing instance of a general theoretic problem was the difficulty of explaining it as merely the calculated handiwork of vested-interests engaged in spreading a contrary-to-fact belief. Generally, when the sociologist with a conceptual scheme stemming from utilitarian theory observes a patently untrue social belief, he will look for special groups in whose interest it is to invent and spread this belief. The cry of "propaganda!" is often mistaken for a theoretically sound analysis.[8] But this is clearly out of the question in the present instance: there are plainly no special-interest groups seeking to misrepresent the age-distribution of Craftown. What, then, was the source of this social illusion?

Various other theories suggested points of departure. There was Marx's postulate that it is men's "social existence which determines their consciousness." There was Durkheim's theorem that social images ("col-

7. Essentially the same discrepancies in age distribution between Craftown and communities of origin are found if we compare proportions of children under ten with those between 10 and 19. If we make children under five the basis of comparison, the disproportions are even more marked.

8. To be sure, vested-interests often do spread untrue propaganda and this may reinforce mass illusions. But the vested-interest or priestly-lie theories of fallacious folk beliefs do not always constitute the most productive point of departure nor do they go far toward explaining the bases of acceptance or rejection of the beliefs. The present case in point, trivial though it is in any practical sense, is theoretically significant in showing anew the limitations of a utilitarian scheme of analysis.

lective representations") in some fashion reflect a social reality although "it does not follow that the reality which is its foundation conforms objectively to the idea which believers have of it." There was Sherif's thesis that "social factors" provide a framework for selective perceptions and judgments in relatively unstructured situations. There was the prevailing view in the sociology of knowledge that social location determines the perspectives entering into perception, beliefs and ideas. But suggestive as these general orientations[9] were, they did not directly suggest *which* features of social existence, *which* aspects of the social reality, *which* social factors, *which* social location may have determined this seemingly fallacious belief.

The clue was inadvertently provided by further interviews with residents. In the words of an active participant in Craftown affairs, herself the mother of two children under six years of age:

> My husband and I get out together much more. You see, there are more people around to mind the children. *You feel more confident about having some thirteen-or-fourteen-year-old in here when you know most of the people. If you're in a big city, you don't feel so easy about having someone who's almost a stranger come in.*

This clearly suggests that the sociological roots of the "illusion" are to be found in the structure of community relations in which Craftown residents are enmeshed. The belief is an unwitting reflection, not of the statistical reality, but of the community cohesion. It is not that there are objectively more adolescents in Craftown, but more who are *intimately known* and who, therefore, *exist socially* for parents seeking aid in child supervision. Most Craftown residents having lately come from an urban setting now find themselves in a community in which proximity has developed into reciprocal intimacies. The illusion expresses the perspective of people for whom adolescents as potential child-care aides "exist" only if they are well-known and therefore merit confidence. In short, perception was a function of confidence and confidence, in turn, was a function of social cohesion.[10]

From the sociological viewpoint, then, this unanticipated finding fits

9. As the differences between theory and general orientations have been considered in Chapter II.

10. Schedule data from the study provide corroborative evidence. In view of the exceptionally high proportion of young children, it is striking that 54 per cent of their parents affirm that it is "easier in Craftown to get people to look after our children when we want to go out" than it was in other places where they have lived; only 21 per cent say it is harder and the remaining 25 per cent feel there is no difference. Those who come from the larger urban communities are more likely to report greater ease in obtaining assistance in Craftown. Moreover, as we would expect from the hypothesis, those residents who are more closely geared in with Craftown, who identify themselves most fully with it, are more likely to believe it easier to find such aid; 61 per cent of these do so as against 50 per cent of those who identify with other communities, whereas only 12 per cent find it more difficult in comparison with 26 per cent of the latter group.

into and extends the theory that social perception is the product of a social framework. It develops further the "psychology of social norms,"[11] for it is not merely an instance of individuals assimilating particular norms, judgments, and standards from other members of the community. The social perception is, rather, a by-product, a derivative, of the structure of human relations.

This is perhaps sufficient to illustrate the operation of the serendipity pattern: an unexpected and anomalous finding elicited the investigator's curiosity, and conducted him along an unpremeditated by-path which led to a fresh hypothesis.

2. THE RECASTING OF THEORY

(New Data Exert Pressure for the Elaboration of a Conceptual Scheme)

But it is not only through the anomalous fact that empirical research invites the extension of theory. It does so also through the repeated observation of hitherto neglected facts. When an existing conceptual scheme commonly applied to a subject-matter does not adequately take these facts into account, research presses insistently for its reformulation. It leads to the introduction of variables which have not been systematically included in the scheme of analysis. Here, be it noted, it is not that the data are anomalous or unexpected or incompatible with existing theory; it is merely that they had not been considered pertinent. Whereas the serendipity pattern centers in an apparent inconsistency which presses for resolution, the reformulation pattern centers in the hitherto neglected but relevant fact which presses for an extension of the conceptual scheme.

Examples of this in the history of social science are far from limited. Thus it was a series of fresh empirical facts which led Malinowski to incorporate new elements into a theory of magic. It was his Trobrianders, of course, who gave him the clue to the distinctive feature of his theory. When these islanders fished in the inner lagoon by the reliable method of poisoning, an abundant catch was assured and danger was absent. Neither uncertainty nor uncontrollable hazards were involved. And here, Malinowski noted, magic was not practiced. But in the open-sea fishing, with the uncertain yield and its often grave dangers, the rituals of magic flourished. Stemming from these pregnant observations was his theory that magical belief arises to bridge the uncertainties in man's practical pursuits, to fortify confidence, to reduce anxieties, to open up avenues of escape from the seeming impasse. Magic was construed as a supple-

---

11. Muzafer Sherif's book by this title should be cited as basic in the field, although it tends to have a somewhat limited conception of "social factors." *The Psychology of Social Norms* (New York, 1936).

mentary technique for reaching practical objectives. It was these empirical facts which suggested the incorporation of new dimensions into earlier theories of magic—particularly the relations of magic to the fortuitous, the dangerous and the uncontrollable. It was not that these facts were *inconsistent* with previous theories; it was simply that these conceptual schemes had not taken them adequately into account. Nor was Malinowski testing a preconceived hypothesis—he was developing an enlarged and improved theory on the basis of suggestive empirical data.

For another example of this pressure of empirical data for the recasting of a specific theory we turn closer home. The investigation dealt with a single dramatic instance of mass persuasion: broadcasting at repeated intervals over a span of eighteen hours, Kate Smith, a radio star, sold large quantities of war-bonds in the course of a day. It is not my intention to report fully on the dynamics of this case of mass persuasion;[12] for present purposes, we are concerned only with the implications of two facts which emerged from the study.

First of all, in the course of intensive interviews many of our informants—New Yorkers who had pledged a bond to Smith—expressed a thorough disenchantment with the world of advertising, commercials and propaganda. They felt themselves the object of manipulation—and resented it. They objected to being the target for advertising which cajoles, insists and terrorizes. They objected to being engulfed in waves of propaganda proposing opinions and actions not in their own best interests. They expressed dismay over what is in effect a pattern of *pseudo-Gemeinschaft*—subtle methods of salesmanship in which there is the feigning of personal concern with the client in order to manipulate him the better. As one small businessman phrased it, "In my own business, I can see how a lot of people in their business deals will make some kind of gesture of friendliness, sincerity and so forth, most of which is phony." Drawn from a highly competitive, segmented metropolitan society, our informants were describing a climate of reciprocal distrust, of *anomie,* in which common values have been submerged in the welter of private interests. Society was experienced as an arena for rival frauds. There was small belief in the disinterestedness of conduct.

In contrast to all this was the second fact: we found that the persuasiveness of the Smith bond-drive among these same informants largely rested upon their firm belief in the integrity and sincerity of Smith. And much the same was found to be true in a polling interview with a larger cross-section sample of almost a thousand New Yorkers. Fully 80% asserted that in her all-day marathon drive, Smith was *exclusively* concerned with promoting the sale of war bonds, whereas only 17% felt that she was *also* interested in publicity for herself, and a negligible 3% believed she was *primarily* concerned with the resulting publicity.

12. Merton, Fiske and Curtis, *Mass Persuasion.*

This emphasis on her sincerity is all the more striking as a problem for research in the molding of reputations because she herself appeared on at least six commercially sponsored radio programs each week. But although she is engaged in apparently the same promotional activities as others, she was viewed by the majority of our informants as the direct antithesis of all that these other announcers and stars represent. In the words of one devotee, "She's sincere and *she really means anything* she ever says. It isn't just sittin' up there and talkin' and gettin' paid for it. She's different from what other people are."

Why this overwhelming belief in Smith's sincerity? To be sure, the same society which produces a sense of alienation and estrangement generates in many a craving for reassurance, an acute will to believe, a flight into faith. But why does Smith become the object of this faith for so many otherwise distrustful people? Why is she seen as genuine by those who seek redemption from the spurious? Why are her motives believed to rise above avarice and ambition and pride of class? What are the social-psychological sources of this image of Smith as sincerity incarnate?

Among the several sources, we wish to examine here the one which bears most directly upon a theory of mass persuasion. The clue is provided by the fact that a larger proportion of those who heard the Smith marathon war-bond drive are convinced of her disinterested patriotism than of those who did not. This appears to indicate that the marathon bond-drive enhanced public belief in her sincerity. But we must recognize the possibility that her devoted fans, for whom her sincerity was unquestioned, would be more likely to have heard the marathon broadcasts. Therefore, to determine whether the marathon did in fact extend this belief, we must compare regular listeners to her programs with those who are not her fans. Within each group, a significantly larger proportion of people who heard the marathon are convinced of Smith's exclusive concern with patriotic purposes.[12a] This is as true for her devoted fans as for those who did not listen to her regular programs at all. In other words, we have caught for a moment, as with a candid camera, a snapshot of Smith's reputation of sincerity in the process of being even further enhanced. We have frozen in mid-course the process of building a reputation.

But if the marathon increased the belief in Smith's sincerity, how did this come about? It is at this point that our intensive interviews, with their often ingenuous and revealing details, permit us to interpret the statistical results of the poll. The marathon had all the atmosphere of determined, resolute endeavor under tremendous difficulties. Some could detect signs of strain—and courageous persistence. "Her voice was not quite so strong later, but she stuck it out like a good soldier," says a dis-

12a. The statistical data will be found in *ibid.*, pp. 87-88.

cerning housewife. Others projected themselves into the vividly imagined situation of fatigue and brave exertion. Solicitous reports by her coadjutor, Ted Collins, reinforced the emphatic concern for the strain to which Smith was subjecting herself. "I felt, I can't stand this any longer," recalls one informant. "Mr. Collins' statement about her being exhausted affected me so much that I just couldn't bear it." The marathon took on the attributes of a sacrificial ritual.

In short, it was not so much what Smith *said* as what she *did* which served to validate her sincerity. It was the presumed stress and strain of an eighteen-hour series of broadcasts, it was the deed not the word which furnished the indubitable proof. Listeners might question whether she were not unduly dramatizing herself, but they could not escape the incontrovertible evidence that she was devoting the entire day to the task. Appraising the direct testimony of Smith's behavior, another informant explains that "she was on all day and the others weren't. So it seemed that she was sacrificing more and was more sincere." Viewed as a process of persuasion, the marathon converted initial feelings of scepticism and distrust among listeners into at first a reluctant, and later, a full-fledged acceptance of Smith's integrity. The successive broadcasts served as a fulfillment in action of a promise in words. The words were reinforced by things she had actually done. The currency of talk was accepted because it was backed by the gold of conduct. The gold reserve, moreover, need not even approximate the amount of currency it can support.

This empirical study suggests that propaganda-of-the-deed may be effective among the very people who are distrustful of propaganda-of-the-word. Where there is social disorganization, *anomie*, conflicting values, we find propaganditis reaching epidemic proportions. Any statement of values is likely to be discounted as "mere propaganda." Exhortations are suspect. But the propaganda of the deed elicits more confidence. Members of the audience are largely permitted to draw their conclusions from the action—they are less likely to feel manipulated. When the propagandist's deed and his words symbolically coincide, it stimulates belief in his sincerity. Further research must determine whether this propaganda pattern is significantly more effective in societies suffering from anomie than in those which are more fully integrated. But not unlike the Malinowski case-in-point, this may illustrate the role of research in suggesting new variables to be incorporated into a specific theory.

3. THE RE-FOCUSING OF THEORETIC INTEREST

(New Methods of Empirical Research Exert Pressure for New Foci of Theoretic Interest.)

To this point we have considered the impact of research upon the development of particular theories. But empirical research also affects more general trends in the development of theory. This occurs chiefly through the invention of research procedures which tend to shift the foci of theoretic interest to the growing points of research.

The reasons for this are on the whole evident. After all, sound theory thrives only on a rich diet of pertinent facts and newly invented procedures help provide the ingredients of this diet. The new, and often previously unavailable, data stimulate fresh hypotheses. Moreover, theorists find that their hypotheses can be put to immediate test in those spheres where appropriate research techniques have been designed. It is no longer necessary for them to wait upon data as they happen to turn up—researches directed to the verification of hypotheses can be instituted at once. The flow of relevant data thus increases the tempo of advance in certain spheres of theory whereas in others, theory stagnates for want of adequate observations. Attention shifts accordingly.

In noting that new centers of theoretic interest have followed upon the invention of research procedures, we do not imply that these alone played a decisive role.[13] The growing interest in the theory of propaganda as an instrument of social control, for example, is in large part a response to the changing historical situation, with its conflict of major ideological systems, new technologies of mass communication which have opened up new avenues for propaganda and the rich research treasuries provided by business and government interested in this new weapon of war, both declared and undeclared. But this shift is also a by-product of accumulated facts made available through such newly developed, and confessedly crude, procedures as content-analysis, the panel technique and the focused interview.

Examples of this impact in the recent history of social theory are numerous but we have time to mention only a few. Thus, the increasing concern with the theory of character and personality formation in relation to social structure became marked after the introduction of new projective methods; the Rorschach test, the thematic apperception test, play techniques and story completions being among the most familiar. So, too, the sociometric techniques of Moreno and others, and fresh advances in the technique of the "passive interview" have revived interest in the theory of interpersonal relations. Stemming from such techniques as well is the trend toward what might be called the "rediscovery of the primary group," particularly in the shape of theoretic concern with informal social structures as mediating between the individual and large formal organizations. This interest has found expression in an entire literature on the role and structure of the informal group, for example, in factory social systems, bureaucracy and political organizations. Similarly, we may anticipate that the recent introduction of the panel tech-

13. It is perhaps needless to add that these procedures, instruments and apparatus are in turn dependent upon prior theory. But this does not alter their stimulating effect upon the further development of theory.

nique—the repeated interviewing of the same group of informants—will in due course more sharply focus the attention of social psychologists upon the theory of attitude formation, decisions among alternative choices, factors in political participation and determinants of behavior in cases of conflicting role demands, to mention a few types of problems to which this technique is especially adapted.

Perhaps the most direct impact of research procedures upon theory has resulted from the *creation* of sociological statistics organized in terms of theoretically pertinent categories. Talcott Parsons has observed that numerical data are scientifically important only when they can be fitted into analytical categories and that "a great deal of current research is producing facts in a form which cannot be utilized by any current generalized analytical scheme."[14] These well-deserved strictures of a short while ago are proving progressively less applicable. In the past, the sociologist has largely had to deal with *pre-collected series* of statistics usually assembled for nonsociological purposes and, therefore, not set forth in categories directly pertinent to any theoretical system. As a result, at least so far as quantitative facts are concerned, the theorist was compelled to work with makeshift data bearing only a tangential relevance to his problems. This not only left a wide margin for error—consider the crude indexes of social cohesion upon which Durkheim had to rely—but it also meant that theory had to wait upon the incidental and, at times, almost accidental availability of relevant data. It could not march rapidly ahead. This picture has now begun to change.

No longer does the theorist depend almost exclusively upon the consensus of administrative boards or social welfare agencies for his quantitative data. Tarde's programmatic sketch[15] a half century ago of the need for statistics in social psychology, particularly those dealing with attitudes, opinions and sentiments, has become a half-fulfilled promise. So, too, investigators of community organization are creating statistics on class structure, associational behavior, and clique formations, and this has left its mark on theoretic interests. Ethnic studies are beginning to provide quantitative data which are re-orienting the theorist. It is safe to suppose that the enormous accumulation of sociological materials during the war—notably by the Research Branch of the Information and Education Division of the War Department—materials which are in part the result of new research techniques, will intensify interest in the theory of group morale, propaganda and leadership.[15a] But it is perhaps needless to multiply examples.

---

14. Talcott Parsons, "The role of theory in social research," *American Sociological Review*, III (1938), 19; *cf.* his *The Structure of Social Action*, (New York, 1937), 328-329n. ". . . in the social field most available statistical information is on a level which cannot be made to fit directly into the categories of analytical theory."

15. Gabriel Tarde, *Essais et mélanges sociologiques*, (Paris, 1895), 230-270.

15a. As appears to be the case now that it has been published: S. A. Stouffer *et al.*, *The American Soldier*.

What we have said does not mean that the piling up of statistics in itself advances theory; it does mean that theoretic interest tends to shift to those areas in which there is an abundance of *pertinent* statistical data.[15b] Moreover, we are merely calling attention to this shift of focus, not evaluating it. It may very well be that it sometimes deflects attention to problems which, in a theoretic or humanistic sense, are "unimportant"; it may divert attention from problems with larger implications onto those for which there is the promise of immediate solutions. Failing a detailed study, it is difficult to come to any overall assessment of this point. But the pattern itself seems clear enough in sociology as in other disciplines; as new and previously unobtainable data become available through the use of new techniques, theorists turn their analytical eye upon the implications of these data and bring about new directions of inquiry.

4. THE CLARIFICATION OF CONCEPTS

(Empirical Research Exerts Pressure for Clear Concepts)

A good part of the work called "theorizing" is taken up with the clarification of concepts—and rightly so. It is in this matter of clearly defined concepts that social science research is not infrequently defective. Research activated by a major interest in methodology may be centered on the *design* of establishing causal relations without due regard for analyzing the variables involved in the inquiry. This methodological empiricism, as the design of inquiry without correlative concern with the clarification of substantive variables may be called, characterizes a large part of current research. Thus, in a series of effectively designed experiments Chapin finds that "the rehousing of slum families in a public housing project results in improvement of the living conditions and the social life of these families."[16] Or through controlled experiments, psychologists search out the effects of foster home placement upon children's performances in intelligence tests.[17] Or, again through experimental inquiry, researchers seek to determine whether a propaganda film has achieved its purpose of improving attitudes toward the British. These several cases, and they are representative of a large amount of research which has advanced social science method, have in common the fact that the empirical variables are not analyzed in terms of their

15b. The statistical data also facilitate sufficient *precision* in research to put theory to determinate tests; see the discussion of the functions of precision in Chapter II.

16. F. S. Chapin, "The effects of slum clearance and rehousing on family and community relationships in Minneapolis," *American Journal of Sociology*, 1938, 43, 744-763.

17. R. R. Sears, "Child Psychology," in Wayne Dennis, ed., *Current Trends in Psychology*, (University of Pittsburgh Press, 1947), 55-56. Sears' comments on this type of research state the general problem admirably.

conceptual elements.[18] As Rebecca West, with her characteristic lucidity, put this general problem of methodological empiricism, one might "know that A and B and C were linked by certain causal connexions, but he would never apprehend with any exactitude the nature of A or B or C." In consequence, these researches advance the procedures of inquiry, but their findings do not enter into the repository of cumulative social science theory.

But in general, the clarification of concepts, commonly considered a province peculiar to the theorist, is a frequent result of empirical research. Research sensitive to its own needs cannot easily escape this pressure for conceptual clarification. *For a basic requirement of research is that the concepts, the variables, be defined with sufficient clarity to enable the research to proceed,* a requirement easily and unwittingly not met in the kind of discursive exposition which is often miscalled sociological theory.

The clarification of concepts ordinarily enters into empirical research in the shape of establishing *indices* of the variables under consideration. In non-research speculations, it is possible to talk loosely about "morale" or "social cohesion" without any clear conceptions of what is entailed by these terms, but they *must* be clarified if the researcher is to go about his business of systematically observing instances of low and high morale, of social cohesion or social cleavage. If he is not to be blocked at the outset, he must devise indices which are observable, fairly precise and meticulously clear. The entire movement of thought which was christened "operationalism" is only one conspicuous case of the researcher demanding that concepts be defined clearly enough for him to go to work.

This has been typically recognized by those sociologists who combine a theoretic orientation with systematic empirical research. Durkheim, for example, despite the fact that his terminology and indices now appear crude and debatable, clearly perceived the need for devising indices of his concepts. Repeatedly, he asserted that "it is necessary . . . to substitute for the internal fact which escapes us an external fact that symbolizes it and to study the former through the latter."[19] The index, or sign of the conceptualized item, stands ideally in a one-to-one correlation with what it signifies (and the difficulty of establishing this relation is of course one of the critical problems of research). Since the

18. However crude they may be, procedures such as the focused interview are expressly designed as aids for detecting possibly relevant variables in an initially undifferentiated situation. See R. K. Merton, M. Fiske and P. L. Kendall, *The Focused Interview,* (Glencoe, Illinois: The Free Press, 1956).

19. Emile Durkheim, *Division of Labor in Society,* (New York: Macmillan, 1933), 66; also his *Les règles de la méthode sociologique,* (Paris, 1895), 55-58; *Le Suicide,* (Paris, 1930), 356 and *passim. Cf.* R. K. Merton, "Durkheim's *Division of Labor in Society,*" *American Journal of Sociology,* 1934, 40, esp. 326-7 which touches on the problem of indices; for a greatly developed analysis, see Lazarsfeld and Rosenberg, eds., *The Language of Social Research,* Intro. to Section I.

index and its object are so related, one may ask for the grounds on which one is taken as the index and the other as the indexed variable. As Durkheim implied and as Suzanne Langer has indicated anew, the index is that one of the correlated pair which is perceptible and the other, harder or impossible to perceive, is theoretically relevant.[20] Thus, attitude scales make available indices of otherwise not discriminable attitudes, just as ecological statistics represent indices of diverse social structures in different areas.

What often appears as a tendency in research for quantification (through the development of scales) can thus be seen as a special case of attempting to clarify concepts sufficiently to permit the conduct of empirical investigation. The development of valid and observable indices becomes central to the use of concepts in the prosecution of research. A final illustration will indicate how research presses for the clarification of ancient sociological concepts which, on the plane of discursive exposition have remained ill-defined and unclarified.

A conception basic to sociology holds that individuals have multiple social roles and tend to organize their behavior in terms of the structurally defined expectations assigned to each role. Further, it is said, the less integrated the society, the more often will individuals be subject to the strain of incompatible social roles. Type-cases are numerous and familiar: the Catholic Communist subjected to conflicting pressures from party and church, the marginal man suffering the pulls of conflicting societies, the professional woman torn between the demands of family and career. Every sociological textbook abounds with illustrations of incompatible demands made of the multiselved person.

Perhaps because it has been largely confined to discursive interpretations and has seldom been made the focus of systematic research, this central problem of conflicting roles has yet to be materially clarified and advanced beyond the point reached decades ago. Thomas and Znaniecki long since indicated that conflicts between social roles *can* be reduced by conventionalization and by role-segmentation (by assigning each set of role-demands to different situations).[21] And others have noted that frequent conflict between roles is dysfunctional for the society as well as for the individual. But all this leaves many salient problems untouched: on which grounds does one predict the behavior of persons subject to conflicting roles? And when a decision must be made, which role (or which group solidarity) takes precedence? Under which conditions does one or another prove controlling? On the plane of discursive thought, it has been suggested that the role with which the individual

20. Suzanne K. Langer, *Philosophy in a New Key,* (New York: Penguin Books, 1948), 46-47.

21. W. I. Thomas and F. Znaniecki, *The Polish Peasant,* (New York: Knopf, 1927), 1866-70, 1888, 1899 ff.

identifies most fully will prove dominant, thus banishing the problem through a tautological pseudo-solution. Or, the problem of seeking to predict behavior consequent to incompatibility of roles, a research problem requiring operational clarification of the concepts of solidarity, conflict, role-demands and situation, has been evaded by observing that conflicts of roles typically ensue in frustration.

More recently, empirical research has pressed for clarification of the key concepts involved in this problem. Indices of conflicting group pressures have been devised and the resultant behavior observed in specified situations. Thus, as a beginning in this direction, it has been shown that in a concrete decision-situation, such as voting, individuals subject to these cross-pressures respond by delaying their vote-decision. And, under conditions yet to be determined, they seek to reduce the conflict by escaping from the field of conflict: they lose interest in the political campaign. Finally, there is the intimation in these data that in cases of cross-pressures upon the voter, it is socio-economic position which is typically controlling.[22]

However this may be, the essential point is that, in this instance, as in others, the very requirements of empirical research have been instrumental in clarifying received concepts. The process of empirical inquiry raises conceptual issues which may long go undetected in theoretic inquiry.

There remain, then, a few concluding remarks. My discussion has been devoted exclusively to four impacts of research upon the development of social theory: the initiation, reformulation, refocusing and clarification of theory. Doubtless there are others. Doubtless, too, the emphasis of this chapter lends itself to misunderstanding. It may be inferred that some invidious distinction has been drawn at the expense of theory and the theorist. That has not been my intention. I have suggested only that an explicitly formulated theory does not invariably precede empirical inquiry, that as a matter of plain fact the theorist is not inevitably the lamp lighting the way to new observations. The sequence is often reversed. Nor is it enough to say that research and theory must be married if sociology is to bear legitimate fruit. They must not only exchange solemn vows—they must know how to carry on from there. Their reciprocal roles must be clearly defined. This chapter is a short essay toward that definition.

22. Lazarsfeld, Berelson and Gaudet, *The People's Choice,* Chapter VI and the subsequent study by B. Berelson, P. F. Lazarsfeld and W. N. McPhee, *Voting,* (University of Chicago Press, 1954).

INDEX OF NAMES

Abe, Junkichi, 61
Abel, Niels, 36
Abel, Theodore, 1
Adams, Romanzo, 113
Allen, R. G. D., 11
Allport, Gordon, 15, 16, 17
Alpert, Harry, 146
Anderson, Bo, 1, 61
Andreeva, G. M., 66
Angell, Robert C., 155
Arber, Agnes, 6
Arensberg, Conrad M., 142
Aristotle, 20
Arthus, Maurice, 142

Bacon, Francis, 4, 5, 8, 30, 56-58
Bakke, E. W., 155
Baldwin, James M., 18, 40
Barbano, Filippo, 60, 138
Barber, Bernard, 117, 137
Barber, Elinor G., 158
Barcroft, Joseph, 101
Barnes, Harry E., 23
Barth, Paul, 27
Barton, Allen, 39, 41
Bateson, Gregory, 81
Barzun, Jacques, 5
Bay, Christian, 138
Bayliss, W. M., 75
Becker, Howard, 1, 23
Bensman, Joseph, 7, 71
Berelson, Bernard, 150, 171
Berger, Joseph, 1, 61
Bernard, Claude, 32, 101
Bernard, E., 32
Bernard, Jessie, 2
Bernard, L. L., 2
Bertalanffy, L. von, 75, 101
Bierstedt, Robert, 62, 63, 64
Blau, Peter M., 61, 117
Blumer, Herbert, 1, 148-149
Bock, Kenneth E., 1
Boissier de Sauvages, 46
Bolyai, Johann, 9
Boring, Edwin G., 13
Bourquet, Louis, 5
Boulding, Kenneth, 138
Boyle, Robert, 40, 41
Branford, Victor, 2
Bredemeier, H. C., 137
Breed, Warren, 138
Brentano, L., 11
Broadus, R. N., 29
Brown, John, 46
Buckle, H. T., 27
Burgess, Ernest W., 155
Burton, P. E., 29
Butterfield, Herbert, 56

Cabot, Hugh, 89
Cajori, Florian, 70
Campbell, Lewis, 31
Cannon, W. B., 75, 101-103, 157
Cardozo, Benjamin, 101
Carrel, Alexis, 101
Catton, William R., 1
Chapin, F. S., 168
Chapman, Dennis, 138
Chapman, Joan, 138
Churchill, Winston S., 99-100
Clagett, Marshall, 3
Clark, Joseph T., S.J., 8
Coghill, G. E., 101
Cohen, F. S., 101
Coleman, James, 61
Comte, Auguste, 1, 2, 24, 29, 33, 34, 46
Conant, James B., 39
Cook, Stuart W., 117
Cooley, Charles Horton, 4, 6, 18, 19, 29
Coser, Lewis A., 23
Croly, H., 127
Crombie, A. C., 3
Crozier, Michel, 61
Curtis, Alberta, 120, 163
Cuvillier, Armand, 59, 60

Dahrendorf, Ralf, 64, 137
Damlé, Y. B., 138
Darwin, Charles, 9, 34, 40
Davis, Arthur K., 59, 117
Davis, Kingsley, 82-83, 117
del Campo, Salustiano, 60
de Morgan, Augustus, 13
Dennis, Wayne, 114, 168
De Roberty, E., 24
Dewey, John, 149
Descartes, René, 4
Dickson, W. J., 120, 152
Dollard, John, 154
Drabkin, I. E., 8
DuBois, Raymond E., 27
Durkheim, Emile, 4, 29, 30, 35, 36, 59, 63, 68, 115, 142, 146, 151, 160-161, 169, 170

Eckstein, Michael, 138
Eggan, Fred, 110
Einstein, Albert, 46, 47, 48, 100-101
Engels, Friedrich, 6, 24, 25, 26, 95
Escalona, S. K., 154
Eucken, R., 27
Euclid, 5, 6

Faraday, John, 28
Fearing, Franklin, 146
Fernandes, F., 138

Feynman, Richard, 48
Fichter, J. H., 45
Firth, Raymond, 137
Fiske, Marjorie, 120, 163, 169
Florence, P. Sargent, 75
Francis, E. K., 65
Freind, John, 32
Freud, Sigmund, 10, 11, 14, 18, 19, 33, 159-160
Furstenberg, Frank, 7

Galileo, 27, 31
Galton, Sir Francis, 12
Garrison, Fielding H., 47
Gassendi, Pierre, 20
Gaudet, Hazel, 150
George, W. H., 157
Gerth, Hans, 65, 66
Gerver, Israel, 50
Giddings, F. H., 24, 46
Gilbert, William, 40, 41
Gillispie, Charles, 3, 27,
Gini, C., 145
Ginsberg, Morris, 58
Glazer, Nathan, 7
Goode, William J., 7, 105
Gouldner, Alvin, 7, 50, 61, 117
Gross, Neal, 43
Guerlac, Henry, 3
Gumplowicz, Ludwig, 46
Gurvitch, Georges, 138
Guttman, Louis, 147

Halbwachs, M., 149
Hall, A. R., 22
Hall, Calvin S., 15
Hall, Marie B., 3
Hall, O. M., 155
Hall, Rupert, 3
Hallowell, A. I., 145
Hamerton, Philip, 19
Hammond, Phillip E., 7
Hankins, Frank, 58, 59
Harvey, William, 22, 31, 49
Hawkins, E. R., 134
Hegel, G. F., 45
Heller, Hermann, 101
Henderson, Lawrence J., 47
Hexter, J. H., 12
Hicks, J. R., 11, 143
Hillery, George, 61
Hobbes, Thomas, 33, 35
Hoijer, Harry, 146
House, Floyd N., 18
Howton, F. William, 50
Hughes, C. C., 138
Hyman, Herbert H., 40, 61

Jahoda, Marie, 7, 117, 120
James, William, 18, 19, 21, 22, 40
Jandy, Edward C., 18, 19
Janne, Henri, 138
Johnson, Alexander B., 33, 34
Joyce, James, 6

Kahn, Robert L., 43, 61
Kant, Immanuel, 45
Katz, Daniel, 43, 61
Kaufmann, Felix, 140
Keebler, R. W., 29
Kendall, Patricia, 169
Kepler, J., 46, 47
Kessler, M. M., 27, 28
Kimball, Solon, 142
Klineberg, Otto, 113
Kluckhohn, Clyde, 76-77, 84-85, 101, 117
Koehler, W., 101
Kolb, William L., 64
Kuhn, Thomas S., 3, 10, 12, 13, 69

Langer, Susanne K., 170
La Piere, Richard, 92-93
Lashley, K. S., 88
Lazarsfeld, Paul F., viii, 7, 50, 140, 150, 155, 169, 171
Leibniz, G. W. von, 4, 5, 27
Leighton, Alexander H., 138
Lesser, Alexander, 75
Lewis, George Cornewall, 2, 57-58
Levy, Marion J., Jr., 137
Lewin, Kurt, 154
Lindzey, Gardner, 15
Linton, Ralph, 41
Lippitt, Ronald, 154
Lippmann, Walter, 19
Lipset, Seymour Martin, 58
Litt, Theodore, 101
Littlewood, J. E., 32
Lobachevsky, N., 9
Lockwood, David, 137
Loomis, Charles P., 23
Loomis, Zona K., 23
Lovejoy, Arthur, 20
Löwe, Adolph, 58
Lowie, R. H., 76
Lundberg, George A., 140, 157

Mach, Ernst, 5
MacIver, R. M., 26, 116, 140
Mack, Raymond, 61
Major, Ralph H., 47
Malinowski, Bronislav, 76, 84, 86, 88, 107, 142, 162-163
Malewski, Andrzej, 60, 61
Mandeville, J., 20
Mannheim, Karl, 58
March, James G., 61
Margenau, Henry, 48
Marsh, Robert M., 64
Marshall, T. H., 50, 51, 58, 63, 64
Martindale, Don, 23, 70
Marx, Karl, 4, 6, 18, 24-26, 29, 44, 68, 93-95, 107, 160
Mason, Ward S., 43
Maxwell, J. Clerk, 28, 31, 47
Mayo, Elton, 121, 152
McPhee, W. N., 171
Mead, George H., 18, 20, 40, 115
Mendelsohn, Everett, 3
Merton, Robert K., 1, 8, 19, 21, 27, 39, 41, 50, 53, 56, 66, 67, 69
Merz, John T., 45
Mill, John Stuart, 16, 17, 20, 57, 58
Miller, S. M., 50
Mills, C. Wright, 60, 65
Mitchell, Larry, 7
Moles, A. A., 5
Moore, G. E., 11
Moore, Wilbert E., 82-83
Mowrer, O. H., 117
Murphy, Gardner, 11
Murray, H. A., 101
Myrdal, Gunnar, 91-92

Nagel, Ernest, 138
Needham, Joseph, 101
Nelson, Benjamin, 65
Nevins, Allan, 3
Newman, S. S., 145
Newton, Isaac, 22, 27, 28, 34, 47
Niemeyer, G., 101

Oberschall, Anthony, 7
Ogburn, William F., 8, 149
Opler, M. E., 110
Ore, Oystein, 36
Osgood, Charles E., 29
Osipov, G., 66, 67

Pareto, Vilfredo, 4, 29
Parker, G. H., 81
Parsons, Talcott, viii, 39, 43-44, 51-53, 68, 88, 96-97, 101, 117, 136-137, 167
Pascal, Blaise, 40
Pavlov, I. P., 10
Peirce, C. S., 148, 158
Pellegrin, R. J., 61
Penrose, Edith, 11
Petrovievics, B., 9
Piaget, Jean, 157
Plato, 7, 56, 57
Poggi, Gianfranco, 60
Popper, J., 11
Price, Derek J. deSolla, 3, 27, 29

Radcliffe-Brown, A. R., 76, 79-80
Redfield, Robert, 101
Reed, Stephen W., 1
Richet, Charles, 32
Rice, Stuart A., 153
Riecken, Henry, 19, 67
Riesman, David, 11, 60, 65
Rigaud, Stephen P., 32
Rivers, W. H. R., 85
Roethlisberger, F. J., 120, 152
Rosenberg, Bernard, 23, 50
Rosenberg, Morris, 140
Ross, E. A., 6
Rossi, Peter H., 59
Rousseau, J. J., 35
Rush, Benjamin, 46
Russell, Bertrand, 10, 46
Russell, E. S., 101

Saintsbury, George, 22
St. Simon, 2, 34, 35
Salvemini, G., 36
Sarton, George, vii, 2, 22
Schneider, Louis, 117
Schofield, Robert, 3
Schumpeter, J. A., 144
Sears, R. R., 168
Selznick, Philip, 61, 117
Sewell, William, 50
Shakespeare, William, 19, 28
Sherif, Muzafer, 160-161
Sherrington, C. S., 101
Shils, Edward A., 7, 121
Simmel, Georg, 4, 16, 17, 24, 29, 35, 36, 44
Simon, Herbert A., 61
Simpson, George E., vii, 97
Slutsky, Eugen, 11
Small, Albion, 18
Smith, Adam, 18, 19, 91
Sorokin, Pitirim A., vii, 23-27, 30, 43, 44, 51, 62, 68, 142, 152
Spearman, Carl, 12
Spencer, Herbert, 6, 19, 29, 33, 44, 46
Spengler, J. J., 20, 25
Spiro, M. E., 137
Steffens, Lincoln, 129-130
Stein, Maurice R., 7, 60, 65
Stephen, Leslie, 19
Sterne, Lawrence, 6
Stoltenberg, H. S., 27
Stouffer, Samuel, 19, 40, 157, 167
Sumner, W. G., 4, 29, 116
Sutherland, E. H., 7, 76-78, 144

Tarde, Gabriel, 24, 167
Temple, Sir William, 31, 32
Thomas, Dorothy, 8
Thomas, W. I., 19, 116
Thorndike, E. L., 10
Thorner, Isidor, 117
Timasheff, N. S., 23
Tocqueville, A. de, 91
Tolman, E. C., 15
Tönnies, F., 24
Trotter, Wilfred, 47
Trow, Martin, 61
Tylor, E. B., 27

Uexküll, J. von, 101

Van Nieuwenhuijze, C. A. O., 58
Veblen, Thorstein, 19, 20, 29, 112, 123-124, 151
Vico, Giambattista, 33
Vidich, Arthur J., 7, 71
Vincent, George, 18
von Wiese, Leopold, 24

Walker, E. R., 153
Wallace, Alfred R., 9
Waller, Willard W., 7, 80, 134
Ward, Lester F., 6, 7, 46
Weber, Alfred, 26
Weber, Max, v, 4, 6, 28, 29, 35, 36, 68, 74
Wedemeyer, Joseph, 26
Weinberg, Alvin M., 55
Weiner, Charles, 3
Wells, F. L., 89
West, Rebecca, 169
Whatmough, Joshua, 146
Whitehead, A. N., viii, 1, 10, 13, 21, 30, 49, 101, 152
Whorf, B. L., 145, 146
Whyte, Lancelot, L., 33, 132
Whyte, William F., 7, 132
Wilensky, Harold, 50
Williams, L. Pearce, 3
Wilson, Edmund, 36
Wilson, E. B., 101
Wirth, Louis, 153
Wolff, Kurt H., 17
Wood, Alexander, 10
Woodger, J. H., 101
Woolf, Virginia, 6
Wootton, Barbara, 50

Xhignesse, Louis V., 29

Yadov, V. A., 66, 67
Yinger, J. M., 97
Young, Donald, 97, 98
Young, Thomas, 10
Yovchuck, M., 66-67

Zdravomyslov, A. G., 66, 67
Zeisel, Hans, 7
Zelditch, Morris, Jr., 1, 61
Zetterberg, Hans L., 60, 61
Zimmerman, C. C., 149
Znaniecki, Florian, 116, 140, 142, 170

SUBJECT INDEX

Accumulation in physical science, 13, 27, 28
  and adumbrationism in social science, 23, 28-29, 35
Action, theory of, 43
Adumbrationism, 20-26, 58
  defined, 20
  in sociology, 22-26
Adumbrations, 8, 17
  and anticipations, 12, 25
  defined, 13
  identification of, 16
  and pseudo-anticipations, 19
Alienation, process of, 53, 54
Analysis, qualitative, 71
Ancients and moderns, battle between, 19, 21, 31-32
Anomie, 41, 63, 117, 163, 165
Anticipations of scientific discoveries, 8, 9, 10, 11, 15, 17, 18, 25, 33n
  and adumbrations, 12, 17, 20, 25
  defined, 13
  and pseudo-anticipations, 15
  identification of, 16
  and prediscoveries, 19
Attitude scales, 170
Authority, theory of, 41

Boss, political, 126-130
Bureaucracy, theories of, 61

Ceremonials, 110, 118-119
Change, social, 94, 101, 135
Civilization, 26
Class, social, 26n, 97
  class conflict, 68
Classical theory, functions of, 34-37
Classics
  in science, 28, 34
  in sociology, 28, 34-35
  scientists' ambivalence toward, 30
Codification, 69-72, 154-155
  defined, 69
  of qualitative analysis, 71
Collective representations, 160-161
Conflict, social, 53, 53n, 54, 68
Comparative sociology, 64, 108
Concepts, sociological, 143-147
Conceptual:
  analysis, 145, 147, 154
  clarification, 144-145, 168-171
  lag, 146
Consequences:
  multiple, 105
  net balance of, 90, 105
  nonfunctional, 51, 105
  objective, 105
  unanticipated, 105, 115-116, 120
Conspicuous consumption, 112, 123-24
Continuities in social theory, 8-14
Correlation, measurement of, 12
Covert cultural patterns, 113-114
Craftown study, 159-161
Crime, 144
Culture, 26, 113-114

Deduction, 154
Demographic uniformities, 61
Derivation, formalized, 154
Deviant behavior, theory of, 61
Dialectical materialism, 93-96
Discontinuities, of empirical research, 153
  of social theory, 8-14
Discoveries, multiple independent, 8, 10, 20, 43n
Dissonance theory, 64
Dysfunctions, 105-107

Empirical generalizations, vi, 66, 149-154
Economic theory of value, 11
Erudition
  vs. originality, 29-34
  scientists' ambivalence toward, 31-33

Fallacy of affirming the consequent, 152
Fathers of sciences, 2n
Formal organization, 43, 68
Freudian error, 159

Function, 74-76, 86, 90-91, 105, 106, 115
(see also latent function and manifest function)
Functional:
alternatives, 87-90, 106
autonomy, 15-17
consequences, 86, 90
equivalents, 106
prerequisites, 87-88, 90, 102-103, 106
requirement, 106
unity, 79-82, 90
Functional analysis: 43, 55, 69
compared to method of dialectical materialism, 93-96
as conservative ideology, 91-92, 93, 96, 108
definition of, 75-77
description of observed pattern in, 109, 112-114
design of studies in, 103-104
logic of procedure in, 102-103
paradigm for, 104-109
postulate of universal functionalism in, 84-86, 90
prevalence in other sciences of, 100-104
as radical ideology, 92-93

General theoretical orientations, vi, 52, 141-143, 154
Group, primary, 18, 114, 121-122, 166

Hawthorne effect, 20, 120-121
History and systematics of sociological theory, 1-37
History of science, 3, 14, 51
and published record of science, 5, 6, 14
Hopi, rain ceremonial, 118-121
"Humanistic coefficient," 142

Ideological superstructure, 26
Indices, 169-171
Induction, 154
Informal groups, 114, 166
Institutional interdependence, theory of, 41, 63
Integral sociology, 43, 68
Integration:
biological, 81
social, 79-82, 90
Intermarriage, 113, 117
Intervening opportunities, theory of, 19
Intervening variables, 146-147, 151
Inventories, propositional, 69

Latent function: 105, 115-121, 122-123
of political machine, 125-127
Logical structure of experiment, 102
Looking-glass self, 18-19

Macro-sociology, 61, 64, 68
Magic, 88, 89, 110, 162-163
Manifest functions, 105, 115-120
Marxian theory, 26, 43, 44, 55, 59, 60n, 68
Mass persuasion, 163-165, 166
Methodology (logic of procedure), 73, 140-141
Micro-sociology, 61, 68
Middle range, theories of the, v, 3-72
uses of, 39
examples of sociological, 39-40, 41, 61, 64
and total sociological theory, 50-53
consolidation of, 51, 61, 65, 68
polarized responses to, 53
stereotypes of theorists, 53
assent to the policy of, 56-62
historical roots of, 56-58
rejection of, 62-67
attributes of, 68-69
Mirriri, responses to, 111
Motives: 114, 123-124
distinguished from functions, 77-79, 113
Multiselved person, 170

Nonfunctional consequences, 105
"Normal science," 12, 13
Nullifiability, 148

Observations:
creative role of, 158-159
protocols of, 105, 114
Occupational subsystem, theory of, 61
Occupations:
social evaluations of, 131
Oedipus complex, 142
Operationalism, 169
Oral history, 3, 3n,
distinct from public record, 5, 6
Out-marriage, taboo on, 113

Panel technique of interviewing, 166-167
Paradigms: codification of theory, 69-72
on functional analysis, v, 104-108, 136
on deviant behavior, 69n
on the sociology of knowledge, 69n
on racial intermarriage, 69n
functions of, 70-72, 109
Participation, differential, 114
Physical and life sciences
compared to sociology, 23
development of, 23n
accumulation in, 27
misconceptions about development of, 46-48
style of exposition, 70
Plausibility, 147-148
Polarization, process of, 53-56

Political machines:
functional analysis of, 125-136
Post factum interpretations, 147-149, 153-154
Power, 127, 170
Prediction, 148, 152
Prediscoveries
defined, 9
and rediscoveries, 13
and anticipations, 14, 19
identification of, 15
Primary group (See group, primary)
Propaganda, 160, 166
Propaganditis, 163, 165
Pseudo-*Gemeinschaft,* 163
Public image, 164
Public opinion, theory of, 61
Punishment, social functions of, 115-116
Puritanism and science, 63n

Quantification, 170

Rediscoveries, 8, 9, 10, 12-14, 35
Reference groups, theory of, 39, 40, 64
Relative deprivation, theory of, 40-41
Religion:
dysfunctions of, 83-84
functional analyses of, 82-84, 89, 90, 96-99, 118-119
indispensability of, 87
integrative functions of, 82-83
Marxist theory of, 98, 99
Research, empirical:
conceptual analysis in, 145-147
discontinuities in, 153
effect on refocusing of theory, 165-168
hypotheses in, 154
indices of variables in, 169-171
interpretative variables in, 154
serendipity pattern in, 157-162
and theory, interplay of, 149-150, 162-165, 168-171
theoretical function of, 156-167
Role-sets, theory of, 41-45
conflict in, 42, 43
mechanisms which articulate, 43
source of mechanisms, 44
Roles, social, 41, 42
conflicting, 40, 170-171
multiple, 42, 44
Romantic love complex, 111

"Scientific revolutions," 12, 13
Self-fulfilling prophecy, 20
Serendipity, 150, 158-162
"Significant others," 20, 40
Social behaviorism, 43
Social change, 94, 135
cohesion, 150, 151, 152, 161
Social differentiation, theory of, 64
Social mobility, 39, 61, 68
Social norms, formation of, 40
Social structure, 41-44, 110, 161
alternative, 87-88
integrated, 79-80
interdependence of elements in, 106-107
Social systems, theory of, 41, 68
Sociological theory (see Theory, sociological)
Sociological theory, total, 45-48, 51-53
stereotypes of, 53-54
utilitarian pressures for, 48-50
Sociologists, Soviet, 66-67
Sociology
public expectations of, 48-49
sociologists' expectations of, 49-50
and social problems, 48-50
Sociology, humanistic, 53
Sociology of science, 3
Solidarity, social, 80, 171
Specification of units, 90
Status, social, 41, 42, 123-124
differentiation, 54
Stereotypes, 19, 54
of theorists, 53-54
Stratification, theory of, 41
Structural:
constraint, 106-107
context, 106-107, 127-128, 131
description, 110
sources of behavior, 131
variables, 142
Structure, social (see Social structure)
Suicide rates, 150-152
Survivals, social, 85-86
System, social, 41

Theory, sociological:
codification in, 154, 155
concepts in, 143-147
conceptual clarification due to research, 168-171
data exerting pressure on, 157-162
defined, 39
empirical generalizations and, 149-150
functions of, 150-153
general sociological orientations, 141-143, 154
interplay with methodology and technique, 140
post factum interpretations, 147-149, 153-154
role of empirical research in development of, 139, 153-154, 162-165
Thomas theorem, 19
Trained incapacity, 19
Trobriand Islanders, 114, 162

Unanticipated consequences, 105, 115-116, 120
Universal functionalism, 84-86, 90
Variables, intervening, 146-147
  indices of, 169-171
  interpretative, 154
Vested interests, 160
Vice, as business, 132-134
Visibility, 41
Voting behavior, 171

White-collar crime, 144
Wishful thinking, 19
Working hypothesis, 39, 39n